The Royal United Services Institute

Global Challenges and
Bridging Divides, Dealing with Perceptions, Rebuilding Societies

Report of the 2004 Tswalu Dialogue

Edited by Richard Cobbold and Greg Mills

www.rusi.org

CO-PRODUCED BY:

First Published 2004
© The Royal United Services Institute for Defence and Security Studies

All rights reserved. No part of this publication may be reproduced, stored in a retrieval system, or transmitted in any form or by any means, electronic, mechanical, photocopying, recording or otherwise, without prior permission of the Royal United Services Institute.

Whitehall Paper Series

ISBN 0-85516-196-5
ISSN 0268-1307

Series Editor: Dr Terence McNamee
Assistant Editor: Alanna Henderson

Whitehall Papers are available as part of a membership package, or individually at £8.00 plus p&p (£1.00 in the UK/£2.00 overseas). Orders should be sent to the Membership Administrator, RUSI Membership Office, South Park Road, Macclesfield, SK11 6SH, United Kingdom and cheques made payable to RUSI. Orders can also be made by quoting credit card details via email to: membership@rusi.org

For more details, visit our website: www.rusi.org

Printed in Great Britain by Stephen Austin & Sons Ltd. for the Royal United Services Institute, Whitehall, London, SW1A 2ET UK

RUSI is a Registered Charity (No. 210639)

Contents

Introduction and Acknowledgements   v
Greg Mills and *Kurt Shillinger*

1. **AFRICAN CONFLICT RESOLUTION**   1
   The Rwanda Genocide – Ten Years On   *Charles Murigande*   3
   Sierra Leone – 'Pregnant with Lessons?'   *David Richards*   9
   Sudan at the Crossroads   *J Stephen Morrison*   23
   Crisis in Zimbabwe   *Tony Hawkins*   31
   Structural Challenges of Transformation in Zimbabwe
   John Robertson   45

2. **DEMOCRATIZATION IN AFRICA**   57
   Democratization in Kenya – Some Observations
   William M Bellamy   59
   The Challenge of Democratization in Ethiopia
   Christopher Clapham   71
   Peace-Building and Democracy – Lessons of Somalia and
   Somaliland   *Rakiah Omaar*   83

3. **AFRICAN SECURITY CHALLENGES AND RESPONSES**   93
   Global Change, Security and Weakened States   *John Mackinlay*   95
   Peace Keeping and Peace Building in the Pacific – Lessons and
   Trends for International Best Practice   *Ian Wilcock*   105
   Old Wine in New Bottles? – US Policy Towards Africa after
   9/11 and Iraq   *John Prendergast*   109
   Perspectives on the AU and Nepad – An Elite Survey in Seven
   African Countries   *Hennie Kotzé*   115

4.	**THE IMPACT OF GLOBAL DEVELOPMENTS ON AFRICA**	**143**
	A Safer World After Saddam? *Richard Cobbold*	145
	The Role of External Actors in Combating Corruption *Jeffrey Herbst*	155
	Impact of Global Developments on Africa *Richard Bouma*	163
	The Importance of Partnership for Peace and Development *Tekeda Alemu*	171
	Bridging Global and National Divides – What needs to be done? *Paul Kagame*	175

Appendix   **179**

Introduction and Acknowledgements
Greg Mills and Kurt Shillinger

The Tswalu Dialogue
The Tswalu Dialogue commenced in 2002 as an initiative of Jennifer and Jonathan Oppenheimer in conjunction with the South African Institute of International Affairs (SAIIA). In 2004, SAIIA entered into a partnership over Tswalu with the Royal United Services Institute for Defence and Security Studies (RUSI). The 2004 event was also part sponsored by the Ford Foundation and the Konrad Adenauer Stiftung.

The Dialogue provides a unique forum for political leaders, diplomats, senior military strategists, business people, policy analysts and academics to discuss matters of critical importance to Africa's development. The opportunities presented to Africa are as great as the challenges it faces, and it is thus a key objective of the Dialogue to promote creative new thinking on Africa by developing a network of the most influential people from across the broadest possible range of constituencies.

The 2002 First Tswalu Dialogue considered three areas relevant to the creation of the logic of stability and prosperity in Africa: (1) The heterogeneous nature of the performance of African states; (2) the problems experienced by the West in developing appropriate policy solutions to assist African countries in meeting such challenges as aid and debt relief; and (3) the role of non-state actors in creating conditions for African prosperity.

Coinciding with the second meeting of a project on 'Big African States,' funded by the Ford Foundation and conducted jointly by SAIIA,

---

Dr. Greg Mills is National Director of the South African Institute of International Affairs (SAIIA) and **Kurt Shillinger** is Managing Editor of *eAfrica: The Electronic Journal of Governance and Innovation*, a SAIIA monthly publication.

Princeton University and the Stiftung Wissenschaft und Politik, the 2003 Second Tswalu Dialogue had a number of aims that included gaining a critical understanding of the failure or dysfunction of large states such as Nigeria, Sudan, Angola, the DRC (Democratic Republic of Congo) and Ethiopia. Other debate themes included the New Partnership for Africa's Development (Nepad) and the consequences for Africa of the war in Iraq.

The theme for the third round of the dialogue, Tswalu 2004, was 'Global Challenges and Africa: Bridging Divides, Dealing with Perceptions, Rebuilding Societies'. This topic was selected as a response to the deepening crisis in Iraq and the Middle East as well as from a general concern about Western perceptions of Africa and African perceptions of the West. In order to examine recent models of external intervention in African conflict and explore new international policy responses to crises on the continent, the Dialogue sought greater participation in this round from top military officials and non-state actors including business leaders. Discussions focused on conflict resolution, security challenges, obstacles to democratization and the impact of global developments on Africa.

The major change in approach for 2004 (and beyond) was the preparation of a formal research agenda in the form of pre-circulated research papers. These provided the foundation for the various discussion sessions. (The Tswalu Dialogue is held according to 'RUSI Rules'. Consequently, beyond the arguments presented in the prepared papers, attributions are withheld from the conference report. A full list of participants and the programme of events are reproduced in the appendix.) This Introduction provides a report of the 2004 Dialogue, highlighting both the contributions of the various papers included in this compendium and those of the participants (on the above 'RUSI Rules' basis), thereby extracting key points made at the Dialogue.

Thursday 29 April 2004

Foreign Minister Charles Murigande of Rwanda presented a concise overview of his government's efforts during the past decade to rebuild a stable, peaceful and prosperous society in Rwanda after the 1994 genocide. The challenge was and remains formidable. When the Rwandan Patriotic Front (RPF) took power, the country had just lost around one million people in three months of ethnic slaughter. Three million had fled across the borders, creating massive humanitarian crises in Zaire (now the DRC) and Tanzania. Hundreds of thousands more were internally displaced, including scores of orphans and widows. All law and order had broken down.

Genocidal militias were still operating inside the country and across the border from teeming refugee camps. The courts, police and civil service had ceased to exist. All economic activity had ground to a halt. Dr. Murigande traced the historical context of the genocide, outlining the deliberate manufacturing of ethnic animosities by Belgian officials during the colonial period.

The mission of the past decade was to lay the foundation for social, political and cultural transformation and restore peace, stability and – above all – trust and hope among the people. The government of national unity had repatriated 3.5 million people and integrated 20,000 officers and men from the old army into the new military. Macro-economic reforms have achieved a sustained 6 per cent growth rate over the past three years, and inflation has fallen from 65 per cent to 5 per cent. A system of traditional courts, known as *gacaca*, has been established to promote reconciliation and clear the huge judicial backlog in prosecuting the perpetrators. Prisoners and the Diaspora have also been engaged in a rolling national discussion about preventing genocide in the future. The government is also investing in human resource development, agriculture and infrastructure as part of a strategy to reduce poverty. First-ever local elections were held in 1999. Following the adoption of a new constitution in May 2003, the first democratic presidential and parliamentary polls have been conducted. Looking forward, the development of integrated regional markets is critical to the ongoing process of rebuilding Rwanda.

Two questions were raised in remarks following the keynote address: (1) What causes violence? and (2) What can be done about it internally and externally? The Rwandan experience underscored the importance of governance as well as the need to understand the pathologies of social phenomena such as leadership and religion.

The Keynote Evening Address was due to be given by Rwandan President Paul Kagame, but late scheduling conflicts prevented his participation in the Dialogue. However, in the text of his prepared speech, which was made available, he considered ways to address divisions that he saw deepening among developed and developing nations. Technology, he argued, is crucial to closing the gap and should permeate every aspect of Africa's development agenda. Long-term investment in infrastructure is equally important. Leaders need to focus on human resources and skills development and gender equality. Science must become an education priority. In the hands of the uneducated, technology is worthless. The constituents of good governance – transparency, honesty, economic liberalization and democracy – are critical to stability and progress and enable closer partnerships between countries. Deregulation spurs entrepreneurship. Better ICT networks will connect peasant farmers with markets, facilitate transnational information sharing and boost trade. Viable regional economic blocs and greater access to international markets are imperatives to development. He concluded by emphasizing 'the need to promote the philosophy of a borderless Africa with integrated regional markets as a means of devising strategic steps to build effective bridges to lessen the gap between the haves and have-nots'.

Friday 30 April 2004

The three main discussion sessions of the first full day of the Dialogue focused on African conflict resolution, democratization and opportunities for external intervention. Five core themes emerged:

- Modern conflict intervention puts a premium on negotiated settlement, but historically, the most stable and enduring periods of nation-building have followed decisive military victory. There is a need to explore why international diplomacy – which in this context includes force intervention – has adopted a negative view toward military victory as a legitimate means of conflict resolution and whether the prevailing imperative to intervene and mediate adequately removes the incentives of warring parties to pursue their objectives through force of arms.
- 'Embedded support' is a highly effective strategy for strengthening young governments in emerging democracies.
- Internal governance is critical to conflict resolution and democratization.
- External consensus is crucial to ensuring that parties seek negotiations as the avenue to political stability.
- External leverage must be created through a combination of hard and soft diplomacy. There is no excuse for failing to cultivate the opportunities to influence the attitudes and actions of conflicting parties.

Four years into the new century, there is hopeful evidence that Africa is experiencing a continent-wide decline in conflict. A number of countries are on the cusp of a possible solution, but continued violence remains a real threat. The first session examined approaches to conflict resolution in three states that posed diverse challenges to external intervention: Sierra Leone, Sudan and Zimbabwe.

Three papers provided the basis for the discussion. In his examination of the external military intervention in Sierra Leone, David Richards argued that the international community repeatedly fails to provide sufficiently coherent and timely pre-emptive action in response to developing crises. Devising a recovery plan from scratch requires active and simultaneous pursuit of the range of interdependent lines of development – political, diplomatic, legal, economic, industrial and humanitarian as well as military – to a defined end. The full range of external and internal actors must be brought into the response team within the framework of a coherent multi-dimensional plan. Tactical considerations alone are insufficient. The building of national security structures – police and military – is vital. So too is tempo. Too often, the international community gets bogged down in bureaucratic inefficiencies and slow decision-making processes.

In drawing lessons from the peace process in Sudan, Steve Morrison also affirmed the centrality of sustained and coherent high-level multilateral engagement. Experiences in Sierra Leone and the Democratic Republic of the Congo showed that the international community too often fails to adequately resource peace and humanitarian missions. Stabilization rests on the quality and strength of sustained external engagement. Peacekeeping operations must coincide with debt relief and reconstruction assistance and should include a Chapter VII mandate to use force as needed. Such intervention in the African theatre places a severe strain on diplomatic resources at a time when stabilizing Iraq is the West's predominate and indefinite foreign policy priority.

John Robertson outlined the extent of the erosion of economic and political stability in Zimbabwe over the past four years, marked by the collapse of the rule of law, the conversion of the national police force into a ruling-party police force and the total disempowerment of the individual.

In the general discussion that followed, it was emphasized that force capacity limitations require sounding the alarm bells earlier. What measures can the international community take to prevent conflict where it has not yet happened? The experiences in Sierra Leone and Sudan demonstrate that the international community has the tools to intervene effectively even at a time when operations in Iraq and Afghanistan diminish the availability of resources for use elsewhere. The multi-dimensional approach is key. Strategies need to be flexible, reactive and, importantly, called failures when they fail. The outbreak of violence in Western Darfur, coming at the fragile critical moment in the Sudan peace process, demonstrates that externally coerced settlement processes are highly prone to breakdown. It also underscores the necessity of forging broad-based, all-encompassing solutions to national crises. Engaging only the key factions in a conflict is insufficient and ultimately costly.

Accountability is essential to effective intervention. It is also important to determine what kind of engagement is most appropriate. Not every situation calls for an external military response – for example, the international community can also punish rogue leaders through international courts. It was noted that despite steps toward the creation of an African Peace and Security Council – an encouraging indication that African states acknowledge the need to review each other and, critically, to create the means for constructive intervention when necessary – the role of African states in conflict mediation and reconstruction remains unexpressed. The surrounding regional players are not telling the parties in Sudan that it is time to close the deal, for example, or applying leverage in Zimbabwe to break the crisis.

Zimbabwe presents a different challenge from those of Sierra Leone and Sudan. Greater leverage remains more important at this juncture than direct intervention. It was argued that negotiations were no longer the most effective way forward and that the international community should now coalesce around a strategy to salvage the March 2005 parliamentary election (see the section below where Zimbabwe is discussed in a separate roundtable session).

Session Two focused on democratization. Most African countries now conduct elections on a regular basis, but the quality of these elections varies enormously. In addition, many countries still have extremely weak democratic institutions: parliaments, parties, courts and the press are often unable to play their democratic roles. This session focused on internal and external approaches to improving Africa's democratic institutions.

Once again, three papers prepared in advance framed the debate. In his examination of political progression in Kenya, Mark Bellamy noted that the December 2002 elections demonstrated the deepening maturity of democracy and a firm and hopefully lasting rejection of autocracy. Three factors place democracy in Kenya on a solid footing. First, Britain as colonial ruler erected durable institutions and educated Kenyans to run them. These generally withstood thirty-nine years of one-party rule. Second, the country has fostered democratic practices from the outset of independence – again, even within the context of long-running strongman governance. There is an established ambivalent relationship between voters and parliamentarians at the local level, reflected in the historical pattern of turnover in the legislature. Even during the height of Daniel arap Moi's 24-year reign, he was still unable to impose members of parliament on the electorate or fail to hold elections. Finally, the country's ethnic diversity means that parties must construct and maintain coalitions to obtain and retain power. Although divisions are now growing within President Mwai Kibaki's administration, Kenyans control their own political future.

No standard model of democratization can be applied in a top-down manner across Africa. Ethiopia, as Christopher Clapham argued, has traveled a unique historical course. He outlined five challenges to stability and democratization in the country, and five reasons for hope. Among the challenges:

- History. No government has ever come to power in Ethiopia by election, and no ruler has ever left power voluntarily.
- Structure. Consensual political structure is frustrated by the country's wide geographical, religious and ethnic diversity.
- Culture. Ethiopian political tradition places enormous emphasis on hierarchy and obedience, which run counter to conventional multi-party democracy.
- Revolution. This tends to lead to dictatorship and both civil and external wars.
- Insurgency. When governments fight their way into power, they tend to have a sense that they have earned the right to retain it.

Even so, optimism is not unreasonable. Dictatorship inevitably fails. The current government has deconstructed hegemony, experimenting with ethnic federalism rather than centralized power. Ethiopians share a strong sense of nationhood dating back centuries. Civil society is emerging and there are signs that the Diaspora is re-engaging.

Finally, Rakiya Omaar drew lessons in nation building from the divergent experiences of Somalia and Somaliland since the collapse of the state in 1991. The critical difference accounting for relative stability in the latter and the elusiveness of peace in the former is the role of the elders in building peace. It is essential to resolve issues critical to a nomadic population initially at the local level. Somaliland pursued an internal course of consolidation from the ground up. Somalia, meanwhile, has been subjected to more than a dozen external attempts at peacemaking, most of which focused almost exclusively on forcing consensus among warring factional leaders in Mogadishu. Political and humanitarian intervention was consequently out of sync with Somali norms and needs. It is vital to give the people a stake in nation building.

Prior to the general discussion, an intervention was made by Ian Wilcock highlighting lessons from Australia's experience in building peace and stability at both the national and regional levels in the South Pacific over the past twenty years. An important approach to external engagement is 'embedded support' – the long-term placement of foreign officials (in this case Australian) into the administrative structures, most particularly the law and order and finance sectors, of weak states. Such activist deployment requires great sensitivity to avoid charges of neo-colonialism, but it can pay substantial dividends in terms of broader regional cohesion and stability.

Discussion led in several directions. It was argued that without economic success, democratization is impossible. This is one of the critical failings of external intervention, which tends to seek quick solutions and quick exits. Prolonged engagement is necessary to help states emerging from conflict to create viable economic and political structures. Often, this requires separating the state and the government so that the one does not collapse when the other changes. The concept of embedded support might provide the framework for ongoing international support for economic stabilization.

Internally, the withdrawal of key elements of regime support can effectively force momentum toward democratic change. This was true in Kenya in the 1990s, when banks closed off resources to the Moi regime and the military refused to be used as a tool for repression. External conditionalities can also be effective, as when the donor community tied economic assistance to multi-party reforms starting in the early 1990s.

One of the thorniest issues in post-conflict reconstruction is reconciliation. Although African societies display an astonishing ability to forgive – South Africa and Mozambique were cited – social healing is a delicate process. Some argued that reconciliation must not be forced. Constant emphasis on the word itself may actually stifle needed debate on past traumatic experience. Others disagreed, contending that national leaders need to be proactive in establishing the framework and incentives for reconciliation. It is doubtful that South Africa would have had a national dialogue on apartheid crimes had it not established the Truth and Reconciliation Commission. Nor would Rwanda clear its massive backlog in dispensing justice for acts of genocide without enabling victims and perpetrators to face each other in the grass-roots courts called *gacaca*.

Three critical issues were identified. First, there needs to be a greater understanding of vendetta. What triggers homicide and what stops it? Second, the inclination to leap toward elections after extended and traumatic conflict is a mistake. There needs to be a pause in order for a society to redefine itself. We may come to regret that this did not happen in Nigeria after the death of military dictator Sani Abacha. Finally, the question of amnesty is pivotal. There was some transmission of informal assurance that Moi could step down without risking prosecution or violent reprisal. That same guarantee of a soft landing, it was widely acknowledged, must be granted to Robert Mugabe as part of a comprehensive solution in Zimbabwe.

Peace in Africa will depend on the immediate cessation of hostilities, the institutionalization of democracy and a halt in cross-border hostilities. African and Western governments and international organizations have roles to play in order to move all these issues forward. Session Three addressed the division of labour in promoting peace on the continent. The discussion considered the separate but symbiotic roles of the international community, regional organizations, national governments and political parties, business and civil society.

When things go wrong in a country, the crisis is usually met by two responses. First, international and/or regional paralysis. Second, late and limited intervention with an emphasis on ending hostilities and moving toward premature elections. At all levels – international, regional and national – lack of leverage is often offered up as an excuse for inaction. This was rigorously denounced. Leverage does not just occur. It must be created through the difficult and sustained application of both hard and soft power. The costs of delay, furthermore, are high: States are at their most vulnerable when new governments come in or old governments are dying out. Much more work needs to be done much earlier in identifying the different roles of different players and in how to co-ordinate them within a comprehensive peace plan. A challenge was raised also about the current orthodoxy of conflict resolution through dialogue. History records that military victory most often results in sustainable peace. Are we undermining lasting stability by imposing coerced settlements before all incentives for conflict have been exhausted?

The peacekeeping mission in the DRC provides a case study in both the challenges and opportunities for building peace from within and without. The United Nations was characteristically slow in intervening, and its response was incommensurate with the complexity of the problem, reflecting the lack of political will to engage in a war of such complexity. But there was and remains an important failure of capacity, too: the UN has no intelligence-gathering unit. The regional response, on the other hand, was more encouraging. Although the UN operation will oversee the country's progress toward elections scheduled for 2005, it was argued that the process has been quintessentially African. South Africa shepherded simultaneous peace initiatives among the warring parties both in the DRC and Burundi. The key challenge now, as indicated in the morning's opening session, is to take a multi-dimensional approach to implementing the peace accords. That requires building state institutions and stabilizing the economy. Once again, the UN's inability to gather intelligence and its failure to put together a coherent strategy in the DRC casts doubt over the viability of the intervention.

In the first decade following the end of the Cold War, decision-making with regard to conflict intervention in Africa – particularly in Washington – was highly idiosyncratic. Levels of US engagement were erratic and episodic; operations were constrained by resource limitations; the administration showed low tolerance for failure and deep distrust of African regional organizations; there was scant commitment to building and using leverage and insufficient strategizing on multilateral approaches to peace. That is beginning to change. Partnership is developing as the model for conflict resolution (see below for a discussion the strengths and weaknesses of partnership), the characteristics of which include: an appropriate division of labour; co-ordination and discipline among parties; use of leverage; enhanced insider knowledge; greater advance planning of peace-keeping operations; and increased interest in dealing with security reform and economic reconstruction. Despite resources limitations resulting from the operations in Iraq and Afghanistan, it was suggested that global terrorism would impel consistent growth in US-Africa engagement.

At the regional level, meanwhile, important changes are beginning to take place. Two elements determine the nature of intervention by regional organizations: One, whether the state in question can maintain peace without the need for intervention from its neighbours. Two, whether the conflict within one state will spill over into another. Prior to the metamorphosis of the Organization of African Unity (OAU) into the African Union (AU), the guiding principle was non-intervention. But over the past fifteen years Africa has gradually moved into a new era defined by the rising prominence of regional and continental institutions: Nepad, the AU, the Peace and Security Council, the African parliament, African courts and so on. While these structures are nascent and still largely ineffective, it is expected that over time they will play increasingly important roles in early conflict warning and post-conflict reconstruction. One of the key limiting factors of regional organizations lies in their origin: as creations of states, their agendas more often reflect national interest rather than a collective agenda. Consequently, not enough work is being done at this level in anticipation of what will inevitably come in a post-Mugabe Zimbabwe.

Concerns were raised about the role and function of donors, which are not to set policy, but rather to assist and advise. Governments must have ownership of the peace plan. The same concerns were applied to foreign non-governmental organizations.

Finally, business needs to be integrated more formally into conflict resolution. Behind every military insurrection in Africa is a business-person seeking political and economic gain. Extractive industries are particularly destabilizing. If they are not alive to their social responsibilities, business-people and companies are probably stalking trouble. That said, business thrives best in politically stable environments, and thus there is a lot that business can bring to the peace table. It should play a role in stabilizing party politics. It compensates for the weakness of governments in archiving the lessons of experience. Part of the equation of bringing business into post-conflict reconstruction plans is gaining a better understanding of corruption. As a rule, big companies are increasingly self-policing. For those that follow long-term strategies, corruption undermines their viability. The two key problems are what to do about the rogue actors, and what to do about indirect corruption – the mishandling of funds paid to the state predominantly through extractive industries like oil and diamonds. Again, the most effective solutions probably lay in coherent, multi-dimensional responses.

Hennie Kotze ended the first day with a presentation of the results of 'African Elite Perspectives: AU and Nepad', a survey of decision-makers in the public and private sectors in seven African countries (South Africa, Nigeria, Senegal, Algeria, Kenya, Uganda and Zimbabwe). The survey found *inter alia* that the success of these two initiatives depends to a large degree on the extent of African ownership and control. Confidence in the AU and Nepad among civil society was generally found to be weaker than support from public servants. In all of the countries except Zimbabwe, the elites surveyed believed their governments had the capacity to implement Nepad policies, but only the respondents in South Africa and Uganda expressed confidence in their leaders to actually meet the goals and pledges of the AU and Nepad.

Saturday 1 May 2004

African police, military and intelligence agencies often function poorly. As a result, many governments are continually at risk of small groups of rebels, organized crime faces little resistance and terrorists are able to find sanctuary. Session Four explored how to promote the effectiveness of African security organizations.

The paper by John Mackinlay outlined how the threat to governance in Africa has changed with shifting geopolitical trends. Insurgencies, once dependent on mass popular support or, during the Cold War, Superpower

clientage, have learned to manipulate the advantages of globalization. Five key changes have fundamentally altered the balance between weak governments and rebel movements in favour of the latter:
- The proliferation of transportation systems in wilderness areas.
- The proliferation of mobile and deregulated communications systems.
- Deregulation of international markets and the simultaneous proliferation of information technology.
- An acceleration of rural to urban migration.
- The transfer of cultural values from one society to another, displacing traditional values and relationships and altering the way in which young people identify themselves.

Consequently, insurgencies are able to loot state resources and engage in direct trade more easily to fund their pursuits. The relationship between insurgencies and civilian populations has also changed dramatically. Popular support, once necessary, is irrelevant and civilians expendable. Guerrilla movements now are also far less idealistic. These changes have rapidly outpaced the international community's ability to respond and have made insurgencies far more dangerous.

Several solutions emerged in general discussion. First and foremost, security was identified as the bedrock of stability and good governance and democracy. That places primacy on building better national armies. African militaries range from the strong to the disorganized and weak. The strong understand their role as servants of the state. They understand the importance of civilian oversight. The weak are found generally to be in service to the regime. Correcting the relationship is the first step. Governments need to openly discuss threats and resources with their militaries. They must also arm, train and pay them adequately. Some states are developing codes of conduct for their armed forces. The lack of ideological drive among insurgencies makes them more unpredictable, but their lack of coherence and principle also renders them easier for strong states to defeat. It should also be understood that globalization provides at least as many new opportunities to strengthen national armies as it does to insurgencies to flourish.

Strong governance is critical to the adequate supply of resources. In economically stable societies, the elite and middle class live off the profits of the productive sector. This ensures growth, opportunity and provision. African societies too often reverse this model, organizing themselves in such a way that the elite and middle class live by taxing the productive sector. This results in a culture of exclusion, loss of economic output and an inability of states to finance their military and security sectors. The right politics are also crucial to international economic and security partnerships. When not a single African state is willing to condemn Mugabe, foreign engagement is less likely. It is, furthermore, impossible to control small arms – the greatest security threat – in weak states that lack the ability to cut supply by regulating intermediary transport and merchandising.

This is where Nepad has a contribution to make. The articulation of commitment to good governance, peace and security, human rights and democracy marks the beginning of Africa's attempt to claim ownership of its problems as well as the solutions to those problems. While there is no blueprint to solving Africa's problems, it was argued that progress cannot be made while there remains a kind of mental rot from within – resignation to negative fate; dependency on external intervention; and leadership that is devoid of vision, confidence and integrity.

These are pivotal concepts at a time when Africa has collectively committed itself to a fundamentally different paradigm of diplomacy. The Constitutive Act of the African Union stipulates intervention. Continental leaders are debating the terms of membership in the African Peace and Security Council – for example, should there be permanent members – but a much more basic issue arises. Whereas the widespread fragility of African states necessitates strong regional organizations, weak states undermine the coherence and capacity of regional structures. The critical challenge lies in theatre, where the making of competent militaries beholden to strong democratic governments remains the cornerstone of stability.

Invariably, international developments affect the poor countries of Africa. New approaches to fighting corruption will affect attempts at governance reform. How Western countries conceptualize security challenges will also alter the opportunities and constraints faced by African leaders. Western evaluations of the international trade regime will have a potentially dramatic effect on the international orientations of many countries in sub-Saharan Africa. Session Five surveyed these and other ramifications of global developments on Africa.

In his preparatory paper, Richard Cobbold presented a synopsis of comparative risks, trends and discontinuities. The actions and reactions of 11 September 2001 changed the world, and currently Africa receives insufficient international attention. If peacekeeping fatigue sets in as a result of over-extension, Africa may become a more dangerous place. Weak states provide linkages to corruption, criminality, ethnic conflict, terrorism and trafficking in people, drugs, arms, diamonds and oil. Small arms and other weapons of aggregated individual destruction – machetes, for example – pose the greatest threat in terms of deaths caused.

Global terrorism is exportable to Africa, but it is also containable. Providing safe haven for terrorists is risky business. Strong governments are needed to combat terrorism. Pragmatism calls for a resilient tough response to crime and the causes of crime. Security is a prerequisite for social security. Intelligence is the key to security in Africa. Information technology and globalization should have a levelling effect in Africa over time. Militaries must be transformed to use symmetrical capacities in an asymmetric environment for peace support operations. International co-operation in both its military and non-military aspects is essential.

The general discussion considered the prospects, conditionalities and influencing factors of international engagement in Africa in the current global context. From the US military's perspective, Iraq and the war on terrorism will have an ongoing impact on Africa as force capacity continues to be stretched. The peace process in Sudan could be a casualty of this limitation. On the domestic side, growing deficits and the 2004 presidential election will complicate budgetary considerations. But that is not to say that the West, and particularly the US, will disengage from Africa. Both the US and Britain have established special executive advisory councils on Africa under their current administrations.

The question is on what terms engagement will take place: Africa of the '*bads*' or Africa of the '*goods*'? In other words, is the case for engagement defined by expectations of potential benefit or threat? The discussion considered responses to this question from the international strategic, diplomatic and business perspectives.

The discussion focused first on the *bads*: the threats of disease, terrorism and corruption. The removal of Saddam Hussein from power has not only created space for change in Iraq but also unleashed a struggle for the future of Islam between moderate and theocratic Muslims. As that struggle becomes more violent, it will also become more polarized. Moderate Muslim governments in African countries like Mali and Mauritania will feel more pressure as radicals infiltrate the polity and society. These and the more hard-line Muslim states are logical places for terrorists to seek refuge. That has not become a large problem yet, but there is evidence of more resilient logistical support and recruitment activity. There is also a discernible rise in rhetoric from radical fringe groups and the corresponding decentralization of Al-Qa'ida. Indicatively, the bombers of Madrid were Moroccan.

Another potentially disruptive trend in Africa that stems from the deepening crises in the Middle East is growing interest in oil. Global price flux is pushing companies to increase exploration of land-based and offshore reserves in Africa. Equatorial Guinea and São Tomé have already manifested the destabilizing effects arising from competition for exploration rights.

These trends are rekindling US strategic interest in ungoverned or weakly governed space – which defines much of Africa. Washington is reposturing its forces globally, with specific attention on strategic choke points. For the first time since 1975, the US is re-establishing a long-term presence in the Horn and has dedicated US$50 million annually to increased counter-terrorism and global security measures in Africa. The Bush administration has also committed to a long-term security relationship in Liberia and is expanding ties with its European partners to strengthen the Economic Community of West African States (ECOWAS).

Diplomatic engagement is marked by the application of both hard and soft power – conditionalities, on the one hand, and investment on the other. Bargaining between the West and Africa is beginning to shift away from a period of high conditionality. It is acknowledged that external micro-management of African economies, exemplified in the structural adjustment programmes imposed by the International Monetary Fund, does not work. Donors are inching toward a healthier relationship influenced by the goals and principles of Nepad. More specifically, the Millennium Challenge Account (MCA), an initiative announced in March 2002 by President Bush, represents a new type of Western evaluation of African indicators. If approved by Congress, the MCA would increase US spending on foreign aid by US$5 billion over three years. As Jeffrey Herbst pointed out in his preparatory paper, participation rests on 'a transparent evaluation of a country's performance on sixteen economic and political indicators, divided into three clusters corresponding to the three policy areas of governance, economic policy, and investment in people'. Countries must score above the median on half the indicators. Corruption, however, is singled out. States that fail to control corruption are automatically disqualified from the MCA irrespective of their performance on the other indicators. The effect this will have on aid distribution is apparent. Countries that are performing well will benefit; countries that are not will be left behind. That, in turn, presents a diplomatic quandary: Aiding the winners raises a question about what to do with the losers.

In what amounts to a significant shift away from the 'African solutions for African problems' approach, the new model for failed small states involves large-scale involvement from the colonial power. But the international community seems far less certain in its response to failed big states. The regional impact of large-state failure is clear: when the anchor state breaks down, the region disintegrates. The consequences for the broader international community are far less certain. Given that terrorists need the same resources as everyone else – transportation infrastructure, communications networks and financial institutions – it may not be true that they will seek haven in large failed states in significant numbers.

Soft-power engagement, meanwhile, is influenced by the vocabulary of the dialogue between the West and Africa. On the positive side, the past fifteen years has witnessed the elimination of virtually all anti-democratic language on the continent. It has become the norm that democratically elected governments should not be overthrown. In that respect, the vocabulary of the dialogue has been harmonized. Africa has also made significant strides in the past few years in harmonizing its response to HIV/AIDS with the West. Economically and strategically, however, Africa still uses a very different vocabulary with regard to personal safety (which has declined immensely) and globalization and market reforms. As a rule, those states that use the same vocabulary as the West will be pulled along, while those that do not will experience a more halting relationship.

Encouraging more equitable and constructive business engagement remains an urgent requirement. On this front the West continues to drag its heels – most notably on the prickly dispute over grossly disproportionate agricultural subsidies. It was argued that greater recognition of Africa's potential is needed. That may be only partly true. American corporate engagement in Africa reflects miscalculations of opportunity, certainly, but it also reflects informed caution. Return and risk are not equal in Africa. If African business does not invest domestically, it sends a negative message to potential foreign investors.

On a more constructive note, joint ventures present one way around the tense US debate over trade *versus* protectionism. Denel and General Dynamics, for example, have partnered to develop responsible security resources in fragile countries to contribute to stability, democracy and protection of human rights. In South Africa, however, rising anti-Americanism has become a barrier to partnership.

Robert Schrire examined the record of the African National Congress (ANC) during its first decade in government in dealing with the legacy of apartheid and establishing the basis of deracialized democracy in South Africa. His paper (which is not included in this volume) noted that apartheid rested on three pillars:

- Policies of prejudice – The Group Areas Act, The Immorality Act,

segregated schools and beaches.
- Policies of power – White control of all aspects of government, including the courts, civil service and military.
- Polices of privilege – White control of all economic concerns, including commerce and land ownership.

The past decade has seen a remarkably smooth transition whereby the edifice of prejudice has disappeared. Although prejudice itself remains, it has been depoliticized and privatized. The only legitimate paradigm now is that of 'non-racialism'. The ANC has generally adopted a cautious approach to transformation marked by compromise and inclusiveness. It has sought a careful balance between creating a just society and promoting economic efficiency. Public and private institutions are being Africanized, but only gradually. Land reform has been marked by no abiding sense of urgency. Black economic empowerment has not derailed the private sector. Labour reform has been fairly radical, but pursued within a sound macroeconomic framework. Corruption is limited. The result is that the ANC has consolidated and centralized power. It grew its majority in the 2004 elections and now controls all nine provinces for the first time. This may continue, but it is not certain whether the ANC's policies have thus far been manifestations of insecurity or whether they reflect inherent values.

The socio-economic system, however, is not reflected in the politics. Most blacks are worse off today than they were 10 years ago. Despite the rise of a small black elite, the prevailing wealth gap remains racially defined: the average black household is 20% worse off in terms of income while the average white household is 15% better off. Unemployment is 60% among blacks, but only 5% to 8% among whites. As a result, South Africa ranks 51st of 173 nations in terms of gross national product, but 107th of 173 countries on the UN human development index. The ANC's hegemony, therefore, is deceptive.

Several questions arise. Can the gap between white affluence and black poverty be narrowed? Can tension between black economic power and white economic power be managed? Can race and ethnicity be kept off the agenda? Is ANC dominance necessary for, or a threat to, democracy? What will be the impact of changing demographics – i.e. youth urbanization? Can unemployment be reduced substantially and the profound implications of the HIV/AIDS epidemic managed? Will opposition emerge from the left or the right inside the ruling party?

On the negative side, the ANC drifts toward authoritarianism in the absence of a strong opposition. The party's strength at the polls masks weaknesses in popular support and the state becomes ungovernable. On the positive side, however, democracy is becoming institutionalized. New alliances emerge and power distribution is redefined. Stability requires either improved life prospects for the poor or an inability of radicals to mobilize the poor. The future has not been written, but there are important reasons to be optimistic. The ANC does not at this point display a sense of entitlement to power. There is an abiding national sense that the people – not the party – liberated the country. South Africa is a sophisticated, self-correcting society with a vibrant civil society and strong commitment to constitutionalism.

Earlier discussions highlighted a need for further specific dialogue on Zimbabwe. A roundtable was assembled for those interested in debating problem-solving approaches. Two strategies were considered. The first was resolution by negotiation. This is the current approach of the South African government, which remained convinced that the people of Zimbabwe must be encouraged to find the solution themselves through talks. That, after all, was the approach that proved successful in South Africa a decade ago. Despite optimistic predictions from some that the two sides were moving closer toward a formal process in Zimbabwe, the roundtable quickly formed a consensus that change through negotiation was a dead strategy. While South Africa continues to work quietly behind the scenes with both parties, Pretoria's rhetoric does not match what the parties themselves say inside Zimbabwe. Zanu-PF has become triumphalist in the wake of a recent urban by-election victory and conveys the attitude that it needs neither to make concessions nor seek external intervention.

The second approach considered was electoral. The next parliamentary poll is due to be held in March 2005. The international community should now work urgently to ensure that this ballot is conducted as smoothly as possible. Zimbabwe must therefore be put on the South African Development Community (SADC) agenda and regional actors, together with their international counterparts, should identify the five or ten key standards, taken from the SADC Parliamentary Forum Norms and Standards for Elections, that must be implemented. These include early and unimpeded access for monitoring teams and the media and UN supervision of the process

This approach would allow the international community to take a more proactive stance. It requires, however, that South Africa take the lead – where Pretoria goes, SADC will follow – and there currently is no indication that the Mbeki administration is open to such a policy shift. Were this strategy to be adopted, the key question would be whether the international community is prepared to uphold the standards it imposes. Significant divergences among observer missions after the 2002 presidential election prevented a coherent judgment, making universal condemnation of obvious electoral fraud impossible and selected team condemnation inconsequential. Elections themselves, it was also argued, would be useless if not part of a broader transitional agreement.

Sunday 2 May 2004

In the closing session, Ethiopian State Minister for Foreign Affairs Tekada Alemu examined the key principles of partnership at the country, regional and international level. Broadly speaking, partnership must be based on mutual co-operation. The interconnectedness of nations and the global nature of security threats results in a situation where even the most powerful states need the co-operation of the manifestly weak to achieve peace and stability. Weaker states, however, must not tend toward seeing the benefits of partnership with their stronger counterparts – and indeed the partnership itself – as an entitlement. Both sides must be worthy of the relationship.

There is no hope of peace and development without strong partnership at the country level among government, the private sector and civil society. National consensus requires even that ruling and opposition parties forge constructive engagement. It follows that if the private sector does not invest in its home country, neither will foreigners. All too often, parties have more confidence in foreign partners than in their domestic counterparts. At the regional level, partnership is critical to establishing and maintaining peace, which in turn is a precondition for economic development. Finally, the escalation of Islamist terrorism provides a self-evident rationale for partnerships at the international level. Economic development in Africa is in the direct interest of the international community and is therefore an international challenge. However, African states must take responsibility for creating conditions for successful development in order for international engagement to have a meaningful impact.

The ensuing discussion identified two primary characteristics of effective partnerships: they are mutual – both sides bring something to the table – and they are voluntary. They furthermore stem from a desire to achieve something greater than either party can achieve independently.

Several factors affect the formation of viable partnerships. Relationships among domestic parties are often more problematic than partnerships between international parties due to internal competition at the country level. Resource constraints hamper the attainment of goals. Differing thresholds of intervention frustrate engagement at the international level. The reluctance of ECOWAS to apply sanctions against Charles Taylor, for example, complicated intervention by Britain and the United States in Sierra Leone and Liberia respectively. Another problem is the temptation to be overwhelmed by the enormity of the task. The parties must be able to take initial steps even if the ultimate solution is not yet apparent. Communication and trust are essential. Partnerships must begin with agreement of interests and intent and identification of tactical requirements. Does the objective require a long-term or short-term partnership? Is the relationship able to adapt to Africa's ever-changing situations? It was generally agreed that consistent, quiet engagement is essential. Turning the tap on and off is counterproductive.

What do we mean by the term 'partnership' in the African context? What are obligation and mutuality? Would the concept of 'embedded support' be accepted by African leaders as a model for partnership or regarded as a form of neo-colonialism? There is a need for Africa to take ownership of problems and solutions. African leaders persist in a mentality of dependence. External funding, however, leads to a condition of lopsidedness in relationships at the international level. Partnerships in Africa, it was argued, should therefore begin at home. Nepad is one such attempt to redefine partnerships according to African conditions. The UN had a special role to play in enforcing the conditionalities of partnership especially when the parties were in dispute or failing to meet the obligations of the relationship.

The meeting ended on a cautionary note. The ascendancy of partnerships as the model for international engagement notwithstanding, it was observed that Africa is, in fact, over-invested in partnerships and the returns were exceptionally low. It is not possible to overcome national deficiencies through international partnership. At the international level, Nepad is in danger of becoming an NGO given its dependence on external funding. At the country level, Nepad is a resource drain. Would the returns not be higher if governments prioritized their own national education systems?

Engagement with Africa has long been defined by a combination of benevolence and historical attachment and sentiment. The breaking down of notions of African uniformity and geography, while counter to African political practice, may well stimulate a new intellectual rather than geographic paradigm of external engagement and partnership, one based firmly on issues and interests, and thus of enduring and dynamic mutual benefit.

Section 1

African Conflict Resolution

The Rwanda Genocide – Ten Years On
Charles Murigande

There is no greater crime than genocide. It is absolute terror, committed against humanity by humanity. The horrific events of 1994 in our country, in which an estimated one million people were murdered, were deliberate, premeditated and cold-blooded. This is not a chapter in the history of our country that can easily be forgotten. That is why the last ten years have been a series of challenges for all of us in Rwanda as we sought to uplift ourselves from the legacy of the genocide and together strive to rebuild a stable, peaceful and prosperous Rwanda.

When the Government of National Unity was formed in July 1994, Rwanda was in utter anarchy. We had just lost one million of our people and most survivors had had many brushes with death and had seen their relatives killed. There was total displacement of the population. Over three million people had sought refuge in neighbouring countries, and many more were internally displaced. There were countless numbers of orphans, widows and widowers, thousands of handicapped people and generally a very vulnerable population. A cloud of insecurity loomed over Rwanda, as the former soldiers and the militia reorganized themselves, intent on continuing their genocidal campaign with the support of the then Zaire, now the Democratic Republic of Congo (DRC), and their many friends in the international community.

Law and order had completely broken down. Large-scale atrocities were still going on in parts of the country. All national law enforcement agencies and judicial institutions had ceased to exist and the system of administration of justice had come to a complete standstill. Social and economic infrastructure was in a state of collapse. All economic indicators showed a desperate situation, with the inflation standing at 65 per cent, and most economic activity having ground to a complete halt. Neither schools nor hospitals were functioning. The civil service had been decimated or its

---

Dr Charles Murigande is the Foreign Minister of the Republic of Rwanda.

membership had fled into exile.

This is the terrible situation we inherited. In fact many diplomats, politicians and scholars around the world doubted that Rwanda would ever become once again one nation and suggested that our country be divided into *Hutuland* and *Tutsiland*. From this account, a casual or distant observer might wish to ask how and why this could happen. At a time when human civilization was celebrating knowledge and numerous achievements never before attained by preceding generations, Rwanda was forcefully engaged in auto-destruction.

Genocide and its aftermath in our country demands an understanding of the context as well as the facts that have shaped our society in a long history that spans centuries. While there is no scope in this paper for a long discussion of Rwandan history, even a brief summary would make clear that our nation was never an aggregate of brute savages, inclined to kill each other at the slightest opportunity. This outlook of a dark continent where primitiveness prevails, long popularized mainly by Western anthropology and sociology, and echoed by some in African scholarship, has evident faults and must be discarded.

The different sections of Rwandans, Bahutu, Batutsi and Batwa, are and were, until the colonial adventure, Banyarwanda – Rwandan people. The governance structures and processes in pre-colonial Rwanda, despite inherent weaknesses and inequalities typical of such a pre-industrial society, offered a minimum of stability and slow, but constant progress.

Never before did those in seats of power engage in premeditated schemes to isolate and destroy a section of the Rwandan society. Neither had ordinary people ever engaged in massive slaughter as they did in 1994, at the instigation of and mobilization by the state machinery.

The 1994 genocide was the result of a failure in the colonial and post-colonial governments' mandate to protect and defend all citizens. It is, therefore, a failure that has both external and local dimensions. The external failure relates to the German and Belgian colonial policies that, like elsewhere in Africa, created ethnic, tribal or clan divisions as an instrument of colonial rule.

The local factors, on the other hand, became predominant after independence in 1962 when the local elite became tools of continuing colonial-era policies, this time for their own benefit. Once terror and mass murder were introduced in 1959 under the auspices of the Belgian administration, subsequent regimes tried genocide in their exercise of power. The period 1959 to 1994 is indeed a history of genocide in slow motion.

Once we fully understood that genocide was a human phenomenon, albeit an ugly and unnecessary one, we were determined to offer a better chance for our society to move beyond death and destruction to post-genocide reconstruction. Against incredible odds, we have succeeded in laying a firm foundation for Rwanda's cultural, social, economic and political transformation. All our eyes are set on the most important prize of the current and successive generations: a united, stable, and prosperous Rwanda; a nation in which good governance and the rule of law are the rule rather than the exception.

To this effect, after 1994, we quickly realized that our mission would be to restore hope to our people and to enable the Rwandan people to be in control once again and to shape their destiny as they had done century after century. Despite these immense challenges, we have restored peace and brought stability to Rwanda through sheer hard work and determination of the Rwandan people, and through the support of our friends.

The Government of National Unity, made up of a coalition of political parties, repatriated and resettled over three and a half million refugees. We have integrated into our armed forces over twenty thousand officers and men of the former army. We have restored public trust in the legal system and were thus able to avoid revenge for the genocide. We have instituted reforms to guarantee independence of the judiciary. Our law enforcement agencies and judicial institutions are now, by and large, evolving to become more and more credible and effective.

The long established culture of impunity, that encouraged past human rights abuses and was in part responsible for the 1994 genocide, has at last been broken. An organic law on the crime of genocide and crimes against humanity was adopted in 1996 to punish all those who committed the crime of genocide and other crimes against humanity. A system of participatory justice known as *Gacaca* has also been established. This system allows Rwandans to establish the truth about the 1994 genocide and contributes to the trial and judgment of those suspected of genocide and other crimes against humanity. Security for persons and property is now at all times guaranteed for everyone and everywhere throughout the country. We have put in place institutions which will make transparency and accountability the cornerstone of our agenda. In the same vein, a policy of decentralization has been introduced in our country, geared for the first time towards putting our people at the centre of decision-making and of our development process.

We have created a stable macroeconomic environment, and have reduced inflation from 65 per cent after the genocide, to under 5 per cent in the last five years. In the last three years we have consecutively registered over 6 per cent GDP growth. We have created an environment attractive to foreign local investors, and we have embarked upon a strategy to invest in human resources development, infrastructure, and the mainstay of our people's livelihood – agriculture. All this is part of our strategy to reduce poverty in our country.

Our strategy has been to adopt an integrated, locally driven approach to solving our problems, in partnership with all the stakeholders. We have paid particular attention to governance issues: unity and reconciliation and human rights. With the social stability slowly recovered, we embarked on an ambitious programme of democratization. In 1999 and 2001 we organized local and communal elections. A constitutional commission was put in place in 2001 and broadly consulted the Rwandan people, including those in prison for the crime of genocide and the Rwandan Diaspora, on how Rwanda should be governed in order to prevent genocide.

The new constitution was adopted in a referendum in May 2003, followed by the first ever pluralistic and peaceful parliamentary and presidential elections in the history of Rwanda. Despite the tremendous progress we have made in the various sectors, Rwanda still has a long way to go. However, the transformation of our country has begun. We will continue to work with our African neighbours to promote the philosophy of a borderless Africa through, among other things, integrated regional markets, based on a development agenda of uplifting the African people from poverty, and as encapsulated in the New Partnership for Africa's Development (Nepad).

The 1994 genocide in Rwanda, our reconstruction effort since then, and the corresponding behaviour of the international community challenge all of us to think and act creatively. We need to create, grow and nurture shared values at national, regional, continental and global levels. But to change the world, we need to understand it as well. We live in times of rapid change in which the conventional norms of international behaviour based on the sovereign nation-state attract divided opinion. The reordering of the new international system evokes debate regarding how our world will look in the twenty-first century. The contending schools of thought that favour everything from the isolated nation-state acting in absolute national interest, to a very ordered world, acting multilaterally, show that the character of the state is one of the central concerns of our challenging times.

Where common threats like terrorism, weapons of mass destruction, and genocide exist, does not a common opportunity exists for us to act together in the interest of all humanity? Was genocide exclusively a Rwandan affair? If we postulate that people and their interests are sovereign, to what extent must the states and the international community deploy their capabilities, individually and collectively, to ensure this sovereignty?

Contrary to the view that the nation-state is in retreat, effective states and national institutions could become the pillars of a just, peaceful, secure, and prosperous world. The case for creating strong and effective multilateral institutions stems from the fact that international public good cannot be produced entirely by lone nation states. The imperative to create a just and effective international order requires us to seek results and not rhetoric. These results include, but are not limited to:

- reforming the international system so that we respond early enough to prevent or stop deadly crises such as genocide and international terrorism;
- creating active and effective global partnerships with local building blocks, against transnational problems such as HIV/AIDS, narcotics and environmental degradation;
- bridging the digital divide, and accelerating poverty reduction;
- redressing the imbalances in Foreign Direct Investment (FDI) and Official Development Assistance (ODA); and
- accessing markets and removing the effects of subsidies in rich countries.

Our view is that a world where the majority live on less than one dollar per day, and a small minority is very rich, is very unsafe. Such a world is dangerously prone to manipulation by those whose interest in violence, terror and genocide outweighs their interest in humanity.

Rwanda's modest triumph over the evil of genocide is not unique. It is still testimony to mankind's will to survive, demonstrated time and time again in human history. Humanity has the capacity to act collectively, and when that capacity is harnessed, we can win together.

Sierra Leone – 'Pregnant with Lessons?'

David Richards

Background

The British academic and strategist Richard Connaughton has described the conflict in Sierra Leone as one that is 'pregnant with lessons'.[1] There are compelling reasons for believing he may be right. Whether one is examining the reasons why Sierra Leone descended into the abyss it did in the nineties, the role of the Economic Community of West African States (ECOWAS) and its armed monitoring group (ECOMOG) in nearly bringing order to the country on three occasions, the UN's initial inability to stabilize the country, the role of the British, or the persistent failure of the international community to build on an improving security environment, there is certainly no shortage of relevant topics to study and from which to learn.

Sierra Leone's civil war began in March 1991 when a small armed group known as the Revolutionary United Front (RUF), accompanied by Liberian fighters and Burkinabe mercenaries, entered south-eastern Sierra Leone from Liberia. Their stated aim was to overthrow President Momoh's corrupt government and they claimed their larger goal was a radical, pan African revolution based upon the Libyan Gaddafi model. Foday Sankoh and other leading figures in the RUF were heavily dependent on Charles Taylor of Liberia. They had all met in the mid 1980s while undergoing guerrilla training in Libya and Burkina Faso. Taylor launched his own attack on Liberia in 1989 but was thwarted in large part by ECO-

---

Major-General David Richards is currently the British Army's Assistant Chief of the General Staff. In the period 1998 to 2001, he commanded the UK's Joint Force Headquarters, in which guise he took part in a number of military operations around the world. These included command of the British force in East Timor in 1999 and command of the British intervention in Sierra Leone in 2000. In his official capacity he has visited a number of African countries, including South Africa, Mozambique, Kenya, Rwanda, Ghana, Guinea, Gambia and Senegal.

MOG, the West African intervention force, led by Nigeria, sent to Liberia. Taylor's support for the RUF was reputedly motivated by a desire to punish the government of Sierra Leone for its participation in ECOMOG. More importantly, he aimed to prevent Sierra Leone from being used as a base by his Liberian opponents, the United Liberation Movement for Democracy (ULIMO), as well as to acquire diamonds and other plunder to finance his own campaign and subsequent regime.

The next nine years of civil war in Sierra Leone consisted of immensely complex and fluid forming and reforming of alliances among the different parties striving to control the spoils of the state. For present purposes it is not necessary to track all the twists and turns of these years, but the broad outline is needed in order to understand how the international community in general and the British in particular came to the aid of President Ahmed Tejan Kabbah in May 2000.

On 29 April 1992, a group of young Sierra Leone Army (SLA) officers, disillusioned with his government, overthrew President Joseph Saidu Momoh in a military coup. However, the new National Provisional Ruling Council (NPRC) administration, consisting of eighteen military officers and four civilians headed by Captain Valentine Strasser, soon adopted a style reminiscent of its predecessors. It also suffered a series of military defeats at the hands of the RUF. Despite military government and the expansion of the SLA from 3 000 to over 13 000, the RUF advanced to within a few kilometres of Freetown, the country's capital. Moreover, it became increasingly apparent that the SLA often avoided fighting the RUF. Some army and rebel commanders even reached informal understandings not to confront one another. Both sides lived off the countryside, murdering, plundering, looting and abusing the civilian population. Militarily, neither side was able consistently to achieve an advantage.

Valentine Strasser was ousted in January 1996 in a bloodless coup led by Brigadier-General Julius Maada Bio. Bio undertook to permit the elections scheduled for February 1996 to go ahead. The oldest political party in Sierra Leone, the Sierra Leone Peoples' Party (SLPP) won 36.1 per cent of the legislature vote. Its presidential candidate, Kabbah, a UN development worker[2] and veteran politician, won 59.49 per cent of the presidential votes

---

[1] Discussion between the author and Richard Connaughton, Freetown Sierra Leone 28 October 2000.

[2] Kabbah had worked for the UN for 22 years before returning to Sierra Leone in 1992.

in a run-off second round election in March. This election and these figures are important because, along with the evidence of the infringement of fundamental human rights (through torture, mutilation and the recruitment of child soldiers), it underpins the international case supporting Kabbah rather than any of the other factions competing with him.

At the end of 1996 a peace agreement was made between Kabbah and Sankoh, but in name only. Kabbah was doubtful of the loyalty of the SLA and used irregular Kamajor 'hunters' and mercenaries from the South African company Executive Outcomes[3] to wage bush war against the RUF, in which good progress was made for the first time. The Kamajor could match the RUF in knowledge of the forest tracks and so block their supply-routes. However, in May 1997 frustration in the armed forces resulted in another coup, led by Major Johnny-Paul Koroma. Kabbah was forced to flee to Guinea and the Armed Forces Revolutionary Council (AFRC), with Koroma at its head, entered into a power-sharing arrangement with the RUF.

There was widespread international condemnation of the coup. The United Nations mandated ECOMOG to intervene in order to restore Kabbah. The Nigerians, who provided the greatest part of ECOMOG, launched a fierce attack on Freetown in September 1997. In October, the AFRC/RUF government conceded. At Conakry a deal was struck which would give immunity to Koroma, a 'role' for Sankoh and a six months' period of transition to restore the Kabbah government. But the Conakry agreement did not hold. ECOMOG continued to fight Koroma's regime until it was overthrown in February 1998. Kabbah was restored in March that year.

However, the violence continued intermittently and with growing intensity. In January 1999 the RUF invaded Freetown and only narrowly failed to secure the city, killing and mutilating thousands in the process. A counter attack by a combination of ECOMOG, loyal SLA and Sierra Leonean irregulars including the Kamajor, known collectively as the Civil Defence Forces (CDF), pushed the RUF back into the countryside before the fighting subsided into months of indecisive stalemate. There were allegations of atrocities committed on all sides. Britain provided material assistance to the pro-Kabbah forces who, assisted by considerable international pressure, were able to force the RUF to negotiations that ended in

---

[3] These were the mercenaries who had restored Kabbah to power – a result which could not be deplored with conviction.

the Lomé agreement of 7 July. At Lomé, the RUF dropped their demand for the removal of the ECOMOG forces, which made way for an agreement to permit power-sharing. The terms gave the insurgents four key government posts and effective control over the country's mineral wealth. Also, significantly, there was to be a total amnesty for the RUF and the death sentence imposed on Sankoh was lifted.

Before being too critical of the government and international community's role in the Lomé Agreement, it should be emphasized just how low the country had fallen in the early part of 1999. The functions of state had practically collapsed with ministries in confusion and officials lacking any direction. The Ministry of Defence staff, for example, comprised three officials. Most businesses and government offices had been looted and vandalized during January's AFRC/RUF attack. There was no water, electricity or any other public services operating in Freetown. Large numbers of armed military, paramilitary, ex-SLA, civilians and CDF roamed the city, occupying buildings, manning checkpoints throughout the town and extorting money from the populace to permit passage. The Sierra Leone Police Force (SLP) was totally ineffective, untrusted and seemingly corrupt at every level. There was no communication to towns outside Freetown other than via radio and satellite telephone and no safe road access to the interior. 'Sierra Leone', stated *The Economist*, 'manifests all the continent's worst characteristics. It is an extreme, but not untypical example of a state with all the epiphenomena and none of the institutions of government. It is unusual only in its brutality: rape, cannibalism and amputation have been common, with children often among the victims'.[4] The life expectancy of the population was only forty-nine years. That population was desperate for peace and, albeit cautiously and with a scepticism born of previous failure, was prepared to give Sankoh a chance.

United Nations Involvement

The international community welcomed the Agreement, because at least it appeared to have stopped the fighting – an assumption that soon proved wrong; but the amnesty was heavily criticized and seen as a major victory for the RUF. On 3 October 1999 Sankoh and Koroma returned to Freetown and held a joint press conference with President Kabbah. They

---

[4] *The Economist*, 13 May 2000.

apologized for the atrocities carried out during the eight years of the civil war and promised to strive for a speedy implementation of the Lomé Agreement. On 22 October the Security Council unanimously adopted Resolution 1270 to establish a 6 000 member peacekeeping force to be known as the UN Mission in Sierra Leone (UNAMSIL) with a six-month mandate to oversee the implementation of Lomé. In December, the International Monetary Fund (IMF) approved 15.56 million SDRs (Special Drawing Rights) for post-conflict reconstruction. The wider international community at last appeared to be paying serious attention to Sierra Leone.

Following the Security Council resolution, the process of putting together the force elements for UNAMSIL began. In February 2000, as it became apparent that there would be a security vacuum with the phasing out of ECOMOG, the Security Council voted to increase the force from 6 000 to 11 000. But UNAMSIL forces[5] encountered difficulty as soon as they entered Sierra Leone; the RUF prevented Indian and Ghanaian elements from deploying to the eastern Bendu region. Furthermore UNAMSIL's commander, despite a Chapter VII mandate, interpreted his brief in a traditional UN peacekeeping manner, as one of neutrality between the parties. This seriously impeded the development of close relations with the democratically elected Kabbah government he had been sent to help and ensured little co-operation between the latter's army and the UN.

Matters did not improve for UNAMSIL. On the very day that ECOMOG officially transferred its duties to the international force, the RUF attacked Kenyan UN soldiers. On 4 May 2000, 208 Zambians who had been sent to relieve the Kenyans were taken hostage and their thirteen armoured personnel carriers were captured. On 6 May, 226 Zambians surrendered to the RUF, bringing the total number of hostages now held by them to over 500. The same day the Secretary-General of the UN requested that the United Kingdom and other countries act to improve the situation. On 6 May the RUF, using the captured APCs, began to advance on Freetown. Lunsar, on the approach road, fell to them and on 7 May the RUF were only forty kms away from the capital.

The UN mandate for UNAMSIL and Kofi Annan's urgent request must be seen in the context of acute and general recollection of the international community's failure to act in Rwanda. The UN report on general

---

[5] Contributors of Force Troops were: Bangladesh, Ghana, Guinea, India, Jordan, Kenya, Nigeria and Zambia.

failures over the crisis, including by its own organs, was widely praised for its candour. Annan in particular was applauded for ordering the enquiry since his own role at the time was subject to criticism. One of the decisions following the Rwandan crisis had been to establish a high-readiness brigade known as the Multinational Stand-by High Readiness Brigade for United Nations Operations (SHIRBRIG), but SHIRBRIG was not to be seen in Sierra Leone. Richard Connaughton cites a letter which he received from the military advisor to the United Nations Department of Peacekeeping Operations, Lieutenant-General Giulio Fraticelli, which explained that SHIRBRIG at that time was only available to Chapter VI (embargo and sanction) operations and that the Sierra Leone mandate was under Chapter VII (enforcement).[6] Since Chapter VI peacekeeping is initiated after due diplomatic process and with the consent of the parties involved, it is arguably the precise circumstance when there is no requirement for rapid reaction.

The British Intervention

The UN appeared powerless to stop the RUF and indeed started to evacuate their civilian staff from the country. The government and UNAMSIL seemed, and indeed believed themselves to be, on the verge of collapse. Into this deteriorating situation, on 5 May 2000 the British Government sent a military team to assess the situation and to recommend whether or not to respond to Annan's request. The team's commander advised in favour of intervention. Within thirty-six hours a sizeable British military force, that at its height grew to 5000 people, started to arrive. The British secured Lungi Airport and much of the Freetown Peninsula, including the site of UNAMSIL's HQ. With their vital ground secured for them, UNAMSIL was given a chance to regroup and reorganize.[7] Although dysfunctional for weeks, it was an opportunity to which, under great pressure from UN HQ in New York, they started to respond. Their evacuation was curtailed and

---

[6] Richard Connaughton, 'Military intervention and peace-keeping: the reality', *Joint Force Quarterly Review*, 26 July 2001.

[7] By chance Bernard Miyet, the head of the UN's Department of Peace Keeping Operations, was in Freetown when the British arrived. There is no doubt that his presence and pragmatism eased the way for what potentially could have been a very difficult relationship between the UN and UK forces. "The arrival of the British is good for us", said a UN spokesman, but there were initial problems, particularly with the Nigerians.

confidence slowly started to return.

What UNAMSIL could not, and would not, do was push the RUF back from their positions close to Freetown. To do this the British coordinated and sustained the efforts of a disparate grouping of Sierra Leoneans, largely CDF and ex-SLA, who remained loyal to their president. Guided at every level by British officers and NCOs, over the next few weeks they succeeded in securing much of the inland road route between Freetown and Lungi, relieving the military and political pressure on Freetown and its beleaguered government. The British themselves fought few battles directly although when they did their overwhelming firepower left no room for doubt in the minds of the RUF rank and file in particular. The RUF started to splinter into different factions and Taylor began to lose his grip. This at first *ad hoc* twin-track operation by the British, giving support to the UN on the one hand and assistance to the government of Sierra Leone on the other, soon became official strategy. To give it further effect, the UK deployed additional forces including a sizeable amphibious force.[8] The result was total psychological ascendancy over the RUF that bought the government and the UN the time they needed to reassert themselves. And perhaps more importantly, in a different psychological sense, was the impact of the UK's role on the mood of the people. They at last felt the glimmerings of genuine hope for the future, a feeling reinforced when many RUF leaders were detained, including, on 17 May, Foday Sankoh himself, taken into custody while trying to escape from Freetown.

By mid-June 2000 the security situation stabilized sufficiently to allow the British operation to be terminated, although the UK agreed to provide additional military support in the form of financial and training assistance to the new SLA, now renamed the Republic of Sierra Leone Armed Forces (RSLAF). Suspicion of the UK's motives dissipated with the departure of the main force. A German journalist who had arrived sceptical of the British a few weeks earlier caught the prevailing mood in Sierra Leone well:

> Intervention in the fate of Sierra Leone has also awakened suspicion of re-colonization. That may be. But this kind of intervention does have a certain charm – especially as the locals have given the Whites such a hearty reception whilst they fear their own soldiers and regard the Blue Helmets as useless. The withdrawal of the main British contingent has allayed any suspicion of over-presumptuousness – and makes the operation appear all the more justified.[9]

---

[8] HMS *Illustrious* arrived off Freetown on 11 May and the HMS *Ocean Group* on 14 May.
[9] M. Tkalec, 'Neocolonialism with a human face', *Berliner Zeitung* 21 June 2000.

Sequel

For a while, the security situation continued to improve as UNAMSIL finally began to deploy troops outside Freetown. But it soon became clear that they had neither the will nor the capability to push home their advantage. Nor, at that stage, was the fledgling RSLAF in a position to do better.

In early October 2000, the situation was deteriorating again. UNAMSIL, far from gaining strength and authority, appeared to be in danger of moving backwards, especially when India announced the withdrawal of its contingent. The RUF remained in control of over half the country and were strengthening their grip on some key areas, including the diamond producing regions needed to finance their operations. They showed no sign of returning to negotiations, and were beginning to expand their operations into Guinea. Charles Taylor continued actively to support them and seemed impervious to ill-coordinated attempts by the international community to bring him into line. The UK's efforts with the RSLAF were beginning to bear fruit but lacked a powerful coordinating headquarters to bring coherence to the work and to develop a plan to defeat the RUF, harnessing and informing other work at the strategic level.

The UK decided to send back to the country the same team that had succeeded in May, this time explicitly charged with developing a coherent plan that would ensure the RUF's defeat while devising a long-term solution that would ensure stability into the future. This work, combined with some bold initiatives by UNAMSIL's civilian and new military leadership, forced the RUF to sign a ceasefire agreement at Abuja on 10 November. The RUF's new leader, Issay Sessay, publicly conceded that the British commitment to Sierra Leone, and the opportunity it had provided the UN, was the distinguishing factor in their decision to seek a peaceful outcome. They had succumbed to the British aim of 'persuading the RUF of the inevitability of defeat'.[10] Although too much time was taken exploiting the agreement, this was a conspicuous success for the UN, the Sierra Leonean government and the UK. It signalled the end of the conflict and an opportunity to start bringing a real improvement to the lives of the long-suffering people of the country.

That process is still in train. Despite the security framework provided by the UN and the British-trained RSLAF and police, the country's

---

[10] The British Commander's direction to his force commanders, and specifically those officers with responsibility for the campaign's information operation – Freetown, 10 October 2000.

situation remains fragile. Although the country benefits from sizeable natural resources and a relatively well-educated populace committed to democracy, inward investment is too low to stimulate self-sustaining economic growth. The UK has so far failed to turn the RSLAF into a force confidently able to secure the country's borders. Five years on, in order to prevent the country slipping back, the UN mandate has had to be extended, albeit on a reduced scale. Standards of governance are only slowly improving and corruption is still endemic. Whilst the omens are broadly good, the jury on Sierra Leone is still out. Huge and continuing international expenditure on UNAMSIL and, by West African standards, on international aid has not yet succeeded in placing the country on a secure long term footing. Why not?

Lessons

The reader will have drawn many lessons from the above account, ranging from the essentially military through to broad issues of international behaviour and competence. My purpose is not to examine the military per se, although there is clearly a huge overlap with other areas. For those who do want to focus on this aspect, Richard Connaughton[11] and Professor Gwyn Prins of London University[12] both offer penetrating and highly readable analyses. How the UN's approach to peacekeeping might improve further is a fertile theme that they both exploit well. Here I want to look at the broader issue of how the international community might better go about assisting deeply failed states such as Sierra Leone. My thesis is, put simply, that in essence the international community is guilty of too much talk and not enough coherent and timely pre-emptive action. There is no shortage of analysis but implementation is something in which we are far less expert. Why are things moving so slowly in Sierra Leone and in many other countries whose populations deserve better? To find the answer requires a stern examination of how, firstly, to produce a coherent multi-dimensional plan tailored to the long-term needs of a particular country and, secondly, how to implement that plan energetically and coherently to ensure success. This absence of coherence has been a key failing in Sierra Leone and other failed or failing states.

---

[11] Connaughton, *Op. cit.* in note 6.
[12] Gwyn Prins, *The Heart of War* (London: Routledge, 2002).

But, before proceeding to offer solutions, what immediate lessons can be gleaned from Sierra Leone's experience?
- First of all, the right security environment (and thus 'the military') is as much a *sine qua non* for success in Africa as it is in any other region of the world. Conflict resolution may just be the start. If there is not enough money spent on a country's army and police, and this means investment in the round, not simply on equipment, then that army will soon bite the hand that inadequately feeds it.
- Secondly, and self-evidently, a good military creating a secure environment will not alone solve a country's problems. It is fundamental to progress but it must be part of a much broader effort across a range of interdependent dimensions – political, diplomatic, legal, economic, industrial, humanitarian, as well as military. Whilst this is well understood, too often the actors in these different areas work narrowly within their own discipline, even parochially; blind to the requirement to ensure their work remains coherent with the overall effort. This need for much greater intra-government and agency coherence is critical to future success.
- Thirdly, when solutions are eventually agreed they are applied far too slowly. In the military, the concept of tempo – acting relatively quicker than one's opponent – is recognized as vital to success. When one fails to achieve this, the initiative is lost and the enemy will surely win. On a variation of this theme, in Sierra Leone it became clear too often that well-intentioned solutions were being overtaken by events. Applied too late, they would become irrelevant, often aggravating the new problem.
- Fourthly, bureaucratic inertia and incompetence is endemic and positively inimical to progress. Worse, it is clear that sometimes those responsible for solving problems deliberately take longer than they might because the problem they are charged with solving is their working life, income and even *raison d'etre*. This is a recurring criticism of many UN workers.
- Lastly, NGOs are often less effective than they should be because they suffer from the same institutional rivalry and bureaucratic inefficiency as government agencies. They too pull in too many directions, undermining each other and failing to see the big picture.

Whilst these broad observations apply to many states at all stages of development, in Sierra Leone they are especially applicable. For example, in 2000, the following specific criticisms applied:

- Massive international investment by West African standards but all focused on the slow implementation of an unimaginative security plan that was very poorly integrated with the wider political, diplomatic, legal, economic and other issues, without which any military success would be, at best, transient.
- There was open and almost anarchical inter-agency rivalry.
- There was no coherent, multi-dimensional plan. Too often organizations that should have been acting in concert were, often unwittingly, actually undermining each other
- A bewildering lack of urgency and of tempo.

Such was the severity of the situation that for once a single actor, in this case the UK, could impose solutions on all the others involved. The Sierra Leonean government, UN and the few NGOs that continued to function needed British help too much and were in no position to argue. The result was the flowering benefits of coherent multi-dimensional action based on a widely understood and firmly directed plan. President Tejan Kabbah, certainly charitably but with some justification, described the British Army as 'the architects of Sierra Leone's salvation'. Indeed it is he who first encouraged the author to expose the approach taken in Sierra Leone more widely. And it is not novel: historically, whilst on a smaller scale, academics[13] have compared the British approach in Sierra Leone with that employed by Britain's Field Marshal Templer in Malaya in the early 1950s.

Two issues are key. How, firstly, does one devise a recovery plan from scratch that ensures coherence over time across all dimensions? And secondly, how does one ensure the plan is implemented efficiently, remaining adaptable and responsive in the process? Here, the military have something to offer their civilian colleagues. When confronted by novel operational or strategic problems, military commanders employ a rigorously logical and deductive analytical tool to produce a coherent plan. By necessity, in recent years it has become highly sophisticated. The result of the analysis in Sierra Leone was a plan in which a number of inter-dependent lines of development (political, humanitarian, economic, financial, reconstruction, industrial, security and humanitarian) were actively pursued, through a number of necessary way points or 'decisive points', to a defined end-state. Success in achieving these points ensures continuing coherence across and through the life of the plan. They are also useful indicators of the pace and depth of progress.

---

[13] Connaughton, *Op. cit.*, in note 6.

But how does one ensure that something so complex remains relevant to developments as they occur and is implemented with the necessary tempo? The key is devolving responsibility to talented, empowered people who understand the big picture, work to clear intent and are authorized, indeed required, to use their initiative and energy to ensure that what they are doing meets their narrow objectives and yet remains compatible with a clearly understood overall plan.

Yet should we expect a country to do all this for itself? Many think not. On a visit to Guinea in 1999, the Finance Minister showed the author yet another sophisticated and highly technical blueprint for recovery he had received. 'I hardly understand it', he said, 'and certainly my team does not. What am I meant to do with it?' The solution is to develop a concept of 'embedded support'. Assume a country accepts it is failing and requires international assistance (although in the case of a deeply failed state what follows might be imposed by the international community). A team of highly-motivated practical people with proven track records – bankers, industrialists, diplomats, civil servants, doctors, and soldiers – drawn from both inside and outside the country is put together. Having formulated an appropriate multi-dimensional plan, the team works with and alongside the host government's departments and agencies over a period that is long enough to teach and train indigenous successors. Donors would agree to devolve responsibility for helping the country to this single team working throughout the government. Crucially, this demonstration of long-term and coherent commitment by the international community, and the high quality of the implementation team, would serve as a vital confidence-building catalyst to inward commercial and industrial investment.

The quality of the embedded-support team means it would be expensive but highly cost effective over time, certainly when compared with the huge rescue packages required (for example) in Sierra Leone, the DRC, and Ethiopia. The team would be authorized to serve as the decisive actor in the country. All other agencies, including NGOs, would be subordinated to it. The team's head, who would play a crucial role in ensuring strong central direction, would report directly to the president or prime minister. This would be a collective effort in which a highly motivated government and its recovery implementation team would be working to common long-term goals across well-regulated and recognizably interdependent lines of development, harmonized by a well-understood, actively managed and properly coherent implementation plan.

This intellectually rigorous analytical and planning tool, accompanied by the dynamism and leadership of the embedded support team throughout the implementation phase, has considerable potential to accelerate progress when applied to the most undeveloped states in Africa. The era of muddled aims, inertia, confusion, and contradictory action could be a thing of the past. And it must be emphasized that external assistance of this type and 'African based solutions' are not inimical, indeed the opposite is true. This is to do with teamwork, playing to people's strengths and, most importantly, the laying of long-term foundations. It offers the real promise of inducing external investment and sustainable growth. The era of fine analyses but inadequate practical help must come to an end. It is time for the practioners to join the team. The international community's watchwords, and its judge, must become implementation and delivery. To paraphrase Winston Churchill, a little 'less jaw-jaw' and a little 'more war-war' is required if the failed or failing state is to recover in a time frame that will satisfy its people and our consciences.

Sudan at the Crossroads

J Stephen Morrison

Khartoum and the Sudan People's Liberation Movement/Army (SPLM/A) signed a final framework agreement to end Sudan's 21-year internal war, the longest-running such conflict in Africa, on 26 May 2004. This historic moment raises the hope that Sudan may finally break free of its legacy of terrible conflict and move to a more stable, open and peaceful existence. Moreover, this moment affirms the centrality of sustained, high-level multilateral engagement comprising (in this instance) the lead Kenyan negotiators, the Bush administration, the UK, Norway and UN Secretary-General Kofi Annan. It also occurred at an acutely delicate moment as an unsteady 45-day humanitarian ceasefire for the western Darfur began to be implemented, and as the ongoing crisis in Iraq continued to consume international attention. Stabilizing Sudan and achieving an enduring postwar reconstruction will face formidable challenges and be highly prone to breakdown.

Sudan, a vast territory, is an impoverished nation. The peace accord is an externally coerced settlement, accepted by two parties who have little trust in one another. By its very design, the accord's core bargain is likely to generate tensions and aggravate mistrust: it proposes to build new national institutions to preserve the unity of Sudan, at the same time it lays the groundwork for an autonomous south, and enshrines the option of secession by the south through a referendum scheduled at the conclusion of a six-year interim period. Many close observers believe this accord will presage an eventual independent, sovereign southern Sudan, and that achievement of that target dominates, and will continue to dominate SPLM/A calculations.

Reconstruction will confront extreme North-South asymmetries of

---

J Stephen Morrison is Director of the Africa Programme at the Centre for Strategic and International Studies (CSIS), Washington D.C., and the CSIS Task Force on HIV/AIDS.

institutional capacity and human skills; over two dozen armed militias; spoilers in the ranks of each side; multiple 'hotspots' where violent instability can flare, most importantly an oil-producing zone that straddles the north and south and will be the subject of continued contestation between the two parties; projected large-scale population movements; an international debt of US$23 billion and arrears of over US$1 billion; a legacy on both sides of poor governance; and the potential for continued destabilizing actions by neighbours.

As steps are taken to implement the accord, the two signatories will simultaneously have to contend with the armed conflict and humanitarian emergency in Western Darfur that has displaced over 750 000 and resulted in an estimated 110 000 imperilled refugees inside Chad. A humanitarian ceasefire signed in Njamena in Chad on 8 April 2004 allows for external monitors and unimpeded access. All parties agreed to neutralize the armed militias, most significantly the government-supported Jingaweit militias responsible for sustained, scorched-earth violence directed at civilians.

Prospects for stabilization and reconstruction will to an important degree rest on the quality and strength of continued outside engagement. The UN, US and other major powers, and African leadership will be called upon to act with conviction on two fronts.

First, immediate pressures will mount to expedite a robust UN peacekeeping operation, and facilitate significant debt relief and reconstruction assistance. For the UN operation to be effective, it will require a large contingent (8 000-10 000), a lead military element provided by a European power, a Chapter VII peace enforcement mandate, and a 500-600-strong Quick Reaction force. As of May 2004, the preparation is for a Chapter VI observation and monitoring force. Who will lead, and what other countries will contribute troops, remains unclear.

The significant accretion of UN peacekeeping commitments elsewhere in Africa – in Liberia, Ivory Coast, Sierra Leone, Democratic Republic of Congo, Eritrea-Ethiopia – may work against the expedited deployment in Sudan of a large UN peace operation with an appropriately robust mandate. If the international community opts to seek peace, stability and humanitarian improvements in Sudan on the cheap, with inadequately empowered leadership, it will risk losing the peace in Sudan and repeating the costly peacekeeping mistakes made in Sierra Leone and the Democratic Republic of the Congo at the beginning of this decade.

Normalizing Sudan's status with the US, international financial institutions (the IMF, World Bank, African Development Bank) and other major bilateral donors will demand clearing accumulated arrears, concluding multilateral agreement on a debt relief/debt forgiveness package, and lifting US sanctions. This process promises to be highly complicated and contentious, will require intensive, protracted multilateral negotiations – for which U.S. leadership will be essential – and will carry substantial financial costs for the United States and other bilateral and multilateral donors.

Second, with respect to Western Darfur, the multilateral coalition will be pressed to take follow-on action that verifies and consolidates the humanitarian ceasefire, reins in the Jingaweit militias, facilitates political negotiations among the Government of Sudan and the western armed insurgents, the Sudan People's Movement/Army (SPLM/A) and the Justice and Equality Movement (JEM), and curbs cross-border arms flows. External support to the SPLM/A and JEM remain uncertain, though Chadian and Eritrean sources are suspected of aiding the SPLM/A.

In the broader, global context, Iraq will threaten to distract and weaken the international response to the fragile gains achieved in Sudan. Further, it is not inconceivable that radical Islamist interests will be drawn to violently challenge a Western-backed Sudan peace accord, UN peace operations, and expansive donor and NGO activities. Little systematic consideration has yet been given to this latter potential threat.

Challenging Sudan's Chronic Intractability

Sudan's current internal war began in 1983. It pits an Arab-oriented Islamist regime in Khartoum against an insurgent armed movement, the Sudan People's Liberation Movement/Army (SPLM/A) chiefly based in southern Sudan. Each seeks to enhance its military position through opportunistic alliances with an array of armed ethnic militias and regional states. In the half-century since Sudan gained its independence in January 1956, there has been only one period of relative (and troubled) peace: 1972-83, during which the Addis Ababa Agreement's grant to the South of substantial regional autonomy was eventually undermined by Khartoum's fiat. Otherwise, Sudan's independent history has been dominated by chronic, exceptionally cruel warfare that has starkly divided the country on racial, religious, and regional grounds, displaced an estimated 4 million persons (of a total estimated population of 32 million) and killed an estimated 2 million persons.

There have been multiple attempts at mediation between the parties that date back to soon after war resumed in the early 1980s. These initiatives range from the first meetings between the SPLM/A and the northern political parties in 1984-85, up to the most recent rounds of the east African regional body, the Inter-Governmental Authority on Development (IGAD), the Joint Libyan-Egyptian Initiative (JLEI) and attempts at facilitation by the Nigerian government. At no point during the war have the parties ceased talking to one another, even in the face of unabated fighting. Nonetheless, before 2002, only the 1988-89 peace initiative and the Nigerian-led Abuja talks of 1992-93 showed any real promise of ending the war. All other initiatives achieved modest gains that initially raised hopes and eventually foundered. These initiatives did generate a dense legacy of written agreements that contained the elements of a possible negotiated settlement. However, the fecklessness of those on both sides who signed these agreements, and their routine non-implementation, discredited mediation efforts and enshrouded them in widespread cynicism.

Several interlocking factors have reinforced Sudan's intractability, most importantly the character of the two principal antagonists. Over time, as the war's duration extended and its human costs worsened, the polarization and mistrust between the Government of Sudan and the SPLM/A steadily deepened. In this period, each side came to be dominated by an autocratic leadership that lacked the coherence, internal unity and clarity of purpose essential to lead Sudan decisively out of war and towards peace. Instead, each settled into a comfortable accommodation with persistent warfare that sustained their respective bases of power and seldom threatened their core constituencies. Each also believed (sometimes correctly, more often erroneously) that military triumph remained within reach and aggressively sold its followers on this ambition. Each typically perceived peace initiatives as mere tactical opportunities to buy time and strike a pose. And each ultimately concluded that achieving peace held too many risks and uncertainties to pursue in earnest.

Powerful external realities further reinforced these leadership choices. Regional mediation efforts have until recently been ineptly managed and insufficiently resourced – in human, financial and political terms. This reflected to a significant degree the internal divisions and institutional weakness within the surrounding region itself. It also reflected the absence of any serious investment by the US and other major powers in a mediation enterprise.

Interestingly, however, during 2001-2 a shift of circumstances appeared to lessen Sudan's apparent intractability and has heightened the opportunity for serious negotiations. The multiple factors underpinning

Sudan's fatalism have been less fixed and more mutable. In July 2002, the parties signed the Machakos protocol that separated religion from the national state and allowed for a southern referendum on unity versus secession after a six-year interim period. This was followed by a security accord in September 2003 that laid down plans for the redeployment of forces to respective sides of the 1956 north-south boundary; the continuation of two separate armies, allowing the SPLM/A to retain a large enough force to defend itself against government actions that undermine the cease-fire, abrogate other aspects of implementation or attempt to upend a referendum outcome that endorses secession; and the establishment of an integrated national force. In January 2004, a wealth-sharing accord was sealed that stipulates an equal split of the nation's future oil wealth earnings.

IGAD, through the Kenyan negotiator, General Lazaro Sumbeiyo, has spearheaded these efforts, supported by a troika comprised of the US, Britain, and Norway. Arguably, the single most important factor in challenging Sudan's intractability has been the Bush administration's increased leverage and focus on Khartoum, accelerated by a global counter-terrorism agenda after 11 September 2001 that placed a premium on coercing sudden co-operation from Khartoum on not just counter-terrorism, but peace negotiations and humanitarian access as well. Implicit was the American threat that if results were not soon manifest on these three fronts, aggressive action to isolate and possibly destabilize Khartoum would follow, endorsed by highly mobilized American constituencies, most importantly evangelical Christians and African-American anti-slavery activists, in league with Congressional allies and hard-line elements within the Bush administration itself.

These twin pressures quickly raised the level of threat felt by Khartoum, and motivated it to seek a new path to avoid American condemnation, normalize its international standing, and preserve its power in the north. For the SPLM/A leadership, it came under newfound pressure from Washington to see an expedited, negotiated settlement, backed by Bush administration guarantees, as its best hope of survival.

Changes in Sudan and the surrounding region followed the shift in American calculations. In Khartoum, President Omer al Bashir deposed his ideological mentor and political rival, the Islamist theoretician and political leader Dr. Hassan al Turabi, in December 1999. This reflected a feeling that the Islamist project in Sudan had reached its limits, and its costs in terms of international isolation and domestic division were too much to bear.

Sudan's radical Islamists were becoming older, and their ranks depleted by the war. Searching for other political constituencies to replace the radicals who had followed Dr. al Turabi into opposition, the Government of Sudan became more politically accommodating. The war was exhausting the government. On the southern Sudanese side, an increasingly organized civil society constituency was becoming less accommodating of the SPLM/A leadership's unending promises that victory lay 'just around the corner.' The internal divisions and internecine strife between southern factions mobilized southern church and community leaders to launch reconciliation initiatives that pressured the SPLM/A leadership to take peace initiatives more seriously.

In the region, the Daniel Arap Moi government in Kenya sought expanded counter-terrorism co-operation (already extensive after the August 1998 bombing of the US embassy in Nairobi) and a diplomatic alliance with the US to achieve peace in Sudan, in hopes that these combined initiatives would raise Kenya's standing internationally and reduce its risks of retributions, as Moi left office in early 2003. Hence the sudden seriousness of purpose shown by the Moi government in 2002 in revitalizing the IGAD process, including pressing the SPLM/A (reliant upon Kenya for its residences, transit of materiel, humanitarian flows and people) to sit at the negotiating table. Since January 2003, the new Kenyan government of President Mwai Kibaki has continued this role without interruption.

Elsewhere in the region, the Ethiopians, Eritreans and Ugandans had mounted a unified campaign in 1996-97 that sought to pressure Khartoum militarily through joint support of the SPLM/A. In 1998, that unity fell apart with the Ethiopian-Eritrea war and conflict between Uganda and its erstwhile ally, Rwanda. In turn, Uganda and Ethiopia each sought better relations with Khartoum.

Sudan's Endgame

In certain respects, it is hardly surprising that Sudan should see an upsurge in new violence as the endgame to the IGAD peace process approached in 2003 and into 2004. That has been the pattern in many other similar situations. Spoilers come forward in hopes of destabilizing the process. Aggrieved parties left out of the process surface suddenly, seeking to win a place at the negotiating table through armed violence. Parties to the negotiations themselves get engaged, overtly or through proxies, as they seek maximum advantage before a final peace agreement is struck.

What is distinct to the violence in western Darfur is the dramatic scale of ethnic cleansing, bordering on or indeed constituting genocide in the views of senior international observers; the conflict's remoteness; the limited outside access and hence limited close knowledge of what is happening; and the acute threat the conflict poses to the IGAD peace process.

The swift onset in 2003 of the SPLM/A and JEM insurgencies has been fed from multiple sources: the brutal disenfranchisement and neglect of Western Sudan's citizens by the government in Khartoum; longstanding ethnic rivalries; pervasive violence against civilians by the government-backed Jingaweit militia; suspected Chadian and Eritrean support of the SPLM/A (with possible encouragement as well by the SPLM/A); and in the case of the JEM, suspected linkages with the radical Islamist Hassan al Turabi.

The situation in Darfur remains fluid, murky, and dangerously volatile. It has hung over the Naivasha endgame talks, stalling progress. It has the continued potential to reignite and escalate rapidly, destabilize Chad, create new space for radical Islamic mobilization, fundamentally reshape international perceptions, and concentrate attention upon government-sponsored allegations of genocide.

What this means, of course, is that the multilateral coalition that has been essential in sustaining progress in the IGAD process has had no choice since early 2004 but to address the Darfur situation at the same time. That in turn has severely tested diplomatic capacities. Even with a peace accord, the imperative for the coalition to concentrate intensively on two complex fronts will not soon fade away. Indeed, integrating action on these dual agendas will remain essential and place excessive demands on an already overstretched core of highly committed international diplomats.

Since late 2003, the Bush administration in league with UN Secretary-General Annan, the Kenyans and other members of the troika have pressed assiduously at the highest levels for the Government of Sudan and the SPLM/A to reach a negotiated settlement. On Western Darfur, they have pressed Khartoum to rein in its militias, open humanitarian access, and enter face-to-face political talks with the SPLM/A and JEM.In an illustration of this diplomatic zeal, President Bush telephoned President Bashir and SPLM/A President Dr. John Garang on 29 March 2004. Secretary of State Colin Powell contacted Vice-President Ali Uthman Muhammad Taha and Garang on 3 April, and National Security Advisor Condoleeza Rice did the same three days later. In early April 2004, at the occasion of the tenth anniversary of the Rwanda genocide, the White

House issued a press statement condemning Khartoum's complicity in the militia violence. Simultaneously, UN Secretary-General Kofi Annan publicly threatened to bring the issue of Western Darfur to the UN Security Council, for consideration of deployment of UN force, and the EU signalled its willingness to table before the UN Human Rights Commission action under Article 9 to appoint a special rapporteur to investigate massive human rights violations in the west by government agencies and proxies.

One difficult issue in the peace negotiations was the application of Islamic law in the capital, Khartoum. In this final round of talks, begun in mid-February, the parties have reportedly reached agreement on the three special territories (Abyei, Blue Nile, Nuba Mountains) and power-sharing arrangements. Khartoum was sensitive to the looming pressure of 21 April 2004 – the deadline set by the US Congress through the Sudan Peace Act under which the Bush administration must report back to Congress on the status of peace talks. It was aware that if, by 21 April, the Bush administration could not claim demonstrable, significant progress towards achieving a framework peace, and that indeed such an agreement was imminent, the Bush administration could lay blame at Khartoum's door and retreat from an activist stance in the peace talks. This step would not only have gutted the talks' momentum but potentially condemned, marginalized and isolated Khartoum.

The White House and others also signalled to Dr. John Garang, head of the SPLM/A, that an accord was essential, and that they would not respond passively to SPLM/A foot dragging.

The 8 April 2004 45-day humanitarian ceasefire for Western Darfur grew out of talks hosted by Chad in Njamena, with observers present from the US, UK, EU, African Union, UN, and France. The week of 19 April 2004, the African Union pursued the organization of the first joint monitoring mission involving the government of Sudan, the SPLM/A, and the JEM, while also exploring the possibility of political talks. Movement of substantial humanitarian relief from Chad or from within Sudan to Western Darfur is, predictably, problematic, subject to persistent obstruction by the government of Sudan. Even if access is improved, relief efforts will continue to be hindered by terrible roads, scant infrastructure, elementary security, seasonal rains and limited UN and NGO presence inside Western Sudan.

Crisis in Zimbabwe
Tony Hawkins

Great Expectations
Notwithstanding the setbacks of the 1970s arising from the liberation war (1972-1979), when Zimbabwe attained independence twenty-four years ago the country turned a fresh page starting out with an inheritance that was the envy of many, perhaps most, Sub-Saharan countries. Although it had lost thousands of skilled, experienced whites in the late 1970s and early 1980s[1], this outflow was offset by the return of many thousands of well-educated and trained black Zimbabweans.

The international community, relieved to have secured a relatively peaceful transition to majority rule, was ready – indeed anxious – to help rebuild the country. The speed and breadth of the economic rebound (real GDP grew 25 per cent in 1980-1981) took donors, lenders and the new government by surprise. Fears that nearly a decade of civil war would constrain recovery were quickly seen to have been misplaced.

With Sub-Saharan Africa's second largest manufacturing sector and second most sophisticated financial sector, a vibrant commercial farming industry, a well-established, broad-based mining industry, a fledgling tourist sector, one of the continent's best-maintained and developed physical infrastructures and thousands of university graduates, Zimbabwe seemed well-placed to become the continent's first Tiger economy.

Bleak House
Yet within twenty-five years the Great Expectations had turned into a Bleak House and today Zimbabwe stands on the brink of basket-case status. More than 60 per cent of the population live in poverty[2] and, on current trends, it will take until 2108 to reach the Millennium Development Goal

---

Tony Hawkins is Professor of Business Studies at the University of Zimbabwe.

of halving income poverty, compared with a target date of 2015. The International Monetary Fund (IMF) estimates that poverty has doubled since 1995, while school enrolments declined to 65 per cent of normal rates in 2003 and the HIV/AIDS pandemic remained 'largely unchecked'.[3]

There are no reliable unemployment figures, but even the most conservative estimates suggest that at least half the workforce does not have a formal sector job. Official estimates suggest that up to three million Zimbabweans have emigrated – mostly as illegal immigrants – to South Africa and the UK, known colloquially as Harare North.[4]

Table 1: Social Indicators

Life Expectancy declined from 62 years in 1985 to 39.5 years (2001)
Infant Mortality rates increased from 51 per 1000 (1990) to 76 per 1000 (2000)
By 2002, population growth was estimated to have turned negative (– 1.1per cent)
Deaths from HIV/AIDs accounted for 1.6 per cent of the population in 2002
The rate of adult HIV-AIDS prevalence is variously estimated at between 24 per cent (Government of Zimbabwe) and 33.7 per cent (UNAIDS)

Sources: Government of Zimbabwe, UNAIDS, IMF, UNDP.

Per capita incomes, which peaked in 1997, had fallen 42 per cent by the end of 2003 and are projected to decline a further 10 per cent in 2004. Even if the economy were to recover and resume growth in 2005, it would take a minimum of fifteen years, and probably longer, to regain 1997 living standards. Zimbabwe's Human Development Index, as compiled by the UNDP, is lower today than at independence in 1980.

---

[1] The white population of Zimbabwe in the early 1980s was estimated at 140 000 – approximately half the peak of around 275 000 in the mid-1970s.
[2] Poverty is here defined as living on less than US$1 a day.
[3] *IMF Statement on the Conclusion of 2004 Article IV Consultation Discussions with Zimbabwe*, Harare, 31 March 2004 (press release No. 04/67).
[4] This estimate is highly questionable because it is based on the mistaken (official) assumption of an unchanged population growth of around 3 per cent a year. In fact, population growth slowed dramatically in the latter half of the 1990s due to the impact of HIV/AIDS, and is officially estimated to have turned negative in 2001-2002.

What Went Wrong?

Economists and political scientists will long ponder the reasons for Zimbabwe's potentially catastrophic, post-independence performance. How and why did one of Sub-Saharan Africa's best-endowed economies fail to exploit the potential it inherited? What went wrong?

There is neither a single explanation nor a single culprit. Ultimately, the blame for Zimbabwe's catastrophic decline lies with successive Zimbabwe African National Union Patriotic Front (ZANU-PF) administrations that have ruled the country since May 1980. But, unsurprisingly, President Robert Mugabe's government accepts responsibility for the crisis only to the extent that it is perceived as the unavoidable consequence of asserting the country's sovereignty, especially in terms of land ownership. Members of the Mugabe administration view the catastrophe as a price worth paying for demonstrating that Zimbabwe had at last taken charge of its own destiny.

They claim too that Zimbabwe has put itself on the African map in demonstrating to other governments and leaders that the capitalist West is not all-powerful and can be shamed and outwitted, if not defeated. In the eyes of some, President Mugabe has transformed himself into an African folk-hero, who took back his people's land that was stolen by the white colonialists and who is not afraid to stand up against the bullying of the Blair government, the Bush Administration and their proxies in the EU, the IMF and the World Bank.

By focusing on the land issue, the Zimbabwe government has successfully portrayed itself to many African leaders and editorial-writers as the victim of Western, especially British, racism. Western – and South African – media preoccupation with land and race has played into the government's hands, undermining the efforts of those who have sought to portray the Zimbabwe situation for what it really is – a failure of governance and democracy.

At home, the government has successfully used its effective media monopoly to scapegoat the British government and its US ally, the fast-shrinking white minority (now down to less than 30 000 permanent residents), the opposition Movement for Democratic Change (which according to the government is no more than a front for white/British influence), venal and corrupt business people, and misguided foreign governments and international institutions, like the IMF, who have been deliberately misled by Whitehall and its allies.

The Lessons of History

The international community cannot escape its share of the blame. In the early 1980s, the Thatcher government – and indeed the entire international community – turned a blind eye to the Matabeleland atrocities. Because Robert Mugabe had espoused reconciliation when he took over as prime minister it was politically incorrect to suggest otherwise, however damning the evidence.

As late as the mid-1990s, the Major government continued to insist that the Mugabe government deserved sympathy and support. Throughout the reform period (1991-1996), the donor community, including the IMF and World Bank, insisted – despite overwhelming evidence to the contrary – that the reform programme was 'on track'. Indeed, as recently as 1999, the IMF made yet another loan to the Zimbabwe government, although its staff must have known that the money would find its way into financing Harare's intervention in the civil war in the DRC. Even when the loan collapsed – within two months – the Fund refused to accept any blame for making what was clearly an ill-advised loan. Any commercial banker who had acted in this way would have lost his job. The IMF official responsible was promoted!

Quite why the international community behaved – and to some extent still does – in this manner is beyond the scope of this paper.[5] What matters is that it did – and still does – and that the lessons of Rwanda, Burundi, the Democratic Republic of Congo (DRC), Somalia, Liberia and Sierra Leone have not yet been learned. While this can be explained by the focus of major players on Iraq and the war against terrorism, such behaviour sits uncomfortably with the international community's repeatedly proclaimed commitment to good governance, the rule of law, transparency and accountability.

---

[5] In early April, an African-Asian grouping voted down a draft resolution on the human rights situation in Zimbabwe for the second year at the United Nations High Commissioner for Human Rights (UNHCHR) in Geneva. The draft resolution, mooted by the European Union and supported by the United States, expressed 'deep concern' at 'continuing violations of human rights in Zimbabwe, in particular politically motivated violence, including killings, torture, sexual and other forms of violence against women ....' Fifteen African countries including the two 'honest brokers' designated by the Commonwealth to find a resolution of the crisis – South Africa and Nigeria – opposed the adoption of the resolution.

Economic Performance (1980-2003)

Table 2: Growth and Decline (% change per annum)

	Real GDP	Population	GDP per Head
1965-1980	4.8	3.2	1.7
1980-1989	4.4	3.1	1.1
1990-1999	1.5	1.9	- 0.4
1999-2003	- 10.0	0.5	- 10.5

Source: Central Statistical Office, Harare

There are two main explanations:
- Donor generosity. Net capital inflows (1980-2002) totalled US$5.9 billion, of which 106 per cent represented official assistance. In other words, foreign donors and the international lending institutions not only provided the entire net inflow of capital but also funded the outflow of private sector, predominantly bank lending and trade finance.
- The economy's capacity to sustain high levels of public spending with modest inflation rates – a classic case of a country living off its past.

Table 3: Zimbabwe – Net Resource Flows (1980-2002) in US$ million

	Foreign Direct Investment	Portfolio Inflows	Trade, Bank and Bond Finance	Aid	Total
1980-1989	(115)	0	(115)	1,950	1,720
1990-1999	420	100	(610)	3,950	3,860
2000-2002	110	0	(112)	321	320
Total	415	100*	(837)	6,222	5,900
Percentages	7.0	1.7	(14.2)	105.5	100

Source: World Bank: Global Development Finance Reports (various issues)

The $100 million portfolio inflow figure is clearly seriously wrong. While there was a net inflow of this magnitude between 1993 and 1997, there has been a persistent net outflow of such funds as a result of net selling of Zimbabwe securities by foreign investors.

By the late 1980s, it had become clear to all but the hardliners in Zanu-PF, which included Robert Mugabe, that a new economic model was needed. Mugabe played a long game, opposing economic reforms as long as he could, but the fall of the Berlin Wall and the collapse of communism forced him to make concessions that he has since repeatedly disavowed.

Second Honeymoon

The period 1991–95 was Zimbabwe's second honeymoon. The donor community, under pressure from the World Bank, the IMF and the British government, convinced itself that Mugabe really had seen the light and been mysteriously transformed from an adherent to a hardline command economy to a forward-looking economic reformer.

Once again Mugabe outwitted the reformers within his own camp, such as Finance Minister Bernard Chidzero, while running rings around the donors and lenders. Economic reforms initially implemented with enthusiasm were subsequently allowed to wither on the vine. Public sector reform, without which there could be no private sector response, was carefully left on the back burner. Military spending and parastatal subsidies were maintained at unsustainable levels. Yet throughout, the IMF and the World Bank insisted 'the programme was on track'.

The Watershed

While unemployment continued to mount, public spending on health and education was cut. Poverty deepened and a classic crisis of unfulfilled expectations developed. The late 1990s was the watershed. Five events – the unbudgeted, panic-driven payout to the war veterans, entry into the DRC war, the launch of a popular opposition party, the Movement for Democratic Change (MDC), the hasty revival of plans for land reform, which had been gathering dust for a decade, and the loss of the February 2000 referendum on a new constitution, finally encouraged Mugabe to return to his philosophical roots. Land and race moved to the top of the political agenda, while hand-wringing donors – the UNDP, the World Bank and the IMF and some Western governments – continued to promote the fiction that once the government's legitimate concerns over land were met, Zimbabwe would quickly regain its status as a fast-track developer.

Having come perilously close to losing the June 2000 parliamentary elections, the government set out to crush all opposition – the MDC, the trade unions, the NGO community, the media and the judiciary. The West watched helplessly, imposing so-called 'smart' (for which read ineffectual) sanctions against individuals and seeking to exert diplomatic pressure through the Commonwealth, the Southern African development Community and bilaterally through Pretoria.

Within Zimbabwe, accelerating economic decline, exacerbated by the AIDS pandemic and the mass emigration of middle and working class

MDC voters, created an unsustainable economic crisis. With no other resources at its disposal the government resorted to unbridled credit creation, pillaged the pension funds and institutional savers with never so much as a word of protest from the country's largest insurer, the South African-controlled Old Mutual, setting in train what is now the world's highest inflation rate in the region of 600 per cent.

Economic Prospects

By the end of 2004, the country's accumulated foreign arrears will be in the region of US$3 billion – approximately equivalent to the country's GDP at current exchange rates. By the end of 2004 too, the Zimbabwe economy will be smaller than those of Botswana and Mauritius, which have little more than one tenth of Zimbabwe's population.

Rising unemployment, the worsening HIV-AIDS crisis, hyperinflation, deepening poverty, ongoing haemorrhage of skills and the erosion of the productive sector all mean that just as other African economies beset by protracted crises (Ghana, Uganda, Mozambique and Zambia) have had to be rescued by the international community, so too will Zimbabwe.

Table 4: Going Backwards

Indicators	1980	Peak (year)	Latest	Percentage Change from Peak
Human Development Index	0.570	0.621 (1985)	0.496	- 20
GDP per head	Z$1850 (1990 prices)	Z$2310 (1997)	Z$1350	- 42
Employment	1 000 000	1 400 000 (1998)	950 000	- 32
Agriculture Value added Z$ billion (1990 prices)	1.89	4.2 (2000)	2.25	- 46
Mining Value Added Z$ billion	0.76	0.98 (1995)	0.65	- 34
Manufacturing Value Added Z$ billion (1990 prices)	3.20	4.85 (1991)	2.80	- 42
Exports (US$ million)	1 300	2 650	1.325	- 50

Source: Central Statistical Office, Harare and the UNDP (for the Human Development Index)

However, it may well be that, like the DRC, the economic slide could continue for several more years yet before there is a political denouement, though ultimately Zimbabwe will have to be rescued. By whom and under what circumstances is impossible to guess. Suffice it to say that South African support alone, assuming that it were to be forthcoming, would not be sufficient to turn the economy around.

That said, South Africa is the only significant foreign investor[6] in Zimbabwe, often on what might be called 'carpet-bagging terms'. A leading South African bank, Nedcor, and its main shareholder, the Old Mutual, are currently engaged in negotiations to take over and restructure a failed Zimbabwe bank, while the country's embryonic platinum industry is effectively controlled by South African mining houses (Implats[7] and Anglo American). South African firms are major players in banking and insurance (Old Mutual, Stanbic, Nedcor, ABSA) in mining, in plantation agriculture (sugar estates), cement and in manufacturing generally. If this trend is maintained, and it is hard to envisage other serious foreign investors showing any interest under current conditions, Zimbabwe will increasingly join Lesotho, Swaziland, Botswana and Namibia as satellite states of South Africa which, in the eyes of cynical Zimbabweans, lies at the very heart of 'quiet diplomacy'.

This cynical interpretation, that economic meltdown of Zimbabwe's US$4 billion economy (no more than 3 per cent of the South African economy) does not pose a meaningful economic threat to South Africa, is rejected by those who argue that the Zimbabwe crisis is causing serious economic dislocation in several South African Development Community (SADC) countries and that Africa's failure to implement the principles enshrined in the New Partnership for Africa's Development (Nepad) threatens to discredit the scheme.

There is however very little hard evidence to sustain the view that Zimbabwe's economic, political and social problems are undermining the regional economy. Indeed, as the crisis has worsened, GDP growth in SADC has accelerated rather than slowed. Those financial analysts who during the rand's meltdown in 2001 attributed the currency's weakness to the Zimbabwe crisis are now unable to explain the rand's strong recovery despite ongoing, accelerating decline in Zimbabwe.

---

[6] One important exception is the decision by the UK-based mining house Rio Tinto to go ahead with the development of a significant diamond find in Zimbabwe.

[7] In 2003 the chief executive of the Implats platinum operation in Zimbabwe famously described the country as 'a great place to do business'.

Attempts at counterfactual analysis – such as that by the Zimbabwe Research Initiative[8] – which seek to identify not what actually happened, but what might have happened had there been no crisis in Zimbabwe, produce a somewhat different result. In its analysis, the Research Initiative estimates that South Africa's GDP at the end of 2002 would have been 1.3 per cent larger had the problem not arisen. The report also suggests that Zimbabwe has cost the SADC region upwards of US$5 billion.

Such efforts at quantification are suspect. The majority of Zimbabwe's SADC partners – Angola, Lesotho, Swaziland, Mauritius, Namibia, Seychelles and Tanzania – have marginal economic relations with Zimbabwe, and the impact on their economies of events in Zimbabwe is minimal. Growth in the SADC economy is driven mostly by exogenous influences such as gold, platinum, oil, copper and tobacco prices, levels of foreign investment and foreign aid, and climatic conditions. Set against these influences, events in Zimbabwe have had only a minor impact.

Nor should the redistributional benefits enjoyed by some SADC states be overlooked. South Africa, Botswana, Mozambique and Zambia have all benefited to some degree from the brain drain from Zimbabwe. Commercial farmers who have relocated in Mozambique and Zambia are boosting production of tobacco, horticulture and food crops. Media reports have probably exaggerated the extent of this flow, which is impossible to quantify, but there is anecdotal evidence of it, as well as evidence from the cross border sales of tobacco and maize seed. Zambia has gained market share in tourism at Zimbabwe's expense, illustrated by the increased number of flights from Johannesburg to Livingstone to cater for tourists visiting the Victoria Falls. In April 2004, Zimbabwe ferrochrome producer, Zimasco, said it was halving production while, almost simultaneously, South African producer Hernic announced plans to expand output by 60 per cent.

The main regional beneficiary of the skills exodus is South Africa, with well-educated, highly skilled Zimbabwean professionals taking up positions especially in the health, tertiary education, information technology and financial services industries. Some multinationals have relocated parts of their operations from Zimbabwe to South Africa. Many Zimbabwean firms have sought to expand regionally, with the most active sector being banking and financial services.

---

[8] Mike Schussler, *The Cost of Zimbabwe to the South African economy* (The Zimbabwe Research Initiative, 2003).

However, positive spillovers of this kind should not be exaggerated. The longer the crisis continues, the worse the regional impact will be, not just in terms of economic growth forgone but in respect of foreign investor perceptions. There must surely also be limits to the willingness of donors to support SADC governments that find no fault with policies and conduct that are anathema in the major donor nations of the OECD.

It is clear too that Zimbabwe has distracted SADC governments from their development agendas. Finance and industry ministries and central banks are far more critical of President Mugabe's policies than their counterparts in the ministries of foreign affairs and defence.

The Nepad Connection

Healthy cynicism is required too in assessing the view that Africa's willingness to turn a blind eye to events in Zimbabwe, while seeking increased aid and trade from the donor community, threatens to undermine Nepad. Put simply, donor support for Nepad is unlikely to be decisive in reviving the continent's economic fortunes. Foreign aid's contribution towards economic growth depends substantially on the quality of institutions and policies in the beneficiary country as well as on the policies of the donors themselves. For the most part African institutions are weak[9] and will take decades rather than years to rebuild and strengthen.

Far more effective in developing African economies are such initiatives as the US African Growth and Opportunity Act (AGOA) and the EU's Everything But Arms trade initiatives. These are not posited on whether or not an African government supports Zimbabwe's atrocious human rights record at the UN, though eligibility for AGOA does depend on the adoption of appropriate policies in respect of economic management and governance.

It follows that, as the April 2004 UN High Commissioner for Human Rights vote on human rights abuse shows, African leaders are unlikely to be influenced by promises of OECD largesse. Not only that but the recent appointment of a Commission for Africa by British premier Tony Blair as part of the UK's chairmanship of the G-8 in 2005 demonstrates that the donors themselves have little intention of allowing the Zimbabwe crisis to derail efforts to revive the African economy.

---

[9] See International Monetary Fund, *World Economic Outlook: Growth and Institutions*, April 2003 (Chapter III).

Those who believe in the efficacy of Western morality need look no further than the charade surrounding the proposed English cricket tour to Zimbabwe at the end of 2004. On the advice of one its leading members, the English Cricket Board (ECB) appeared to have taken the view that the tour should be cancelled on moral grounds. However, once the full impact of the financial cost of cancellation – put at some £50 million – became clear, the ECB's qualms vanished overnight, to be replaced by pleas to the British Government to ban the tour.

Endgame Scenarios

Notwithstanding the precipitous decline of the Zimbabwe economy, the collapse of the rule of law, the disregard for property rights, the stark deterioration of institutions at all levels – health, education, the police, the judiciary, the media, the public service and parastatals – none of the players seems to have an endgame strategy. Indeed, the nearest to having such a strategy is probably Zanu-PF itself, which is increasingly confident that it can ride out the storm, underpinned by African, and especially South African, backing, as well as that from some Asian nations, notably China and Malaysia.

Zanu-PF, which draws its inspiration and structures from Soviet communism, believes that in winning the liberation war, it has won the right to rule Zimbabwe indefinitely. Accordingly no serious political opposition is tolerated and limited democracy is allowed only to an extent that is compatible with the ruling clique's view of the future. Government, parliament and state institutions (the Central Bank, the Judiciary, the armed forces and police) are subservient to the party. Crucial policy decisions are made at Politburo and Central Committee level and rubberstamped by parliament when deemed necessary. Similarly, the electoral process is controlled by the party. The state has monopoly control of radio and TV and the only daily newspapers are either owned by or support the government. The government closed down the only independent daily newspaper, *The Daily News*, last year.

Given this mindset, free and fair elections are simply impossible. The recent by-election in the previously safe MDC seat of Zengeza, which was won easily by ZANU-PF, has convinced many opposition politicians that there is no point in contesting the next parliamentary elections scheduled for March 2005. Without radical electoral reform, including international involvement in the conduct of the elections and the counting of votes, the

MDC is likely to lose most of its seats in parliament. The Mugabe government would win a comfortable two-thirds majority enabling it to alter the constitution, allowing the party to sidestep the electorate and bypass presidential elections at least until 2008.

This scenario assumes that the international community would be forced – partly by pressure from South Africa and other African states – to accept the outcome of the poll and the subsequent constitutional changes. It assumes too that South Africa and other African states would use their influence at the IMF and World Bank to secure an IMF facility for Zimbabwe that would enable Harare to reschedule its foreign debts as a prerequisite for economic recovery.

Given the prevailing mood of downright despondency in Zimbabwe, it is all too easy to understand why opposition and human rights activists, businesspeople and diplomats, believe that the endgame in Zimbabwe is still some years away, meaning that ZANU-PF could maintain its hold on power for the foreseeable future.

Four Scenarios

Such an assumption, however, is deeply flawed because it implies that the already-ravaged economy can recover without substantial foreign aid and foreign investment. Because this is just not credible, four possible scenarios are suggested.

1. Assuming, as seems highly probable, that ZANU-PF comfortably wins the 2005 elections and amends the constitution, the international community could accept this as a valid expression of the will of the Zimbabwe people. As of April 2004, this seems inconceivable, but in politics nothing can be ruled out. The solution to which the international community is presently committed – the holding of fresh elections under international supervision and conducted in an atmosphere conducive to a (relatively) free and fair poll – will become feasible only if the stalemate is broken in one or a combination of three ways:

2. The retirement or incapacitation of the 80-year-old Mugabe. This would break the logjam, quite possibly with devastating repercussions within the ruling party, which is deeply split on a successor and which is unlikely – certainly on present form – to unite behind a single candidate. The downside with this scenario is that it could

degenerate into a chaotic struggle for power, conceivably culminating in military intervention.

3. It could be that the combination of economic decline and international diplomatic pressure will force Mugabe to accept that the game is up and go along with whatever face-saving compromise Pretoria is able to cobble together, agreeing to step down and allow free and fair elections. It appears, however, that ZANU-PF is prepared to sacrifice the economy to its determination to hang onto power, conscious that, as in the DRC, the collapse of the formal economy could take decades during which time there could be enormous scope for rent-seeking exploitation by those in power. That being so, this scenario depends on Pretoria taking a far tougher line against the Mugabe government than it has been prepared to do hitherto. Without that pre-requisite in place, the probability is that ZANU-PF will preside over continuing, protracted economic decline.

4. A final possibility is a breakdown in law and order as a result of the people taking to the streets against the government. Efforts to generate such popular unrest have failed dismally. So long as opposition activities continue to vote with their feet and so long as the authorities maintain their iron-fist control, such a scenario is highly improbable.

None of this makes cheerful reading – except possibly for the Zimbabwe government and its allies. But the speed with which change can occur should never be underestimated. Those who remember the dark days of Zimbabwe (Southern Rhodesia) at the end of the 1970s, when all seemed lost, or South Africa a decade later, or Nigeria prior to the death of Sanni Abacha, know full well that even seemingly hopeless situations are susceptible to remarkably positive transformation.

Whatever form the endgame takes, hopefully the international community will have learned a lesson. By failing to take a stand, by repeated, transparently untruthful claims that programmes were on track and that events on the ground were exaggerations by human rights groups, opposition politicians, church leaders, NGOs and the media, it has contributed to an outcome that will be vastly more costly – in financial and human terms – to resolve than would have been the case had the West, and indeed Zimbabwe's neighbours in SADC, taken a longer-term view.

Structural Challenges of Transformation in Zimbabwe

John Robertson

In her farewell speech to Zimbabwean guests a few months ago, a diplomat about to leave Zimbabwe paraphrased Winston Churchill's speech on the pilots who fought the Battle of Britain. On Zimbabwe's mounting agonies, created by bad economic and political policies, greed and corruption, she said, 'Never in the field of political endeavour has so much been wrecked by so few so quickly.'

Her comment was fitting, even though many people who know Zimbabwe well still cannot believe what has happened. The country is still one of the most industrialized in the third world, it mines at least three dozen different minerals, it has one of the best climates in the world, and people who know what they are doing can grow just about anything. Adding to these a list of world-class tourist attractions makes it all the more important to ask: 'What went wrong?'

Economic Mismanagement

Without doubt, a great deal has gone wrong. Basic statistics show that, since 1997, Zimbabwe's economy has shrunk by a third, employment has fallen by 35 per cent, export revenues have fallen by about 50 per cent and half the population of the country has become dependent on food aid.

Typically, only out-and-out warfare would do this much damage to a country's economy, but no other country has declared war on Zimbabwe. Perhaps the best way to sum up the situation is to say that Zimbabwe is a country at war with itself. But Zimbabwe is not engaged in a normal civil war. The attacks in progress have been engineered to bring about a change of ownership of assets, rather than a change in political leadership.

John Robertson heads Robertson Economic Information Services in Zimbabwe.

That said, it must be acknowledged that the political hierarchy has taken extraordinary measures to secure its power-base. They might prefer to argue that the transfer of ownership of assets is simply one of the strategic building blocks it has chosen to retain the political support of the electorate. However, the moves made to transfer ownership of assets have been highly disruptive and, in fact, have been the cause of the declines in production in export revenues, in food security and in the country's ability to attract any financial assistance from abroad.

The International Monetary Fund (IMF) has been particularly unimpressed with the Zimbabwe government's policy choices and it has shown no inclination to accept Zimbabwe's moves to nationalize commercial farmland. Many African countries have found the IMF to be a difficult mentor. It asks for very heavy commitments to recovery procedures, and gets impatient when the countries agree to terms and conditions but repeatedly fail to meet them. However, if the response to the first Economic Structural Adjustment Programme is examined, Zimbabwe did meet one of the IMF's requirements – it dispensed with import licences and foreign exchange allocations at the beginning of 1994.

This meant that the government had to abandon the chosen beneficiaries of its earlier affirmative action-related measures, its currency allocation schemes. Some of the affected individuals were not too concerned as they were able to capitalize on the surge in commercial activity that was financed by the changes, but many found that they did not have the business skills needed to compete. Some felt that they had earned the right to generous advantages and should not have to work to retain them.

Transfers of ownership of assets therefore became their main preoccupation, and by 1997, they had vigorously revived demands for free land. When it was discovered that many had received payments from the War Victims' Relief Fund on the strength of fraudulently issued disability claims, the activists took defensive action by going on the attack. They claimed that cash payments and pensions as well as land were owing to every single war veteran, not just the disabled or the politically powerful.

These ideas were taken up with such vigour and gathered so much momentum that President Mugabe was forced to concede, first to the demands for money and then to demands for land. In August 1997, he launched a series of political rallies at which he promised that the redistribution of land would start in earnest that year. Within weeks, notices were sent out to about 1 800 white farmers advising them that their farms were designated for acquisition and would be taken over before the end of the same year.

These events steered Zimbabwe into mounting uncertainty. The money to pay the promised gratuities and monthly pensions for life to 60 000 war veterans did not exist, so it had to be printed. The threatened takeover of a quarter of the country's most productive farms was seen as a threat to foreign earnings as well as every supplier of farm inputs, every processor of farm outputs and every business supplying financial and professional services to commercial farmers. More directly at risk were the hundreds of thousands of people who earned direct incomes from these businesses, the country's export revenues, the millions of people who depended on the country's foreign earnings and the stability of the banks.

Not surprisingly, the announcement of the policies led to a collapse in confidence. This led to a run on the Zimbabwe dollar and a sharp decline in the exchange rate. Interest rates and import duties were stepped up sharply to defend the dollar and shortages, together with rising import costs, pushed up prices, which led to demonstrations and rioting. The seeds were sown for the creation of the first strong opposition party since independence in 1980.

When the President sent troops to the Democratic Republic of Congo in August and September 1998 to help bolster the threatened Kabila government, the Zimbabwean dollar fell heavily again. It dropped to a quarter of the value it had before the start of the problems in 1997 and inflation rose even more steeply. The new opposition party captured even more ground and the ruling party chose to react by re-introducing regulations and controls that it had abandoned earlier in the decade.

It then fixed the exchange rate from the beginning of 1999, but inflation reached 70 per cent, interest rates doubled to 80 per cent, business activity slumped and unemployment increased. To win back the initiative, the ruling party commandeered a new movement to redraft the constitution, and the results of this exercise were presented to the population in a referendum in February 2000. Included in it were the provisions considered necessary to speed up land acquisition procedures, mainly by nullifying property rights. But the proposed constitution was defeated.

The government then separately enacted the constitutional amendments needed to remove commercial farmers' rights to challenge it in court. However, its referendum defeat was immensely disturbing to the party and to the war veterans. With the parliamentary elections due within months, Zanu-PF saw the possibility that the war veterans could spearhead their election campaigns in the rural areas. By giving them a free hand to move onto commercial farms and instructing the police not to intervene, the party was seen to be progressing the land acquisition policy and securing the political support of the farm-workers and other rural populations.

As widespread occupations of white-owned farms gathered momentum, the original property owners found that they had no recourse to the law as the activities of the land occupiers were defined as political demonstrations. When the general election in 2000 gave the ruling party only a few more elected seats than the opposition, efforts were made to push the boundaries out even further by stepping up the pace of farm occupations. The government then formally extended these boundaries by announcing that more than 3 000 farms were to be compulsorily acquired.

With the coming Presidential election in mind, part of the war veterans' mission appeared to be to re-indoctrinate the voters among the workers on the farms and in the rural towns. The Presidential election in 2002 was even more disturbing to the social fabric and court cases challenging the results are still pending. Zimbabwe was suspended from the Commonwealth, the overseas bank accounts of senior party officials were frozen and Zimbabwe found itself further isolated from the international community.

In response, the government designated virtually all the remaining white-owned farms for expropriation. Now, all but about 400 commercial farmers have been dispossessed of their farms and this land has been reclassified as the property of the State. It now has no market value and no collateral value, and the people to whom it has been allocated have no ownership rights, no security of tenure and neither the means nor the incentive to invest in production. Meanwhile, the attack on property rights has brought private sector investment virtually to a stop throughout the economy. The government's growing budget deficits have generated hyperinflation, foreign earnings have shrunk to about half the sums of a few years ago and the vastly bigger food imports ran the country's foreign reserves down to zero and then into negative numbers.

Unfortunately, many individuals have profited enormously from the distortions and scarcities in the market. Some in privileged positions have had access to scarce food, foreign exchange and imported luxuries that can be traded at huge profits. Trading in unofficial markets at prices that feed off scarcities has become a more attractive option than production in any industry. Under these conditions, food shortages are acute, job security is crumbling, employment levels are falling by the day and the prospects of serious social unrest are mounting steeply. Industry is being severely damaged by the same policies and the job losses and decline in product volume will become much more serious if the policies are kept in place for much longer.

Many separate crises are coming to a head, including possible financial sector failures due to interest rate policies that have destroyed most of the country's savings. Many exporters are threatened by the exchange rate policy and the whole population faces mounting food shortages and uncertainties over fuel and electricity supplies, while vastly higher charges for electricity are affecting the production of minerals and irrigated crops. The inflation rate remains well above 500 per cent a year, generating uncertainties and social stresses that have become very much more severe with business closures and the increasing possibility that a large proportion of the labour force could soon be thrown out of work.

With all of these issues working against the country at the same time, together with escalating debt, rising inflation and serious food shortages in the second half of 2004, the need for far-reaching policy changes is becoming more urgent by the day. Zimbabwe has felt some benefit from the serious attempts by the new Reserve Bank Governor, Dr Gideon Gono, but he would be the first to agree that a great deal more has to be done. At the heart of the difficulties is the massive reduction in the country's foreign earnings, which has left a gap that cannot be filled by borrowing money or by encouraging the Zimbabweans working abroad to send home whatever money they can save. Exporters have to earn the revenues needed, and the country can achieve this only by fully re-engaging the existing skills and by making Zimbabwe an attractive destination for new investment inflows.

In these regards, Zimbabwe does not seem to be on the right track. The government has announced its intention to ensure that up to 49 per cent of all foreign mining investments is to become the property of indigenous Zimbabweans. This is likely to bring to a halt all new foreign currency inflows to support mining exploration and investment. Minerals that have been underground for millions of years will remain undiscovered and unmined for as long as it takes for Zimbabwe to accept the realities of the financial requirements of large-scale mining. The small-scale mining and gold-panning that will dominate future mining activities will not overcome foreign exchange shortages. All that can be expected of them is that they will damage the environment and cause the more rapid siltation of dams.

For agriculture, the government has recently announced its intention to declare all farmland to be the property of the state. To try to overcome misgivings over farmers' security of tenure, the government intends to offer them lease-hold agreements of up to ninety-nine years. However, the government intends to retain full control over who will be allowed to take over a lease, so lease-hold agreements will not be marketable documents.

As things stand now, this will remove all prospect of leases being bankable. The agreement will not be transferable in the market, so it will not be acceptable as collateral for bank loans and the occupiers of the land will remain as financially disabled and de-motivated as they are today in the communal areas. On this basis, Zimbabwe will not succeed in rebuilding its food security or its former export earnings from agriculture.

As a result of the changes in monetary policies, a start has been made in achieving the needed shrinkage in the number of financial institutions. However, the massive loans to support the less secure banks have still to be repaid and the sharp rise in interest rates is making the recovery process difficult. However, even higher interest rates are needed, given the level of inflation. Savings institutions and pension funds are being endangered by the deeply negative rates still being paid to savers, and the banks are being endangered by every borrower's eagerness to take advantage of loans at only 30 per cent. As loans at very low interest rates cannot make up for the losses being incurred because of the country's over-valued exchange rate, the banks face the prospects of serious loan defaults if exporters are driven to bankruptcy.

Some of Zimbabwe's most important parastatal organizations have experienced marked downturns in their ability to meet the country's needs. Electricity generation is less than installed capacity because of inadequate maintenance and almost no new investment. Efforts to extract the needed revenues from customers have resulted in plans to move productive capacity, such as mineral refineries, into South Africa for cheaper power. If these plans are put into action, Zimbabwe will lose an important source of revenue from current value-adding processes.

The railway services are erratic at best and no longer dependable enough for most users. Conditions on the lines have become so dangerous that the insurance companies serving the railway systems of neighbouring countries have withdrawn the cover offered if any of their rolling stock or locomotives enter Zimbabwe's network.

Flights into Zimbabwe's airports have fallen by more than half in recent years and Zimbabwe's own carrier, Air Zimbabwe, now offers a much reduced service route. Claims that tourist inflows have increased only reflect the large inflows of cross-border traders last year. Regrettably, they did not stay at hotels, go on camera safaris, try bungie-jumping or pay for white-water rafting. They only bought goods at huge discounts for resale outside the country, but they were less eager to come when the exchange rate made their trips less profitable and they stopped coming altogether when police at road-blocks started to confiscate all the foreign currency in their possession. That is why the shops were left with large stocks of unsold goods at the end of 2003.

Under current conditions, other service sectors are struggling too. Wholesalers who hoped to export consumer goods also became victims of the strengthening of the Zimbabwe dollar. With confidence falling and prices rising, the construction industry has too few customers and the transport industry has a large part of its capacity and warehouse space standing idle. Schools are experiencing sharp declines in enrolments and the medical services sector is experiencing serious skills losses as well as cost increases that they cannot pass on to patients.

Role of International Community

Right now, it might be true to say that Zimbabwe has never before been in such dire need of friends and financial support. Whatever might be thought of whether the population's conduct in the past has been or has not been justified, the simple fact is that those who can offer support are not persuaded that the right things have been done, or are being done now. In April 2004, a no-action motion was passed by the members of the United Nations High Commission for Human Rights on the question of human rights in Zimbabwe. This was by a roll-call vote in which twenty-four voted to have pressure applied to Zimbabwe to respect human rights, but twenty-seven voted in favour of no action. Two countries abstained.

The resolution that was rejected in this way expressed deep concern at what it said were continuing violations of human rights in Zimbabwe, in particular politically motivated violence, including killings, torture, sexual and other forms of violence against women, incidents of arbitrary arrest, restrictions on the independence of the judiciary and restrictions on the freedoms of opinion, expression, association and assembly; and at the failure to allow independent civil society in Zimbabwe to operate without fear of harassment or intimidation. Had it been passed, the resolution would have urged the Government of Zimbabwe to take all necessary measures to ensure that all human rights were promoted and protected.

The twenty-seven countries that voted that no action should be taken were mostly African countries, but several Arab countries together with China, Cuba, Russia, Indonesia, India, Pakistan and Sri Lanka supported them. The twenty-four who wanted action taken were entirely outside Africa. They included all the European member countries of the Commission plus the United States, Japan, South Korea and about half a dozen South or Central American countries. It is worth summarizing the arguments made to demolish the human rights case put forward in the motion, because the basis for this divide between the African and Asian grouping and the world's most industrialized countries becomes a little more apparent in the choice of words.

From the DRC representative came the claim that the Zimbabwe government had been demonized because of its redressing of the uneven distribution of land that had been perpetuated since colonial days, and he claimed this redistribution process was completely unrelated to the human rights issues. The Cuban representative said that although the resolution was drafted on human rights issues, it was totally unrelated to human rights. It was aimed at undermining the right of the 'heroic people of Zimbabwe' to land. Nigeria said that, 'without prejudice to its own commitment to human rights and fundamental freedoms', Nigeria would endorse the position of the African Group on the no-action motion. China supported the no-action vote because it said that China believed the resolution had nothing to do with the promotion and protection of human rights. It was simply the product of the politicization of international standards. Finally, the Zimbabwean representative said that human rights problems in the country were not out of the ordinary and the allegations should not be allowed to take up the Commission's time.

The US said the government of Zimbabwe was conducting a concerted campaign of violence, repression and intimidation against its citizens, clearly demonstrating the leadership's gross disregard for the full range of human rights. The international community should resolutely condemn the repressive policies of the Mugabe regime, which denied the people their inalienable human rights. The US also pointed out that the idea of no-action motions amounted to approval of human rights abuses being perpetrated by nations serving on the Commission for Human Rights, but choosing to disregard the principles of the Commission.

These samples of the official thinking of developed and developing countries throw only a little light on the major distinction between them. But that 'developed' and 'developing' distinction is not accurate, neither is a north-south distinction, and an east-west distinction does not work either. For example, developing South and Central American states sided with the rich Western and Far-Eastern countries in the Northern Hemisphere, so the issue is more complicated.

Perhaps the best labels for the two compartments would be 'democratic' and 'non-democratic'. Of course, we would have to make sure we are not fooled by the inclusion of the word Democratic in the official names of various countries, such as the Democratic People's Republic of Korea or the Democratic Republic of the Congo. Under the Khmer Rouge, Cambodia was known as Democratic Kampuchea and East Germany used to be called the German Democratic Republic. But perhaps this misuse of the word also shows up one of the principal common features of such countries – dishonesty so deep that they have lost the ability to recognize it.

At the core of the real difference between these groups of countries is the eagerness of the one to accept, and the complete rejection by the other, of the very idea that ordinary people should have a voice, have power and have a say in the choice and conduct of their country's leaders. In other words, have rights.

Removing Individual Rights in Zimbabwe

I attempt to trace the events in Zimbabwe through this concept of rights by linking two facts, which are that at the start of the land reform programme, people had rights, and that today, most of these rights have been stamped out. I also hope to show that the alleged moves made to empower the masses has actually led to their disempowerment and that, in other ways too, the government of Zimbabwe has achieved exactly the opposite of its claimed successes.

When the first compulsory land acquisition orders were issued, the property owners were able to seek the protection of the law in several ways. Their property rights were constitutionally protected to start with, and the rights of others to whom money was owed if the payments for the land were still in progress were also protected in law. The farmers threatened with dispossession were able to take the government to court. In terms of the law, the judges were right to find in favour of the farmers, or more accurately the formally constituted and registered limited liability companies run by the farmers. Very quickly, legal precedents were set and by the first anniversary of the original batches of land acquisition papers, when the government had acquired those properties owned by absentee landlords and only a few others, hundreds of other cases did not have to go to court.

President Mugabe was deeply angered by the fact that his presidential powers could be challenged by farmers and by the fact that the courts could find in their favour. He announced his intention to change the law and to change the constitution to accommodate his legal requirements. With rather ominous clouds threatening the constitution appearing on the horizon, a private initiative was launched to propose a new constitution that would carefully enshrine and more effectively entrench the rights that seemed to be most at risk.

This initiative was seen by the ruling party as a threat, so it was hijacked by the party and repackaged as a government exercise. A Constitutional Commission was established, inputs were sought from the public and the commission assembled proposals that reflected a wide consensus. However, a much more narrowly drafted constitution was presented to the electorate in a referendum, and this would have given the government sweeping powers to expropriate land by removing property owners' legal rights to contest acquisition orders. Many of the constitutional commission members dissociated themselves from the proposals, saying that they did not represent the views they had gathered from the public.

The referendum was held early in 2000 and it was defeated. The ruling party at that time had not had to contest any election against a strong opposition party, so it still had an overwhelming majority in parliament. However, by the beginning of 2000 the new Movement for Democratic Change party was becoming a potential threat and a new parliamentary election was to be fought within a few months. Zanu-PF used its majority in the House to quickly pass constitutional changes to give effect to the provisions that had been rejected in the referendum.

While this process was taking place, the ruling party, in its guise as the government, authorized the war veterans' movement to occupy commercial farms and instructed police to assist them. Police were specifically instructed not to assist the farmers or their families in any form of conflict that might arise. Effectively, the commercial farmers were denied the protection of the law. As the constitutional amendments were pushed through, the property laws themselves were changed, but many other laws concerning protection against physical molestation and personal rights were simply flouted. Knowing that they could keep anything they could pinch, opportunists descended upon the unprotected families. Many dreadful accounts of abuse stemmed from these events.

When the parliamentary elections resulted in the biggest opposition party wins in Zimbabwe's history and many of the claimed victories of the Zanu-PF candidates were shown to be highly suspect, the party set about deepening its resolve to eradicate any power groups that could challenge its authority. Judges who had found in favour of opponents on any issue found themselves being threatened, and appointments to the bench were stepped up to dilute their influence. Then a sequence of forced resignations followed until almost the entire judiciary was composed of judges selected by the party.

To get to the core of what has been achieved by the Zimbabwean government, it has to be pointed out that each move has been designed to remove the power that any individual or interest group might have had to challenge a government decision. Property owners used to have legal power because of their property rights, so these rights had to be withdrawn at the constitutional level. At a less formal level, the ruling party has given itself the right to deny anyone the protection of the law if they choose to oppose anything the party decides to do. The cases in point could fill many hundreds of pages, but they include the destruction of the independent daily Press, the conversion of the national police force into a party police force, the establishment of a party youth militia with extrajudicial powers and the establishment of a party-political structure that is anything but democratic.

The people have been told that they have been empowered by being given back their land. In fact, the collective rights conferred upon them, which might be common to North Korea or Cuba, have wiped out their rights as individuals. Even if they have the land in some figurative sense, they have no individual rights of ownership, no security of tenure and no right to express support for any system that would diminish the government's absolute power over them. In fact, they have been totally disempowered.

The countries that voted to suppress the debate on human rights in Zimbabwe almost all appear to share the same belief that their own populations should be kept in their place of subservience to the power of the ruling party. India might appear to be an exception, but that could be more in theory than in fact.

The effects on Zimbabwe's economy extend across the full range of the country's productive and social sectors, but the focus can be left where the debacle started – on agriculture. Big efficient farms have been broken up into small farms that would need subsidies even if the farmers were very experienced. The subsidies needed by experienced farmers on small farms all over Europe provide ample proof of this. European countries can afford subsidies, but Zimbabwe cannot. Furthermore, the majority of the new farmers are far from experienced. Food production has been cut to a third of its former level and foreign earnings have been cut by more than half. Zimbabwe can no longer afford to buy what it is now regularly failing to grow.

The damage done to property rights, to the monetary system, to the country's competitiveness in foreign markets, to its international credit rating and to its standing with development agencies has brought new investment almost to a halt. Mining has been the only important exception, but new proposals to enforce indigenization could soon change that.

Zimbabwe has always been proud of its transport, power, health, education and tourist infrastructure, and its citizens used to boast that its skills base was the best in the Third World. Now its infrastructure is in a very sorry state. State health facilities and schools can no longer perform beyond the most rudimentary levels, power cuts are frequent, rail and air transport services are highly uncertain and the hotels and holiday resorts are almost empty. Skilled people are now Zimbabwe's biggest export. The Zimbabwean economy has shrunk by more than a third, meaning that both the people have experienced a severe fall in average standards of living and the country has suffered a sharp decline in its ability to provide for its needs. The population is too big and too well educated to be expected to settle for a smaller and less sophisticated economy, but unless the situation changes rapidly, a much smaller economy might soon be all that is left.

An acceptable solution to the crisis in Zimbabwe would have to include the full restoration of human rights, property rights and the rule of law, plus the creation of a genuinely democratic constitution. However, the attempts made so far by domestic as well as international groups to force the pace and direction of change in Zimbabwe have brought forth nothing but ridicule and derision from those in power. If the unrestrained powers of Zimbabwe's ruling clique, or of the similarly motivated rulers of other countries, remain more than a match for the best that internal and external forces are prepared to raise against them, then far more serious tragedies await us in Africa.

Section 2

Democratization in Africa

Democratization in Kenya – Some Observations

William M Bellamy

The December 2002 Presidential election victory of Mwai Kibaki, and the parliamentary majority won by the 'Rainbow' coalition of parties he headed, are landmark events in modern Kenyan history. With this vote Kenyans put an end to twenty-four years of one-party rule under the autocratic Daniel Arap Moi and raised expectations of major changes in the way Kenya is governed. Indeed, President Kibaki's promises to voters included completion of a new constitution, as well as wide-ranging actions to begin to redress the devastating legacy of economic decline and social neglect left behind by the Moi regime.

For all the celebration, both in Kenya and internationally, that followed the December 2002 elections, it would be inaccurate to conclude that Kenya has undergone a democratic transition.[1] In reality, Kenya has functioned formally as a democracy since the first days of its independence. Long before Kibaki's election, Kenyan voters had acquired the habit of voting regularly, and especially voting in and out of office their legislative representatives. Kibaki himself had twice run for the Presidency in the 1990s. His victory in 2002 was as much the result of lessons learned, and of savvy coalition building among Kenya's diverse political leaders and parties, as of popular disenchantment with Moi's and the Kenya African National Union (KANU)'s governance failures.

The advent of the Kibaki administration is an important step forward in Kenya's progress towards a more mature democracy. For the first time, Kenya is governed by a coalition of parties that reflects the ethnic and regional diversity of the country. Unlike under President Moi, Parliament will be called upon to play a central role both in shaping policy and in legislating the many political, economic and social reforms promised by the Kibaki government. There is no guarantee that Kenya will successfully

---

His Excellency **William M Bellamy** is the US Ambassador to Kenya. The opinions expressed are those of the author's alone.

consolidate this gain. It is not clear that the Kibaki government will actually be able to translate its popular victory into meaningful, sought-after reforms. Should he falter, however, events of the past several years have served to implant more deeply in Kenyan society the demand for, and expectation of, democratic governance. Among many ordinary Kenyans, there is a belief that, whatever the political future holds in store, 'the bad old days' of autocratic, one-man rule are definitively behind them.

All Politics are Local – and Ethnic

Kenya's unfinished democracy rests on two historical pillars. The first is the legacy of British colonial rule. Whatever errors were committed by Britain in its withdrawal from Kenya, it cannot be argued that it failed to leave behind viable institutions. Prior to independence, educated Kenyans were recruited and inserted into the provincial administration, the eyes and ears of the central government: its administrative and police apparatus and its instrument for the delivery of governmental services to the grassroots. Throughout the early years of Kenya's independence, the provincial administration served professionally and well. Though much abused during the Moi presidency, the provincial administration remains an important instrument of future effective governance. Britain also left behind a functioning parliamentary system. Four legislative elections were held in the six years leading up to independence in 1963 precisely for the purpose of normalizing the connection between voting and the creation of representative government free of colonial interference. By the time Kenya became independent, Kenya's voters already had considerable experience in the polling stations. Finally, and somewhat less relevant to this discussion, Britain instituted a massive land settlement and loan scheme at independence to transfer land from white settlers to the indigenous population. The land issue, still a critical one in many respects today, was de-racialized and largely divorced from the colonial experience at the outset of Kenyan independence.

With this inheritance in hand, Kenya embarked on a 14-year period (1963-78) of Presidential rule under founding father Jomo Kenyatta, a period best described as a mixture of active democracy at the local level and

---

[1] Throughout this paper I have drawn heavily and unashamedly on the work of Joel D. Barkan, Judith K. Geist, and Njuguna Ng'ethe contained in the draft monograph *Kenya in Transition* (23 January 2003).

semi-authoritarian practices at the national level. The key characteristic of Kenyan politics today was evident at the outset: the tendency of Kenyan citizens to define their economic, social and political interests in terms of where they live, and not on the basis of their occupation or economic class.

This tendency is common across most of Africa and other agrarian societies, and gives rise to a distinctive form of politics regardless of the formal structures of the state. In this context, local and ethnic considerations are uppermost in people's minds. The result is that parties are little more than shifting coalitions of local organizations created to mobilize local electorates on the basis of appeals made to local interests and ethnic identity.

This is the second pillar of Kenya's democratic experience: all (or almost all) politics are local and ethnic. Political parties only exist to represent the interests of individual leaders and the residents of particular geographic communities. The political process in this context is one of perpetual coalition building – of the formation and reformation of coalitions of local organizations that have no common interests other than the control of the state and its resources. The objective is to control the state for the purpose of funnelling state resources back to one's supporters and local communities.

This characteristic of Kenyan politics is both a weakness and strength. It is a weakness because it is an open invitation to patronage politics, clientelism and corruption, and because it subordinates nationhood and national interests to neighbourhood and parochial interests. Even before Kenyatta's death in 1978, corruption had become a significant problem, although it was not until the early years of the Moi presidency, in the mid-1980s, that the monopolization and appropriation of state resources reached truly alarming proportions. Diverting state revenues into private accounts, operating parastatal enterprises as private fiefdoms and packing the civil service with trusted if not competent ethnic kinsmen were some of the hallmarks of the neo-patrimonial system perfected by President Moi. It is noteworthy that this corruption was not practiced primarily as a matter of personal enrichment, although many of President Moi's associates became very wealthy men in the 1980s and 1990s. The neo-patrimonial system's main purpose was to maintain the President in power by ensuring a steady flow of patronage and largesse to local political chiefs, members of parliament and key government officials.

One of the most telling elements in this system was the low pay accorded members of parliament. Until recently, elected members of parliament earned a little over US$1000 per month. MPs were meant not only to support themselves and their families on this sum, which is admittedly far in excess of the average Kenyan's income, but also to pay all official expenses from it – including food, travel, lodging while in Nairobi, salaries for staff, and constituent services. Surveys showed that most MPs spent more than US$1000 per month in constituency services alone, ranging from paying school fees, helping with medical bills, issuing small loans, contributing to small development projects. MPs are expected to perform these small services for voters; those who do not seldom win re-election. One of the more enduring images of the Moi years was the line of MPs at State House on Friday mornings, waiting for their brief interview with the President and the envelope of cash they would take back to their constituency for the weekend.

Paradoxically, the strongly local and ethnic nature of Kenyan politics is also a boon to democratic development in some ways. It creates an important check against the centralization of power under an authoritarian leader. These countervailing tendencies were visible in the early years as Kenyatta gradually but inexorably co-opted or sidelined his political opponents to create, by 1969, a virtual one-party state. Though he had informally eliminated competition from political parties at the national level, Kenyatta was never able to completely control or channel grassroots political energy. Partly this was due to Kenyatta's own sponsorship of the time-honoured Kenyan tradition of 'Harambee' – self-help committees at the local level that raised funds and provided labour to build basic infrastructure, with assistance expected from the locally-elected MP. The Harrambee system resulted in a vibrant civil society in the most densely populated rural areas of Kenya, and created a special bond between local communities and their elected leaders. Even at the heyday of his power in the late 1980s, when he was dispensing envelopes of cash to MPs heading back to their constituencies for weekend Harambees, President Moi was not in a position routinely to impose his choice of an MP on any particular constituency. The primacy of the peculiar relationship between communities and their elected leaders trumped Presidential power at the local level.

Kenyan voters are, moreover, extremely demanding of their elected representatives. From the earliest days of Kenyan independence and continuing to the present day, voters have routinely ejected more than 50 per cent of incumbent MPs at election time. (The percentage of incumbents defeated in the 2002 parliamentary elections was close to two-thirds.) Even though one party (KANU) totally dominated Kenyan politics for two decades, no KANU officeholder was spared the requirement of campaigning for and winning his seat at the local level, usually in competition with other KANU aspirants in what amounted to 'primary' elections.

Perhaps another paradox in the Kenyan system of governance has been the fact that ethnicity, which is so often considered a source of divisiveness, has also worked to keep in check the centralizing and authoritarian tendencies in the Kenyan presidency. Depending on the criteria one uses in counting, Kenya contains as many as forty-nine distinct tribes or ethnic groups (although only a dozen can be considered numerically significant). The largest of these groups, the Kikuyu, number about 23 per cent of the country's total population. Thus, if only local/ethnic considerations are considered, any attempt at coalition-building at the national level must combine at least three or four different groups to achieve a majority. Both Kenyatta and Moi experimented with different combinations of ethnic coalition-building at the national level. The conclusion one draws from these experiences is that it is extremely difficult to build enduring coalitions across multiple ethnic boundaries, particularly in a system that depends heavily on trickle-down patronage from governments that have prioritized the diversion of public resources to partisan use and are thereby unable to stimulate or sustain real growth in the economy. One of the major constraints faced by the Moi Presidency by the late 1980s was that the demands of patronage had outstripped the system's ability to divert funds from a weakened public sector.

Repression Under Moi

The constitutional and institutional framework inherited at independence, a strong measure of active democracy at the local level and a dispersal of power due to ethnic diversity were factors that mitigated dictatorship in Kenya. Nonetheless, for many Kenyans these factors made little obvious difference in the 1980s and 1990s. Kenya suffered enormous damage over this period in terms of human rights abuses, bad governance and economic decline. The descent became most noticeable following a failed coup attempt by a handful of air force officers in 1982. Thereafter, President Moi took few chances. Repression against suspected opponents intensified, including the use of torture. Legislation was passed turning Kenya formally into a one-party state. The packing of the civil service with ethnic loyalists – and the weeding out of certain suspect ethnic groups (especially the Kikuyu) – accelerated dramatically. More power was centralized within the office of the Presidency, most notably control over regional and local development funds, drought assistance and food aid. Attempts were made, not altogether successfully, to transform KANU into an omnipresent force in political and social life.

By the end of the 1980s, Moi had effectively throttled most open forms of opposition to his rule, gathered enormous power into the Presidency and appropriated broad swathes of the economy for his own political purposes. Although few could see it at the time, his system was at the zenith of its influence and would soon begin to unravel. Poor governance, disastrous declines in the functioning of the civil service, runaway corruption, crumbling infrastructure, loss of investor and donor confidence and mounting resistance to the regime's heavy-handed suppression of the opposition combined to put Moi under heavy pressure by the beginning of the 1990s. Importantly, as the Kenyan economy languished, sources of regime patronage dried up.

It was at this juncture that interventions by the international community played a critical role in transforming the Kenyan political scene. Although Moi had been a valuable ally of the United States and the West throughout the Cold War, the effect on Kenya's stability as well as the dire human consequences of continuing bad governance and economic decline could no longer be ignored. Initially, only a handful of donor states, including the US, were willing to publicly call for an end to repression and to the one-party state. Others joined later and, by 1991, the International Monetary Fund (IMF) suspended its lending programme as a result of the Kenyan government's failure to address human rights and economic governance issues. While the Moi government denounced donor and International Financial Institutions (IFI) interference in Kenyan affairs and vowed not to bend to such pressure tactics, within a month of the IMF suspension parliament had repealed the 1983 law that established Kenya as a one-party state.

Many in power today in the Kibaki government were opposition figures at that time and recall the role played by embassies, donor states and international institutions in applying pressure on the Moi regime. There is little doubt in their minds that domestic pressure alone would not have sufficed to open up Kenya to multi-partyism, at least not by 1992, when the first multi-party elections took place. It is also true, however, that were domestic conditions not right – had not a pattern been established of internal resistance to one-man and one-party rule – then outside pressures would have been of little effect. Together, internal and external pressure forced an opening of political space in Kenya which allowed genuine multi-party competition in elections in 1992, 1997 and 2002.

Kenya in the 1990s: The Gradual Triumph of Democracy
The story of Kenya in the 1990s is one of diverse democratic forces gathering strength, thanks in part to the protection and sponsorship of the international community, and of a corresponding loss of control by President Moi as a worsening economy and defections from KANU ranks progressively limited his room for manoeuvre.

In remarkably similar fashion, Moi was able to win the Presidency in both the 1992 and 1997 elections by a narrow plurality. In both elections, opposition candidates and parties were divided along geographic and ethnic lines and thus splintered the vote. However, these elections brought to the fore a new generation of political leadership, both in opposition ranks and within KANU itself. This successor generation was often foreign educated, computer literate, experienced in grassroots activism and well connected to the global NGO network. When a prominent Kenyan NGO, backed by foreign donors, sponsored a series of parliamentary workshops in the late 1990s, crowds of new MPs showed up. These workshops marked the final transformation of parliament from a backwater where elected representatives bided their time between visits to their constituencies to an effective counterweight to the executive power of the presidency. In these workshops, new MPs from all parties, including KANU, openly debated policy issues, a practice practically unheard of during the Moi heyday. More importantly, these workshops set a course towards thoroughgoing parliamentary reform, which included legislation formally separating parliament (and parliamentary salaries) from the Office of the Presidency, creation of a parliamentary personnel office (to separate parliamentary staff from the civil service), establishment of a committee system and increased funding for staff and facilities. By the time of the 2002 election, this alliance between civil society, the donor community and the Kenyan parliament had created a legislature that was empowered, independent and a growing check on Presidential power.

Throughout this period, President Moi's poor governance and the nation's mounting economic woes increased Kenya's vulnerability to pressure from the IMF and World Bank. Three IMF programmes were started and suspended from 1990 to 2000. The unwillingness of the IFIs and the donor community after 1990 to countenance the Moi government's worsening human rights and economic record limited the regime's room for manoeuvre.

As the 2002 Presidential elections approached, there were many doubts within Kenya that Moi would respect the Presidential two-term limit imposed by constitutional amendment a few years earlier. In a final effort to escape mounting internal and international pressure, Moi undertook a series of coalition-building efforts in early 2002 that carried him well across ethnic lines. Despite some initial successes, these efforts to enlarge the ruling party ended up exacerbating tensions within KANU. When Moi anointed as his successor Uhuru Kenyatta, son of the founding father but a political newcomer, many KANU members left the party to join the opposition. Moi's and KANU's fates were sealed when, unlike in 1992 and 1997, Kenya's ethnically diverse opposition parties coalesced into a single presidential and parliamentary ticket. Had they instead repeated past errors by failing to unite, it is entirely possible that Uhuru Kenyatta would have won despite his connection to Moi and widespread disenchantment with KANU's governance. In the event, Kibaki's 'Rainbow Coalition' swept to power with more than 60 per cent of the vote.

Kenya peacefully achieved multi-partyism in 2002 after years of repressive and corrupt rule. The path followed was a long and at times uncertain one. If there is a lesson to be learned, it may be that gradualism can work. In Kenya's case, constraints on executive power were built up slowly over time, with increasing help from outside the country. The President's room for manoeuvre was slowly narrowed as the stage was set for his peaceful ouster.

The Future

The challenges facing the Kibaki government are daunting. Two decades of misrule under Moi caused enormous fundamental economic and social damage. These were the 'wasted years of nationhood', in Kibaki's words. Slow economic growth, huge drops in public sector capital investment (and corresponding increases in public sector wages and patronage payments), and overall mismanagement of the economy throughout this period produced an alarming human balance sheet:

- Per capita annual income declined from US$271 in 1990 to US$239 in 2002
- The percentage of Kenyans living in poverty rose from 48 per cent in 1990 to 56 per cent in 2002
- In 1990, 11.3 million Kenyans were poor. In 2001, the number was 17 million
- Life expectancy declined and infant and child mortality rates rose in the 1990s

Expectations are high in Kenya that the Kibaki government will deliver on its campaign promises and attack these ills. In its first year, the new Kenyan government marked a clear departure from its predecessor. Kibaki instituted free primary education for all, launched an ambitious road-building programme, regulated the fearsome private taxi industry upon which most Kenyans depend for transport, and set up anti-corruption machinery within government that soon produced a housecleaning of Kenya's corrupt judiciary. The IMF and World Bank have both announced renewed lending to Kenya. Relations with donors are excellent.

Yet these gains have been offset by political setbacks. Battles within the governing coalition began almost as soon as Kibaki announced his new cabinet in January 2003. Kibaki's main rival, Luo politician and Liberal Democratic Party (LDP) leader Raila Odinga and his followers insist that Kibaki has failed to honour the pre-election memorandum of understanding that called for an equal division of ministerial portfolios between Kibaki's National Alliance Party of Kenya (NAK) and Odinga's LDP. Moreover, Kibaki is alleged also to have reneged on his promise to create a prime ministerial position for Odinga. The dispute has spilled over into the process of drafting a new constitution (a process that began in the latter Moi years) and resulted in its virtual deadlock. The Kibaki-Odinga rivalry has gradually escalated to the cabinet level, where the conduct of government business has slowed.

Spreading beneath this rivalry are whispered concerns that Kenya is witnessing a revival of tribal politics. Kibaki is a Kikuyu, most of his closest advisers and colleagues in cabinet are Kikuyu: the Moi years were hard on the Kikuyus, and now it is payback time – or so the popular reasoning goes. Without actually joining the Odinga camp, other Kenyan parties and politicians have expressed similar misgivings about what they see as the exclusiveness of Kibaki's so-called 'Mount Kenya mafia' and the secrecy with which this mostly Kikuyu group seems to operate within government.

These problems have been compounded by what some consider a hands-off style of governance by President Kibaki. While there is much virtue in Kibaki's practice of delegating responsibility to ministers (Moi, by contrast, micro-managed every ministry), the frequency and severity of public clashes between ministers has created an image of chaotic government. Part of the problem may be related to Kibaki's health. The President was slow to recover from a motor accident in December 2002 and from complications related to the treatment of his injuries. The infrequency of Kibaki's public appearances and his apparent reluctance to wade into the fray and restore order may be due, some argue, to diminished physical or even mental capacities. Kibaki and his advisers insist that his health is normal.

Whatever the truth, the Kibaki government is splintered by internal conflicts that have little to do with ideology or programmes but appear more related to geographically and ethnically based rivalries. The conflicts have stalled and possibly killed the process of constitutional revision and greatly slowed the pace of day-to-day government business, including movement of legislation through the National Assembly.

Kibaki has promised Kenyans they will have a new constitution by June 2004. That deadline, like all earlier ones, will not be met. Although the Constitutional Review Commission of over 600 delegates completed its work and agreed by a two-thirds majority a new draft constitution in March, the courts, at the instigation of elements in the Kibaki government, have blocked parliament from taking up the draft. Kibaki's followers are concerned that the draft constitution goes too far in limiting the powers of the President and that it sets up a devolution of power to local governments that is both unnecessary and ruinously expensive. Both complaints have some merit. However, with the constitutional draft now in limbo, the Kibaki administration has opened itself to charges that it is trying to manipulate the review process to produce a constitution tailor-made for the incumbent President.

Constitutional debates have been the focal point of the bitterest infighting in the Kibaki government. The government now finds itself in a cul-de-sac, with a stalled process and no clear way forward. Because of factionalism in the governing coalition, the government does not have the votes in Parliament needed to push through its own constitutional amendments, assuming it chose that route.

Already, less than two years into the Kibaki administration, there is talk of the coalition falling apart, possibly to be replaced by a different combination of parties. Several of Kibaki's supporters have pushed, thus far unsuccessfully, to disband all the constituent parties of the 'Rainbow Coalition' in favour of one overarching Party, the National Rainbow Coalition (NARC). This has been bitterly resisted by Odinga and other component parties of the coalition. At the same time, feelers have gone out to the opposition KANU to determine if it might consider joining government in the event Odinga's LDP quits the coalition. These and other reactions to the current political crisis all, unfortunately, point backwards to earlier periods when Kenyatta and Moi sought to absorb or co-opt opposing parties. These efforts testify to the difficulties Kenya is having in adjusting to government by multi-party coalition. As one prominent

KANU member remarked recently: 'It's hard to know what the role of the Official Opposition is supposed to be when the most vociferous opposition is coming from within government itself'.

The real danger of governmental infighting is that it makes it much harder for the Kibaki government to the concentrate on governance and delivering on its electoral promises. Legislation is needed now to combat terrorism, fight financial crime and pave the way for privatization of failing state-owned enterprises. This work is not getting done. The longer the government takes to put in place enabling legislation and actually to launch its promised reforms, the harder it will be to do so in the future. In particular, the steps the Kenyan government must undertake to get rid of loss-making parastatals, restore basic services (communications, power, water and sanitation and transport) and generate badly needed foreign investment all involve pain and sacrifice. For example, jobs must be shed in government and inefficient sectors of the economy, at least in the short run, if there is to be sufficient revenue to rebuild infrastructure and provide basic services (and thereby make Kenya competitive as a site for foreign investment). No Kenyan government can afford to wait until the year before the next election to make these moves.

Whatever its shortcomings, the Kibaki government is still enjoying a honeymoon with the electorate. This hiatus could continue for months. Most Kenyans accept that they are much better off today than under the previous KANU government, even if their lives have not changed dramatically since December 2002. There is a palpable sense in Kenya that there can be no turning back to old practices, and that any attempt by a political leader or party to do so would be met with significant popular resistance. And while there is comfort in this for most ordinary Kenyans, there is also the realization that resistance alone does not point the way to the future.

Looking to the future, it is hard not to agree with the summary views of Joel D. Barkan, Judith K. Geist and Njuguna Ng'ethe when they note that Kenya is a much younger country today than in 1992, that a new generation of leadership is in power or on the fringes of power and that opportunities to practice old style, neo-patrimonial politics, with all of the ethnic and patronage considerations that are built into it, are declining. Considerations of policy are more prominent than ever before. This newer group of Kenyan politicians spans the ethnic spectrum. It is not shy about questioning presidential authority and will subject the executive to demands for oversight and better governance. Kenya has never had a better opportunity to change for the better the manner in which it is governed.

The Challenge of Democratization in Ethiopia

Christopher Clapham

Introduction

The rapid transition to multi-party democracy of many African countries over the last fifteen years has been one of the most encouraging developments in the continent. In every region of the continent, there are now states where it has become normal for citizens to participate, every four or five years, in elections at which they are free to vote for the party that they wish, and where the victory in those elections of an opposition party leads to a peaceful change of government. Though inevitably it takes time for changes in political arrangements to be reflected in long-term changes in social and economic conditions, there is also now mounting evidence that democratic governance does indeed contribute significantly to improving the often miserable condition of Africa's peoples.[1] The often self-serving claim that Africa was in some way unsuited to democracy has been convincingly rebutted.

It would, however, be unreasonable to expect democratic habits and institutions to be adopted equally easily and unproblematically in every part of the continent. There can be no single blueprint. Political arrangements everywhere – and especially democratic ones, since these necessarily reflect the cultures and identities of the peoples to which they are applied – must be adapted to specific circumstances, which may be far more conducive in some places than others. Most obviously, the existence of a structure of order and government must logically precede the way in which that government is chosen; and though a government chosen by the people whom it governs is likely to be far more effective than one that is imposed on them, it has been amply demonstrated that one cannot simply use elections as a means to create a viable and legitimate government,

---

Professor **Christopher Clapham** is an Associate of the Centre for African Studies at Cambridge University.

under circumstances where the basis for such a government does not already exist. No-one can plausibly expect states that have collapsed like Somalia or Liberia, or peoples who have been brutalized by vicious civil wars, to be rescued by the instant application of democracy. Equally, different states have different histories, cultures, sizes, and economic and demographic structures that at the very least have to be taken into account in the construction of democratic formulae, and that may make any form of democracy more or less easy to achieve.

Ethiopia illustrates this truism with particular clarity. It certainly does not belong in the category of collapsed states, and though in recent decades it has suffered from an appalling level of both civil and external war, it is now nonetheless a country broadly at peace. Its transformation into an effective democracy is not, therefore, simply ruled out from the start. It does, however, suffer from a set of legacies that have made democracy particularly difficult to achieve, and that must require any process of democratization to be carefully crafted to fit its distinctive circumstances. It is no responsibility of mine to tell Ethiopians how to achieve this. It may however be helpful if – as an external observer of over forty years' standing – I attempt to outline some of the features of the country's history and development that must inevitably affect it. I will do so by outlining some of the 'challenges' to democratization in Ethiopia, together with recent developments that have made its achievement both more possible and more necessary.

Challenges to Democratization

The Challenge of History[2]
The past does not determine the future. Few countries start as democracies, and some (Germany and Japan, for example) have managed astonishingly rapid transitions from brutal autocracies to stable democracy. Nonetheless, history does establish patterns than may guide people's expectations, and make democracy harder or easier to achieve. In

---

[1] See, for example, Rod Alence, 'Political institutions and developmental governance in sub-Saharan Africa', *The Journal of Modern African Studies* (Vol. 42 No.2, June 2004, pp.163-187).
[2] For background reading on Ethiopian history, see Paul Henze, *Layers of Time: a history of Ethiopia* (London: Hurst & Co, 2000); and Bahru Zewde, *A History of Modern Ethiopia, 1855-1991* (Oxford: James Currey, 2nd ed. 2001).

Ethiopia's case, it makes it harder. Throughout the distinguished past that makes it Africa's oldest state, it has never (prior to the accession of the present government in 1991) had any regime with the slightest plausible claim to democracy, and it has lacked much of the basic experience that we tend to take for granted in other parts of the continent. Though elections were held to a powerless House of Representatives in the period between 1957 and 1973, no political parties were allowed to form; and though a vanguard single party, the Workers' Party of Ethiopia, was established under the Derg regime (Amharic for 'committee', the abbreviation of the Coordinating Committee of the Armed Forces, Police, and Territorial Army) in 1984, not until after 1991 did Ethiopia hold its first elections to be contested between rival parties.

No Ethiopian government, consequently, has ever gained power by election, and over the last century and a half succession to power has almost invariably been determined by force. Rulers have been overthrown by external invasion (1868, 1936, 1941), by civil war (1855, 1871, 1889, 1991), and by coup d'état (1916, 1974 (twice), 1977). Only in 1913 and 1930 were there 'legitimate' successions, in each case after the death of the incumbent. Ousted leaders have been killed (1868, 1889, 1974 (two), 1977), imprisoned (1916) or gone into exile (1936, 1991); no Ethiopian ruler has ever continued to live peacefully in the country after losing power, as happened even after transitions as momentous as those in Zimbabwe in 1980 and South Africa in 1994. This is a tough record to break, and makes it difficult to establish the expectation of peaceful succession on which democracy depends.

The Challenge of Structure

Different countries are fitted together in different ways, in terms both of the ways in which they were formed, and of the range of geographical features and social demographies that they encompass. In both respects, Ethiopia's experience has been difficult.

Though it has been widely assumed in Africa that 'artificial' states formed by external colonialism have particular difficulties in establishing the basis for stable governance, the problems are in some ways greater in a country like Ethiopia that was established by internal force. The 'historic' core of the Ethiopian state lies in the northern highland zone, stretching from the region of Addis Ababa to present-day south-central Eritrea, which has long been inhabited by Orthodox Christians speaking the Amharic and Tigrinya languages. Though it has never been an 'ethnic' state, in which membership of a particular group has been an essential qualification for political power, its leaders have been expected to assume the cultural traits associated with this core. The rapid expansion of the country's territory, especially in the late nineteenth century, therefore led to the incorporation (and in many places, the ruthless exploitation) of other peoples, who were generally regarded as inferior, and had very limited (if any) opportunity to participate in government. Many of these people were Muslim.

Ethiopia was therefore dogged by a premise of inequality, in which full incorporation into the state required the abandonment of one's own indigenous culture and identity, and the assumption – in terms of name, religion, food and dress, language – of those historically associated with the state. Many individuals made this transition, and rose to the highest positions in government; but many more were alienated from and oppressed by the state in a way that would inevitably deeply affect political attitudes once they gained the democratic ability to express them.

The country's geographic and demographic range is also enormous.[3] One of Africa's largest countries by population, it encompasses every ecological zone from highland plateau through rainforest and savannah to areas below sea level, every economic system from ox-plough agriculture to nomadic pastoralism, and every social system from feudal hierarchy to egalitarian anarchy, including substantial longstanding Christian and Muslim populations, in an area of the world where religion has been a primary social and political marker. A number of African countries certainly enjoy a comparable diversity, though few have such rugged topography or such poor communications, but when combined with other factors, this diversity makes the maintenance of consensual political structures considerably more complex.

The Challenge of Culture

'Culture' is a tricky concept to grasp, and Ethiopia in any event has a wide range of cultures, corresponding to its ecological, ethnic and social diversity. Nonetheless, ways of thinking about issues of power and authority are often deeply entrenched, and profoundly affect the ways in which politics works in any part of the world. Despite its diversity, moreover, Ethiopia has

---

[3] For a discussion of the implications of Ethiopia's size and diversity, see Christopher Clapham, 'Ethiopia', in Christopher Clapham, Jeffrey Herbst and Greg Mills, eds. *Africa's Big States* (forthcoming 2004).

a 'state culture' derived from its long imperial history and from the societies especially of the northern highlands, which, despite the upheavals of revolution and social change, continue to exercise a strong influence.[4]

In sharp contrast to that misleading stereotype that sees African societies as inherently egalitarian and democratic, Ethiopian state culture has placed enormous emphasis on hierarchy and obedience. Entrenched in language, dress, socialization practices and the exercise of authority down to the local and indeed familial level, it has taught Ethiopians that people are not equal, and that those in authority are worthy (at least in public) of unremitting deference, obedience and respect. These attitudes bear a major part of the responsibility for many of Ethiopia's greatest achievements, including the maintenance of effective government over many centuries and over a huge area, the military capacity that ensured the country's independence from colonial rule, and the ability to absorb upheavals that would have shattered a less solidly established state. The change of regime in May 1991, for example, when the Derg's forces crumbled in the face of the advancing Ethiopian People's Revolutionary Democratic Front (EPRDF), was achieved with minimal bloodshed and destruction, and only the briefest hiatus between the collapse of one government and the installation of its successor.

This culture of obedience does however place considerable obstacles in the way of conventional multi-party democracy. The idea of voting against the government is for many Ethiopians, especially in rural areas, a strange and disturbing one – and to many officials, whose primary responsibility has always been the maintenance of obedience to the established order, it is downright subversive. It has been extremely difficult to express opposition to the existing authorities, without implicitly challenging their right to rule and opening the possibility of a resort to violence. The idea of a 'loyal opposition', seeking to displace the government by peaceful and constitutional means, has been equally difficult to grasp from the viewpoint either of the government itself, or of its would-be opponents. Nor do Ethiopian attitudes to power readily lend themselves to bargaining and compromise. Levels of interpersonal trust, which have been identified as a critical element in building the institutions on which democracy depends, are characteristically low.

Such attitudes readily become self-reinforcing. When governments

---

[4] For a discussion of Ethiopia's 'state culture', see Sarah Vaughan & Kjetil Tronvoll, *The Culture of Power in Contemporary Ethiopian Political Life* (Stockholm: Swedish International Development Cooperation Agency, 2004).

have only ever been removed by violence, it is difficult both for opposition movements to regard any other way of proceeding as likely to be effective, and for governments to accept their assurances of constitutional behaviour. When trust is (as it has been) betrayed, it cannot readily be restored. The establishment of democracy in Ethiopia correspondingly requires not merely the installation of appropriate constitutional mechanisms, but radical changes in the ways in which Ethiopians have conceived basic questions of governance and authority.

The Challenge of Revolution
In the years after 1974, Ethiopia experienced the only major social revolution yet to have occurred in Africa. Not only the monarchy but the entire structure of government was swept away, all major productive assets (notably all land) were brought under state control, and the country was transformed like Russia from an Orthodox Christian empire to a Stalinist dictatorship.[5] As in France after 1789 or Russia after 1917, this process was viciously bloody. A reign of terror ensued, on the streets of Addis Ababa and other towns, and in much of the countryside. Resistance movements sprang up in much of the country, most of which were brutally suppressed. An invasion from Somalia was defeated with Soviet and Cuban aid. Hundreds of thousands of Ethiopians died.

In the longer term a revolution like this, no matter how horrifying at the time, may contribute to the development of democracy. It sweeps away entrenched structures of privilege, creates a measure of equality, and incorporates the masses into political life in a way that was never possible before. Its immediate impact, however, is very different; all major revolutions have led to dictatorships, and most of them (like Ethiopia's) to civil and external wars. Intense hostilities and resentments are almost bound to follow. The bases for trust, already fragile, are further eroded. The foundations of democracy, even if they are forged in the heat of revolution, will inevitably need a long cooling and healing process before they can be built on.

---

[5] See Andargachew Tiruneh, *The Ethiopian Revolution 1974-1987: a transformation from an aristocratic to a totalitarian autocracy* (Cambridge: Cambridge University Press, 1993).

Global Challenges and Africa

The Challenge of Insurgency
Africa now has a significant number of regimes – Angola and Mozambique, Rwanda and Uganda, Ethiopia and Eritrea, to name six obvious ones – in which rulers have eventually assumed power after a long period of rural insurgent warfare. This is an experience that deeply affects those who undergo it, not least when many of their friends and colleagues have died before victory is eventually achieved. It is difficult for the victors not to feel that the power that they have gained at such cost is theirs by right, and very difficult indeed for them to abandon this power as the result of democratic procedures to politicians who have not in their view earned it, and who may well have spent the period of the struggle in comfortable exile, or as the associates and collaborators of a vicious regime overthrown at the cost of much blood and suffering. Though guerrillas who have come to power have certainly ruled in very different ways, some with far greater wisdom and tolerance than others, it is easy to appreciate that they do not make natural democrats.[6]

This may seem a depressing assessment of Ethiopia's prospects for democracy. It is however essential that we should not treat democracy simply as a formula that can be readily and successfully applied, regardless of the circumstances. Different countries, in Africa as elsewhere, come to it with very different experiences that must be fully taken into account. At the same time, there are also elements in the Ethiopian experience, notably since 1991, that have greatly improved the prospects for democracy, and are bringing about important and very largely positive changes in the way in which Ethiopia is governed.

Sources of Hope

The Failure of Dictatorship
While Ethiopia's recent past certainly contains much that militates against democracy, it also has elements that can only encourage it. The most basic of these, in my view, is the obvious and abject failure of the Derg regime's attempt after 1974 to construct a hierarchical system of government ruthlessly controlled from above. The Derg took the authoritarian tradition of Ethiopian government, and the values of deference that had historically

---

[6] For the guerilla origins of the present Ethiopian government, see John Young, *Peasant Revolution in Ethiopia: the Tigray People's Liberation Front, 1975-1991* (Cambridge: Cambridge University Press, 1997).

helped to maintain it, to the point of destruction and beyond. The dictatorship built on the imperial legacy of autocracy, but swept away the impediments that had in practice prevented the imperial regime from exercising the virtually limitless powers that it claimed. The Derg was far more efficient than Haile Selassie's ramshackle empire: it was ruthlessly organized, heavily armed, fortified by massive external military aid and by an ideology that assured it inevitable ultimate victory, and engaged in ambitious projects of social engineering and economic transformation.[7] It sought to destroy all those who opposed it. When it failed, this was more than the defeat of a single repressive regime: it signalled the inadequacy, indeed the impossibility, of attempting to govern Ethiopia from the top down, and left some form of government that ultimately rested on the consent and participation of the governed as the only remaining option. It likewise alerted Ethiopians, in the most traumatic manner, to the dangers of autocracy and the need for some kind of constraint on those in power. Democracy in many countries has developed from a recognition of the failure of dictatorship, and Ethiopia may be no exception.

The Deconstruction of Hegemony
The political structure erected by the EPRDF government since it assumed power in 1991 has been quite unique in Africa, and is far from unproblematic. In seeking to build explicitly on the different 'nationalities' (to use the term commonly employed in Ethiopia, or alternatively ethnic groups or even tribes) of which the country is composed, it has parted company dramatically with the instinct of virtually all other African governments, which has been to play down or delegitimize the separate identities of different internal ethnic groups to the greatest possible extent. In Ethiopia, on the other hand, these groups have been elevated into the building blocks from which the new federal system has been constructed. Not only are the units in the federation ethnically based – designated for Afars, Tigrayans, Amharas, Oromos, Somalis, and distinct territories for each of the numerous southern and western peoples – but political parties seek only to represent the claims of different ethnicities.[8]

---

[7] See Christopher Clapham, Transformation and Continuity in Revolutionary Ethiopia (Cambridge: Cambridge University Press, 2nd ed. 1990).

[8] For a collection of studies of this process, see Wendy James, Donald Donham, Eisei Kurimoto & Alessandro Triulzi, eds. *Remapping Ethiopia* (Oxford: James Currey, 2002).

The difficulties that this system creates scarcely need to be enumerated. It has led to numerous conflicts over the demarcation of ethnic territories, which are now of cardinal importance; it has imposed a crude division into nationalities on a changing society in which – even more than in many other parts of Africa – ethnic identities had become blurred by intermarriage, internal migration, social assimilation, and the development of a national economy and consciousness; and it has converted many Ethiopians living outside their areas of ethnic origin into foreigners within their own country. It has encouraged the development of an ethnic politics which in some regions, notably Oromiya, has acquired a worrying tone. Its great merit, on the other hand, is that it has sought to tackle explicitly the underlying assumption of hegemony on which the Ethiopian state has historically been built, and in the process to lay the foundations for an Ethiopia constructed on the basis of equality between social groups and cultures, not merely between individuals. By far the most important challenge facing Ethiopia is whether this bold experiment will succeed.

A Sense of Nationhood

Despite its unique system of ethnic federalism, Ethiopia has a sense of national identity that can draw on its long history, and that is emphatically not just the property of a single group within the country. Its peoples have much in common, and distinctively Ethiopian characteristics – including food, dress, and the use of the Amharic language – have spread throughout almost the entire country. Despite the provision under the current constitution for each of the country's nationalities to enjoy a right of self-determination, up to and including secession, I can detect no serious demand for secession even among groups that are least enthusiastic about the current political order. A more positive sense of belonging was very strikingly illustrated in May 1998, when Eritrea occupied by force a fairly small area of territory in the extreme north of Ethiopia, and a deep sense of national outrage spread throughout the country – to an extent that may have surprised even the national government – and volunteers for the army that had to be raised to restore its territorial integrity were readily forthcoming, even from such distant areas as Gambela in the far south-west.[9] For any democracy to take root, certain basic assumptions about the

---

[9] See Tekeste Negash & Kjetil Tronvoll, *Brothers at War: making sense of the Eritrean-Ethiopian war* (Oxford: James Currey, 2000).

nature and legitimacy of the state, and the extent of its national territory, must be shared by a substantial majority of its population, and there are encouraging signs in Ethiopia – which has historically been subject to secessionist claims, both from Eritrea and from the Somali territories in the south-east – that this is now being achieved.

A Nascent Civil Society
In the 'third wave' of democratization that had spread round the world in the wake of the collapse of the Soviet Union, much emphasis has been placed on the need for 'civil society', in the form of a complex of organizations, outside the state but nonetheless impinging to a significant degree on public life, as a means to ensure the development of habits of peaceful participation in public affairs on the part of the population, while at the same time placing constraints on the arbitrary exercise of power by the government. Key elements of this civil society have included an independent press and other media, wide participation in voluntary organizations, the development of trustworthy independent arbiters of public behaviour such as election and human rights monitoring, and a complex of organizations such as businesses, trades unions and professional associations that help to regulate economic life, and whose views governments need to take into account.

Even though much of the literature on civil society betrays a simplistic assumption that mechanisms that have developed in Western societies can readily be transferred to very different parts of the world, there is nonetheless a great deal of value in the basic idea that democracy depends not just on establishing state-level institutions, but on a wide range of supportive elements in the society as a whole. In Ethiopia, these elements have until recently been very weak indeed. As already noted, the idea of peacefully restraining government has had very little resonance in the dominant state culture. Though there have been widespread forms of self-help organizations, such as the savings associations known as *equb* and *idir*, these have not had the public role required of 'civil society' in the sense outlined. During the Derg regime, even those feeble organizations that had emerged under the imperial government were ruthlessly suppressed and subordinated to the ruling power.

Nonetheless, things are changing. One key development since 1991 has been the emergence of a genuinely independent press. This has its deficiencies, to be sure, and is largely restricted to the major cities, but still serves not just as a source of information independent from government, but also (perhaps more important) as a guarantor of independent thought. The importance of the press as a demonstration that it is permissible to comment on public affairs independently (and even critically) of government spreads well beyond its often very limited readership. A striking illustration of this was the complete closure of the independent press in Eritrea in September 2001, following a public conflict between President Isaias and many of his former colleagues in the ruling Eritrean People's Liberation Front/People's Front for Democracy and Justice (EPLF/PFDJ); no such measures have taken place, or can plausibly be imagined, in Ethiopia. Beyond that, however, the period since 1991 has seen a burgeoning of independent organizations, including not only the more prominent Addis Ababa-based ones (like the Ethiopian Human Rights Council, or the Ethiopian Women Lawyers Association), but extending widely into provincial towns and beyond. Federalism has led to the development of an active local politics, in which rival parties and associations compete for attention and support at the local level. There has been a considerable expansion likewise in autonomous economic organizations, extending into areas (such as tertiary education) that were previously the preserve of the state. Ethiopia, in short, has developed a level of pluralism that extends well beyond the state's capacity to control.[10]

The Ambivalent Role of the Diaspora
One result of Ethiopia's traumatic recent history is that many Ethiopians have fled the country at one time or another, and have now established substantial diaspora communities, especially in North America and Europe. Others have followed in search of economic opportunities unavailable at home. This is very far from an unmixed blessing. Many skills that are desperately needed within one of the poorest countries in the world have been lost to the wealthiest. The attitudes of exiled Ethiopians towards developments within the country are also often naive in the extreme; Americo-Ethiopians, in particular, often seem quite unable to understand why politics in their country of origin should not immediately assume the same characteristics as in the United States. The extensive linkages

---

[10] For the recent emergence of an Ethiopian 'civil society', see Sarah Vaughan & Kjetil Tronvoll, *The Culture of Power in Contemporary Ethiopian Political Life* (Stockholm: Swedish International Development Cooperation Agency, 2004).

between Ethiopians within the country and outside – and any flight between Europe and Addis Ababa now contains a fair contingent of 'outside' Ethiopians revisiting their roots – have nonetheless brought new openings and ideas with many positive elements. A small but often extraordinarily dedicated number of exiles have returned to put their skills and experience to the benefit of their fellow countrymen and women, and are having an impact well beyond their numbers. Ethiopia – a country used to isolation – is now very much part of the greater world, and democracy is in turn part of the way in which that world increasingly operates.

Conclusion

At present, Ethiopia cannot be considered a democracy. It has yet to pass the acid test of a new government peacefully assuming power as the result of fair elections, and it seems unlikely to do so in the near future. Its human rights record, massively improved though it is since the Derg regime, is still mixed. Deeply entrenched attitudes to power and authority – on the part of opposition groups and not just the government, and most basically in the population as a whole – continue to impede the development of attitudes and practices on which democracy must ultimately depend. Ethiopia still lacks an adequate political process, through which its diversity can be accommodated within a set of effective and consensual mechanisms of governance. The development of such a process is the most important task that the country faces. Scarcely less important, though beyond the scope of this short survey, is the massive task of transforming Ethiopia's desperately impoverished economy – a task which in the view of many observers, both Ethiopian and foreign, must encompass the granting of freehold in agricultural land, in place of the state ownership which the present government has maintained from the ousted Derg regime;[11] smoothing the path for external investment likewise remains a major priority. Enormous progress has unquestionably been made in both political and economic fields, by comparison with any previous system of government that the country has experienced, but it is still unknown whether it will be possible to bring them to completion, and how long these tasks might take.

---

[11] For a forthcoming study, see Berhanu Abegaz, 'Escaping Ethiopia's poverty trap: the case for a second agrarian reform', *The Journal of Modern African Studies* (Vol. 42, No. 3, September 2004).

Peace-Building and Democracy – Lessons of Somalia and Somaliland

Rakiah Omaar

There are a number of obvious connections to be made about the war in Iraq and the situation in Somalia. It has been widely reported, for instance, that the first attacks organized by Al-Qa'ida were against US military forces in Somalia in 1993, that groups linked to Al-Qa'ida continue to operate in Somalia and that Somalis were involved in the deadly raid upon the resort in Kenya. There has even been speculation that the recent murder of four foreigners in Somaliland was the work of Islamic extremists. The rush to appear tough on terrorism makes it difficult to establish the facts and to make a sober judgement.

Meanwhile, the US 'war on terror' has had its own direct impact upon the life of Somalis. Besides the persistent rumours that Somalia might be on the list of targets for US military action, the welfare of thousands of Somali families has been affected by the US decision, in November 2001, to freeze the assets of Somalia's largest financial company, al-Barakaat, because of its alleged association with Al-Qa'ida terrorists. There is no evidence to prove this link, but the freeze has been hugely damaging as people across Somalia depended on this company for transfers of money from relatives in the large Somali Diaspora.

Beyond the obvious, however, and little considered in mainstream dialogue, is what the experiences and initiatives of the Somali people might suggest about the prospects of building peace and democracy world-wide. One evident reason is that we remain so far from achieving a durable solution to our own conflicts; Somalia remains, in the eyes of the world, a failed and dangerous state. But our failures, along with a number of key peace-making successes, illustrate some of the costs of international involvement and the possibilities of local participation and hint at the nature of the struggles required to craft a sustainable democracy that takes account of unique realities.

Rakiya Omaar is the Director of Africa Rights.

I share the view that the promotion of democratic systems of governance offers the best hope for more peaceful and stable societies in Africa. But to rely, as many in the West have done, on the assumption that the content, meaning and form of democracy is uncontested and that models of democracy can be imported and imposed, has led to disappointment and setbacks. Moreover, there seems to be a general agreement that democracy, in and of itself, delivers peace, contrary to the evidence in Africa and elsewhere. With regard to Iraq and wider international conflict resolution endeavours, the lessons of the 1992-93 US/UN intervention in Somalia may be that international interventions, even when humanitarian in conception, can create their own destructive dynamics. Amongst other problems, they can erode people's spirit of ingenuity and self-reliance, hamper local initiatives, wound their sense of self-respect and nationalism, create conflict over aid resources and allow external priorities and deadlines to dominate.

By contrast, the relative success (so far) of Somaliland in achieving stability occurred in a context of international neglect. Somaliland's achievements are home-grown, not only independent of international involvement and encouragement, but in spite of international indifference, hostility and occasionally destructive interference. It has been a long and arduous road, a journey marked by periods of collective despair, jubilation, fear and hope. The progress made here is due entirely to the will of ordinary people. Weary of war, want and displacement, their determination to live in peace dictated the political agenda. Their accomplishment, however limited and precarious, is a powerful antidote to the seemingly endless cycle of violence and dependence in Africa.

Ongoing efforts to resolve conflict in Somalia and now to build democracy in Somaliland, which has yet to be recognized as an independent state, indicate that these struggles are not only fragile and lengthy processes, but that they are also uniquely determined by cultural and historical influences and local circumstances.

When over 30 000 American troops arrived in Somalia in December 1992, speculation about President George Bush's true motives was rife. No-one believed that the humanitarian impulse provided the whole story. Was it Somalia's oil reserves? The threat of Islamic fundamentalism?

The arrival of billions of dollars worth of military hardware was a grand spectacle, and the belief that the military investment would be matched by a political and aid commitment raised hopes dramatically. As with Iraq today, the intervention appeared to promise the wholesale reconstruction of Somalia, or at least generous resources to the individuals or group who were internationally recognized as having the clout, if not the legitimacy, to rebuild the country.

It did not, of course, happen like that. Ill-informed about the political situation on the ground, unaware of its complexities and sensitivities, and with no apparent interest in the priorities and perspectives of Somalis, the US-led force was immediately caught in a quagmire. The refusal to work with local people quickly soured relations; disillusion turned into resentment as Somalis encountered fearful and suspicious soldiers who looked upon them as the enemy. The prophecy came true as the atmosphere deteriorated and Somali politicians exploited the volatile situation to strengthen their power base. The bloody clashes between Aideed's men and US/UN soldiers is now the stuff of history. Much has been said about the consequences, in particular for the tragedy in Rwanda in 1994, of the US disengagement from international affairs in the wake of the gruesome murder of its soldiers in Mogadishu.

For Somalis watching Iraq reel from one explosive crisis to another, there is a painful sense of *déjà vu*. What Somalia showed graphically – that military intervention creates as many humanitarian and political problems as it solves – is being proved every day in Iraq. And it also highlighted that agreements reached under the shadow of an occupying force are unlikely to hold when that force withdraws, making conflict inevitable. Our past may well be Iraq's future.

The international community began peacemaking efforts in Somalia in 1993. Eleven years and millions of dollars later, and after more than a dozen marathon meetings in neighbouring countries, peace, a power-sharing agreement and the establishment of an effective central government remain elusive. The Transitional Government, established after a meeting in Djibouti, barely governs more than a corner of Mogadishu.

The negotiations got off to an inauspicious start. By reinforcing the impression that major financial resources were available, and by making straightforward payments to the signatories, the scene was set for manipulation and exploitation by wily politicians. The negotiations were themselves resource-rich; delegates had been put up in hotels in foreign countries for months on end. The agenda, timing and venue have been set in large part by donors. This has allowed them, the hosts and governments and institutions in neighbouring states – each with its own perspective, interests and its alliances with client warlords to protect – to push their own concerns.

Many Somalis have called for the talks to take place in Somalia itself, as a way of putting self-appointed warlords to the political test of acceptance by their own citizens, to give the Somali people the opportunity to influence the discussions and decisions and to put an end to grandstanding in foreign capitals.

Perhaps most importantly of all, despite the payment of lip-service to innovative constitutional arrangements, the negotiations have been directed at the re-establishment of government with the 'normal' accoutrements of sovereignty. The explicit concern of both the former and the current Secretary-General of the UN with maintaining the territorial integrity of Somalia has reinforced this view.

At the outset of the intervention, the United Nations Operation for Somalia (UNOSOM), in charge of the peacekeeping operation after the departure of US forces, made a policy of restricting political representation on the envisaged national council to factions existing at the time. This was a major political blunder that reflected a gross misunderstanding of the political dynamic at work. The main factions had become little more than sets of initials, referring to clans and clan-families, which were rapidly breaking down and being reconstituted into inter-clan alliances. This course of restructuring was following more and more localized fracture lines. Though the proliferation of political groups made national-level diplomacy more complicated, it reflected a real political momentum whereby people were beginning to grapple with local issues. By bringing the established factions to the negotiating table in Addis Ababa during the first round of talks in March 1993, and forbidding the formation of new factions, UNOSOM halted this development and indeed set it into reverse. If seats at a new transitional council were to be awarded on the basis of certain factions, then these factions certainly had to exist, and there had to be a struggle for control of them. Rather than focusing attention on the basic issues of conflict at the local level, UNOSOM centralized political competition. Combined with the promise of international aid to the winners, the effect was to sharpen conflict.

Much time has since elapsed, but little has changed. No group has proved strong enough to take unchallenged control of the capital, let alone of the country. Insecurity is widespread amidst the proliferation of groups headed by different warlords, including prominent war criminals. For ordinary Somalis, life is a daily battle of wills in the context of hardship and fear. The absence of a central government has made life harder for the public, but it has created a vacuum for politicians and businessmen bent on self-interest. They have prospered and are accountable to no-one. The impact of the 1992 intervention has been enduring and continues to colour the efforts at peacemaking between Somalia's various factions. Peace negotiations, including the latest session in Nairobi, have become an expensive and embarrassing ritual defined by arguments over per diems and hotels. Leaders represent themselves and, lacking legitimacy, they rely on the power of coercion. Insecurity increases abruptly in Mogadishu whenever a deal looks imminent as the warlords scramble to claim the crown.

Somalia was born in 1960 out of the hasty marriage of Italian-ruled Somalia and the British Protectorate of Somaliland. Until it seceded in May 1991, the region that today comprises Somaliland was known as northwest Somalia. It was the site of horrendous human rights abuses in the 1980s, during the rule of the late President Mohamed Siad Barre. A well-organized campaign of terror, directed principally at the majority Isaaq clan, provoked a backlash when military officers, backed by civilians, established the Somali National Movement (SNM), with bases in Ethiopia. The government's determination to root out support for the SNM knew no bounds: businessmen, civil servants, nomads and schoolchildren were equally targeted. The intensity of the repression swelled the ranks of the SNM, which in turn hardened the government's resolve to crush the rebellion. When, in May 1988, the SNM, deprived of its bases in Ethiopia, invaded the main towns of the northwest, a full-scale war broke out, a war in which the government turned its full fury on the Isaaq civilian population. Within days, most of them became refugees in Ethiopia; homes, towns and infrastructure were demolished, leaving behind an empty terrain encircled by landmines. In the meantime, other rebel movements had sprung up in south and central Somalia, making it increasingly more difficult for the government to hold the country together.

Victory came to the SNM in January 1991 when Siad Barre fled Mogadishu. Within days, the SNM took far-reaching steps to reconcile with its former opponents, including those who had fought alongside the forces of Siad Barre. The rapidity and comprehensiveness of this reconciliation meant that there were few significant military clashes between Isaaq and non-Isaaq clans in Somaliland. Reconciliation was helped by the military supremacy of the SNM.

The unity of the northwest was also assisted by the virtually unanimous opposition to the self-declared interim government of Ali Mahdi Mohamed, announced in Mogadishu on 27 January 1991. As the factional fighting intensified in Mogadishu, northerners were increasingly confirmed in their belief that involvement with the south was best kept to a minimum. Meanwhile, political momentum was dictated by popular pressure. At a meeting in Burao on 18 May 1991, the SNM was forced by public insistence to declare the formation of the independent Republic of Somaliland.

Celebrations were short-lived. The refugees' dreams of returning and rebuilding their shattered homeland evaporated when a series of bloody internal conflicts erupted in 1992, first in Burao and then in Berbera. Those who had barely settled in were again on the move, losing what little resources they had accumulated. The government took no action to prevent or contain the Burao and Berbera wars, and seemed to be helpless as Somaliland threatened to slide towards wholesale civil war, as had happened in the south. Early on, however, clan elders stepped in and took on the responsibility abdicated by a divided government. This began one of the most remarkable political processes, that in less than a year was to lead to a complete, non-violent change in government in 1993, and the establishment of nation-wide peace, with the beginnings of a structure to enforce it.

The elders used their moral authority and their experience as traditional arbiters of disputes to end the fighting and to defuse tensions through painstaking negotiations that began at the grassroots, dealing initially with the specific material and local issues that sparked hostilities or aggravated misunderstandings. The emphasis on resolving local tensions was not accidental. In a semi-nomadic society where the environment is inhospitable, peace is not the mere absence of armed conflict or social tension, but living in harmony with one's neighbours. Survival – the perpetual search for pasture and water – depends on fostering good relations with other communities.

Once they had stopped the bloodshed and secured the semblance of peace at the local level, they initiated a series of regional meetings to prepare the ground for building national political consensus for a new and representative government. Through an alliance with a grateful public, they were able to disarm and rein in militia groups who had brought the people of Somaliland to their knees. There was no timetable to decide the pace of talks, no foreign donor or actors to exert pressure and no external schedule to influence the outcome. The fact that the talks were taking place in Somaliland itself, and were financed by Somali communities, at home and in the Diaspora, was critically important. It made everyone feel like a participant, not just a stakeholder, and gave them the incentive and the opportunity to be involved, informed and protective of their investment.

The government and political system that emerged from this political experiment was not democratic by any Western yardstick. It was not based on 'one man, one vote', women were left out altogether and it did not include the conventional checks and balances. But it was widely accepted as legitimate and viable because it reflected existing cultural norms and because it had delivered peace and promised security. A Council of Elders, known as the *Guurti*, was set up in addition to parliament and the executive branch.

With the establishment of peace, a spirit of enterprise took over. All over Somaliland a robust private sector is flourishing. Shops are well-stocked, hotels are thriving, communications and the airline industry are functioning well and private schools and clinics exist.

When President Mohamed Ibrahim Egal, who had taken office in 1993, died in May 2002, he was succeeded in a smooth transfer of power by his vice-president, Dahir Rayale. In December 2002 municipal elections, the first free elections in more than thirty years, took place in an atmosphere of calm, contested by different political parties, followed by presidential elections in April 2003 which were won by the incumbent. Again, the elections were peaceful, but were marked by controversy and accusations that the president's party had secured victory by influencing elders and by resorting to bribery. The press is uninhibited and contentious, despite the evident need for training and equipment. There are no armed men on the streets, there is security in the towns and travel throughout Somaliland is largely without incident, notwithstanding the unfortunate recent killing of a number of foreigners.

Unlike most other African countries, there has been no serious pressure on Somaliland to democratize, mainly because few countries are engaged with Somaliland in any meaningful sense. The decision to move from a clan-based system of political dispensation to multi-party politics grew out of local circumstances and the emerging consensus that, ten years after secession, a group of elderly men should not continue to mould the political destiny of Somaliland. Younger men wanted a shot at political leadership and women chafed at their exclusion.

Impressed by this record, and conscious that countless governments in Africa have done little for their people, many visitors to Somaliland question the need for international political recognition. But the lack of recognition comes with a heavy price. In an era of globalization,

Somaliland is peculiarly isolated and voiceless. People interact with the outside world on their own initiative, but do so against the odds. Travel abroad is a nightmare because passports issued by Somaliland are not considered valid. It is not possible to send or receive post from overseas. International banking and insurance facilities are essential to unlock external investment in business and job-creating opportunities as well as to build trade relations, but enticing foreign companies in the current diplomatic vacuum is an uphill battle. Without its own representatives at the UN, the Somaliland government has not found it easy to protest the crippling ban imposed by the Arab world on the export of livestock, the economic lifeline of a largely nomadic population. Government institutions – the central and local administrations, the judiciary, schools, hospitals, roads, the water supply system, agriculture and many other sectors – are starved of resources and unable to deliver services. And yet, unless people's fundamental needs are met, the long-term prospects for growth and stability in Somaliland cannot be taken for granted. Nor indeed, can the preservation of security.

People complain that they are hostages of their hard-won success. They ask why the outside world refuses to help them consolidate their gains. For the UN, the African Union and the Organization of Arab States, Somaliland raises thorny questions about self-determination and secession. They fear that giving the green light would hinder efforts to bring order to Somalia and would encourage secession elsewhere in the continent. Arab countries are worried about the impact on southern Sudan and its ambition of independence from Khartoum. But the people of Somaliland find it illogical that they should be punished, rather than helped, for achieving what the world is seeking in Somalia – to make peace and build on it.

And while this indeterminate status persists, people are reluctant to do or say anything that could adversely influence the case for recognition. This is a reality which gives leaders room for political manoeuvre domestically, an opening they have not been slow to exploit. Haunted by their long experience of war and dislocation, expecting little of governments except trouble, and only too aware that even a minimalist government can wreak havoc, there seems to be no limit to what people will tolerate from their leaders, even when their behaviour threatens that most precious of commodities, peace. They get nervous when the opposition does what it should do, namely question government actions and policies. The government's campaign during the 2003 presidential elections was blatantly corrupt, discriminatory and divisive. Tension in the wake of the disputed results was met by a show of force reminiscent of the brutal tactics of Siad Barre's forces. People were angry but remained silent.

Sadly, but perhaps not surprisingly, the political landscape of Somaliland today resembles the multiparty politics of the early 1960s. An ineffectual government is emerging, intent upon claiming the meagre resources of the country to fund its own political interests. Because the hiatus of thirty years stunted the development of political structures that cut across clan lines, politics remains dominated by clan issues, discouraging accountability by allowing politicians to hide behind the cover of clan identity.

The elders should have withdrawn from active political service once they had delivered peace. Unfortunately, their extraordinary success in the early 1990s proved too strong a temptation. With time, they have transformed their role from community representatives and peace-makers to power-brokers. They received material advantages they had never seen in their lives and they are now perceived more as an adjunct of the government. This shift was engineered by the government which regarded the independence of the elders as a threat. Given weak governmental structures, a poor legal system vulnerable to political manipulation and the absence of other strong civic groups and opposition parties, the disappearance of institutions with the authority and tradition of bringing communities together in the search for peace poses a grave threat for the future of Somaliland.

Although clan solidarity is a major impediment to the emergence of strong political parties based on a shared political vision and programme, on a day-to-day basis it is the economic and psychological glue that holds society together, the only existing form of social security. In an impoverished country where life is a struggle for basic survival, and there is no public service ethos, dependence on family and clan is a necessity, not a choice.

Confronted with the demands of modern life, the breakdown of family structures and social norms as a result of war, the huge exodus from rural areas to urban centres and the changes in the standing of elders, and challenged by women who are seeking political representation, the clan system no longer offers a very real mechanism for accountability. The decision to continue the development of political parties reflects this ambivalence, but lack of experience and, much more importantly, lack of resources means that these parties themselves continue to be heavily influenced by clan politics.

More than ten years after American and UN soldiers arrived on Somali soil to help move the country towards peace, reconciliation and democracy, Somalia remains a potent symbol of the perils of an ill-informed military intervention, a casualty of the politics of international involvement without responsibility. And as we look into the future not only of Iraq, but also of Afghanistan, it might be helpful to reflect on the Somaliland experience, which hints at the nature and length of struggles required to establish a democracy in the arid ground of a post-conflict situation even where peace prevails and some form of national consensus exists. As my friend, the late Nigerian social scientist Claude Ake, pointed out, there are no 'blueprints' for democracy. It has to be defined, fought for and defended by the people upon whose participation it ultimately depends. Grounded on their practical experiences and aspirations, the process must, as he argued, engage their energy and commitment, enabling them to set the goals and make the decisions.

Section 3

African Security Challenges and Responses

Global Change, Security and Weakened States

John Mackinlay

Prior to its invasion and colonization, sub-Saharan Africa was ordered and regulated by a rich variety of indigenous political and social structures. On colonization, these were replaced in many cases by what appeared to be replicas of the European nation state. After the departure of the colonial regime, African leaders were reluctant to abandon their inherited structures of governance, for without them there appeared to be little guarantee that they could survive as heads of newly emerged states. However, in some cases the panoply of statehood concealed the fragility and limitation of their governance. Moreover, a head of state's ability to enforce its writ over a territory was constantly challenged by local war leaders and insurgent movements which had flourished during the colonial period. Although the fiction of the state was reinforced by economic surges of the 1960s and 1970s, in reality a government's ability to control revenues and impose law and order seldom reached beyond the state capital.[1]

Several separate strands of development impacted on both the insurgents and the government forces that sought to contain them. Globalization changed the nature of the conflict area, strengthening some parties and weakening others, expanding the definitions of portable wealth and resources and altering the military equation between government forces and insurgents. Distant developments at the strategic level reached down to local communities in the conflict zone, changing the context of the struggle for power and wealth.

The effect of globalization was to project social, political and economic values across frontiers, and from one region to another,[2] speeding the transmission of ideas, goods, information, capital and the migration of populations. Thus distant events altered the lives of isolated communities, whose dependence on foreign investment and influences had increased.

Dr John Mackinlay is a lecturer at the War Studies Department of King's College London.

This paper concerns five individual strands of development, which had for some time been altering local communities: improvements in transport technology; the proliferation of information and communications; the deregulation of the international economy and markets; urbanization; and culture.

Although the pace of change was initially gradual, over several decades the pressure on weak governments increased. Arguably, the end of the Cold War was a trigger mechanism which in weaker states released tensions that had been building for some time. The end of the zero-sum game affected remote communities and villages in regions far from the Central Front of the Cold War armies. By the late 1980s, diminishing US–Soviet interest left client regimes of both sides without support. This made insurgents realize that their war economies had to change from relying on political assistance from abroad to becoming more business-oriented.[3] Both government forces and insurgents became illegal dealers in precious woods, gemstones, protected antiques, ivory, jade and the production and trafficking of drugs.[4] In doing so, they rapidly discovered and exploited the advantages presented by global change. At the same time, some of their expectations were met by a surge of war materiel onto legal and illegal markets. This went beyond increasing the obvious availability of small arms; entire military units were for hire, with Russian garrisons searching for a raison d'être in former Soviet space, and more immediately for a means of subsistence. Logistics aircraft from the disestablished Soviet air force appeared on the air-charter market, and individual mercenaries gravitated towards the new crisis areas of the 1990s. Individually benign developments had coalesced to alter the structures of governance, the possession of wealth and the disposition of military power.

This paper argues that the controlling instruments that had allowed the fiction of statehood to survive were disastrously weakened by the corrosion of global changes. Furthermore, although globalization has been a factor of change since early history, its pace and persuasiveness intensified

---

[1] Jeffrey Herbst, Responding to State Failure, *International Security* (Vol. 21, No. 3, Winter 1996-7), pp. 120-144.

[2] David Held and Anthony McGrew, with David Goldblatt and Jonathan Perraton, 'Globalization', *Global Governance* (Vol. 5, No. 4, 1999), pp. 483–96.

[3] Jean-Christophe Rufin, 'The Economics of War: A New Theory for Armed Conflicts', *Forum*, Series 2 (Geneva: International Committee of the Red Cross, February 2000).

[4] *Ibid.*

in the last three decades and, above all, had altered the balance between the government and the insurgent in favour of the latter.

Transport

In the wilderness areas, a potent development was the advance in transport technology and the proliferation of new transport systems.[5] Where roads had not yet been developed, traditional porterage along rivers and footpaths still moved at the speed of a handcart. The ability to override the limitations imposed by terrain and poor technology was a monopoly that lay in the hands of international corporations and the more powerful armed forces. These were the only actors who could afford to use the large helicopters and heavy transport systems that reached into the heart of the wilderness.

By the end of the Cold War, several developments were eroding this monopoly. In the 1980s, overland communications in developing wilderness areas were improved. Engineering companies came to build or improve road systems, introduced better vehicles and, more importantly, sealed roads which increased the tempo of movement and interaction. New and more powerful cross-country vehicles were reaching isolated areas. They arrived in the form of military equipment, as commercial carriers and as cheap and easy-to-maintain logistics vehicles introduced by the development agencies. Effective commercial vehicles reached remote areas directly from the retail market, in particular the Nissan minibus, the Isuzu 10 MT truck, the Indian Tata series of logistics carriers and European vehicles such as Mercedes and Fiats.[6]

In the air, deregulated Soviet tactical-support helicopters and strategic transport aircraft were ideally suited for remote areas and tended to operate without elaborate support facilities, consequently costing far less. Chartered strategic aircraft from the Soviet military fleets and small, privately-owned aircraft[7] connected remote airfields in conflict zones directly

---

[5] In a Maoist insurgency, 'wilderness areas' referred to an extensive refuge so wild that the technical and numerical advantages of government forces were greatly reduced, and combat would therefore be on the insurgent's terms.

[6] From information supplied by Paul Molinaro, Department of Defence Management and Security Analysis, Cranfield University, 6 August 2001.

[7] Popular models were the small ten-seaters such as the Cessna series, which had an increasingly better short take-off capability. These and the smaller *Antonovs* tended to be run by entrepreneurs, who now operate in the remotest areas from very primitive airfields.

to the international systems beyond, introducing a two-way traffic that had either never existed before, or had been the monopoly of governments and international corporations.

At sea, containerization dramatically lowered costs, speeding up the movement of cargo. The small entrepreneur could ship large, illegal cargoes around the world with greater ease than before. In some cases, the transport costs of moving bulk materials against the stream of international export traffic were considerably lower than the real expense of the journey.[8] Containerization was anonymous: an illegal cargo cased along with 6 000 other containers and stacked on the deck of a ship was unlikely to be found, and in most cases impossible to open, until its turn came to be unloaded.[9] The speed of delivery through the docks onto the ship was swift and at the destination, despite its size, the container was inconspicuous and easily moved over long distances by truck. Physical checks tended to be fruitless and anticipatory intelligence became more important. In many cases, weak governments whose authority barely extended to the edges of the capital city did not have the information or power to regulate this movement.[10]

As long as the transport of bulk materials and passengers remained the monopoly of the government or their international contractors and clients, the definition of 'portable resources', which could be used to fund violence, was limited to the small amounts of precious minerals carried or smuggled out on a person. The proliferation of a new generation of transport was altering and expanded the definition of portable resources in favour of the insurgent.

Communications

The second strand of technical development that altered the conflict area is described by some as the communications revolution.[11] Universally, com-

---

[8] The cost of container traffic is dictated by the popularity of the route. A 'heavy leg', for example exporting Western goods to the Gulf and sub-Saharan Africa, is heavily subscribed and therefore operating at cost, whereas the returning or 'light' leg, in which many containers would be empty, would offer transportation at less than cost. This favoured small entrepreneurs seeking to export on the light legs.

[9] 'The Perils of Packet Switching', *The Economist*, 6 April 2002, p. 13.

[10] Interview with David Hall, 6 January 2002. Hall is a consultant and former vice-president of several container-shipping lines.

[11] Frances Cairncross, *The Death of Distance 2.0: How the Communications Revolution Will Change Our Lives* (London: Texere Publishing, 2001).

munications devices became smaller, more portable and easier to conceal. In the remote areas of weakening states, users enjoyed vastly improved access to networks, any of which could be increasingly interactive and carry other audio and visual services. Once a system had been purchased, distance no longer decided the cost of communicating electronically. The consequent tidal wave of information in most cases overwhelmed a controlling organization's capacity for absorption and collation. Regardless of geography and political constraints, new ideas now took much less time to reach an optimum audience. In this way, culture and new technology moved more swiftly from the rich world to the poor, where in the past it could have taken decades.

This acted against governments that were already weakening for other reasons. The freedom of access and the surge of ideas and information could not be controlled, and laws preventing the circulation of subversive material were impossible to enforce. The control of movement and communication, which underwrote the exercise of authority in a weak state, was disintegrating. Government failure and malpractice became increasingly exposed. Rigorously investigated by international non-government researchers, it was now published and made globally visible on the internet.

Access to network television also challenged weak governments. Satellite communications meant that local leaders opposed to government forces could be interviewed from their rural bases by overseas television stations, which beamed their imagery and manifestos onto screens around the region. Radio interviewing via insurgents' mobile or satellite telephones removed the need for the foreign correspondent to be in the same wilderness location as the interviewee. Stations like the BBC World Service and Voice of America were respected in the crisis zones to which they broadcast, and international correspondents in English-language services were vested with a towering stature and credibility that local politicians seldom enjoyed. Media deities conferred a statesman-like aura on local insurgent military leaders that exaggerated their real significance. Interviewing them on an equal footing to national leaders was an acceptable device in rich, safe countries, but in a weakening state, it elevated local war leaders, even warlords and road bandits, to a political importance they neither understood nor deserved.

Although information technology-generated countermeasures threatened individual privacy and the insurgent users, the compilation of voice features, technical fingerprinting and even tracking credit-card records were expensive surveillance methods. In states where electronic surveillance was beyond the purchasing power of the government, the communications revolution favoured the small entrepreneur, the criminal and the insurgent. The cost of starting a new business was falling dramatically, and small companies with almost no capital now offered services that in the past had been the monopoly of the international giants. The internet opened up a new highway of evasion for criminal and seditious transactions; it could

> carry illegal material across international borders, covering its electronic tracks, and delivering it straight to the desktops of millions of individuals. Criminal organizations could migrate to countries where laws were lenient or weakly enforced, creating offshore havens for pornography, gambling and tax evasion, and breaching international rules on intellectual property.[12]

Deregulation of the international economy

The third strand of development was the weakening of international commercial systems and markets. During the 1980s, many newly-emerged nations had fallen into debt. In some cases, their fragile economies were disrupted by civil conflict, while others were weakened by the collapse in the price of their exports. Debts attracted huge loans which had to be repaid on a regular basis. Meanwhile, in the rich nations the proliferation of IT and digitization meant that viable profits could be made increasingly easily from the mere circulation of money, rather than its transfer into goods and services.[13] For poor and developing states, this meant that capital became disconnected from social relationships. In the past, obligation and trust had to be established between borrower and lender as an essential element of dealing. Now, as borrowers, developing states found themselves increasingly shut out from, or let down by, the international lending system. Wealth had become more mobile, but borrowers were no longer linked to lenders. New investment policies meant that it was

---

[12] *Ibid.*, p. 215.
[13] In David Harvey's description of hedge-fund dealing, the tiny profits in each transaction would not in normal circumstances have been worth picking up.
However, with computer-assisted data processing money could now be made from 'gathering up infinitesimally fractional differences in the movement in prices'. David Harvey, *Conditions of Post Modernity*, cited in Ankie Hoogvelt (ed.), *Globalization and the Post Colonial World* (Basingstoke: Palgrave, 2001).

becoming increasingly unlikely that capital would move 'from where it is concentrated and politically and strategically safer, to where it is scarce and subject to political and strategic risks'.[14]

The combination of loan-repayment obligations and the diminishing value of state resources removed executive power from governments. Whereas during the Cold War developing states in Latin America, Africa and Asia could manipulate the competing superpowers and extract favourable deals, now the situation was reversed. In sub-Saharan Africa, the indebtedness of poor states gave international lenders and the International Non-Government Organizations who acted for them enormous leverage. Debt reduction, which might have redressed the balance in favour of weakened governments, made no real progress as there was still a strong conditional linkage between reduction and the imposition of apparently 'sound' policies.

Above all, it was increasingly possible for communities to see how deprived they were in the global scale of social endowment, and in particular the inequality between the wealth of the rich nations and the wretchedness of the poor. The speed and volume of capital flows from one country to another had no antecedent. Electronic money passed from one side of the world to another at the click of a mouse at the rate of more than a trillion dollars each day, destabilizing the economy of one state in favour of a market trend in another.

Urbanization

In African countries, the population increased more rapidly after the 1960s with the introduction of foreign medical-development schemes that eradicated malaria and lowered child-mortality rates. In broad terms, the population in the north African region increased from 280 million to 640 million in thirty years. In some countries, the rate of increase was more dramatic; in Kenya, for example, the population soared from 6 million to 12 million in the same period, and in Côte d'Ivoire from 3 million to

---

[14] A. Sampson, *The Midas Touch: Money, People and Power from the East to the West* (London: Hodder and Stoughton, 1989), cited in Ankie Hoogvelt (ed.), *Globalization and the Post Colonial World* (Basingstoke: Palgrave, 2001) p. 88.

[15] Paul Kennedy, 'Preparing for the 21st Century: Winners and Losers', *New York Review of Books*, 11 February 1993, cited in Patrick O'Meara, Howard Mehlinger and Matthew Krain (eds)], *Globalization and the Challenges of a New Century: A Reader* (Bloomington, IN: Indiana University Press, 2000).

12 million.[15] Although the population was still largely rural, a greater proportion was becoming urbanized and by 2025 and an estimated 61 per cent of the world's population will be living in cities.[16] The pressures of rural unemployment, environmental damage to their former homelands and climate change spurred migration to the cities, where expectations of greater opportunity and better services were seldom fulfilled.[17] Some cities ceased to function as civil societies as families moved outwards to the suburbs, leaving a lawless vacuum behind them. Inflation, disease, starvation and banditry became normal. Survival depended on self-sufficiency.[18]

Culture

The projection of goods and capital across borders brought with it new ideas through radio, film and television, exposing people everywhere to the presence of other values.[19] Branded merchandise and 'celebrity' lifestyles collectively advocated a 'McWorld' culture.[20] McWorld was the antithesis of a pre-modern community and, in a dully insistent manner, it dictated a way of living: how to dress and what to eat, as well as business conventions and social mores. In some cases these foreign mores were actively resisted, but nevertheless they eroded and challenged local or traditional values.

Before this cultural invasion, young people maintained their identity and self-respect as part of a traditional or communal structure. Life was brutal, but it could be endured with the help of traditional structures such as the extended family, in which the individual had a sense of place, an identity and a degree of support. Chiefs and clan elders imposed themselves as a ruling class, which valued age and traditional authority over youth.

The invasion of global culture disturbed these local communities. The lyrics and images that assaulted young people arrived via the internet, public hoardings, cinema screens and the radio, telling them that their conservative values were irrelevant in the globalized world. In the bright

---

[16] Eugene Linden, 'Exploding Cities of the Developing World', *Foreign Affairs* (Vol. 75, No. 1, 1996), cited in O'Meara, Mehlinger and Krain (eds), *Globalization*.

[17] *Ibid.*

[18] Eugen Linden, 'Exploding Cities', cited in O'Meara, Mehlinger and Krain (eds), *Globalization*, p. 411.

[19] Held *et al.*, 'Globalization', p. 486.

[20] Benjamin Barber, 'Jihad vs McWorld', *Atlantic Monthly*, March 1992, cited in O'Meara, Mehlinger and Krain (eds), *Globalization*.

images of a consumer culture, they saw young people of both sexes presented as heroes, leaders and role models, and certainly not fastened down by communal conventions and family expectations in which youth deferred to age. The same media also highlighted their poverty and the fact that they were destined to be excluded from the McWorld lifestyle. The reactions to global culture, particularly by young people, were highly exploitable. Images of consumerism told them there were options to their harsh lifestyle in rural areas, and many migrated towards urban areas or crossed state boundaries searching for something closer to the attractive visions they had seen.

Young people rejecting the communal lifestyle became a rich source of recruits for local gang leaders. When they rejected the traditional lifestyle, the overwhelming motives were not uniformly political or ideological, but also stemmed from a personal need to find an alternative to the grind of subsistence living. Observers and retired insurgents speak of the need to 'make a statement'.[21] Making a statement might involve a gang of armed boys looting an isolated settlement, burning houses and ransacking a bar. The status quo was increasingly threatened: young people had always been inherently lawless and political regimes inherently unjust, but the nagging lyrics of the rapper from another world[22] helped to make it all seem unbearable.

Conclusion

For an authoritarian regime in a weak state, exercising control over movement, electronic communications and the state's natural resources sometimes made up for a lack of competence and legitimacy. But the proliferation of transport, new means of communications and the impact of a less regulated global economy gradually eroded these monopolies.

For the same reasons that governments became weaker, anti-government forces grew stronger. The changes that eroded the government's power also gave the insurgent international freedom of movement, association and communication. The demobilization of Europe's military stocks

---

[21] Much of this account is from Lieutenant-Colonel Joe Poraj-Wilczynski, UK Defence Advisor, British High Commission, Freetown. Interview, September 2001.

[22] For example the rapper Tupac Shakur who made records under the name 2Pac. His lyrics were nihilistic, rebellious, anti-authoritarian, sentimental and very violent. Interview with Mansel Fletcher, arts correspondent, 1 February 2002.

lowered the price of weapons and war material on the international market. Above all, insurgents were immensely richer than before, trading natural resources as well as farmed products directly onto international markets and in much greater quantities. The invasion of a global culture became their recruiting sergeant, eroding the traditional social structures that had been the controlling devices of a weak government.

The insurgents' survival strategies and modus operandi altered. The Cold War insurgent had relied on the local population for logistic supplies, intelligence, concealment and funds. Mao's success as an insurgent leader depended on cultivating a positive relationship with the local population so that, when events turned against them, his forces could return to the people and hide. In his logic, a movement that lost the support of the population would ultimately fail. But in the post-Cold War world, the trend was moving away from a 'people's war' strategy to one based on meeting the demands of international commerce. The successful insurgent had to secure sources of wealth and the facilities to move goods onto the international markets. When these facilities also became military objectives they corrupted the political integrity of the movement. The profits from stripping the state's resources and trading them onto the international market were so enormous that they, rather than any political intent, became the reason for war.[23] The principles of survival and success had altered; popular support was no longer a requirement for the exploitation of a state's resources and so the local population was used manipulatively, as shields against attack and to attract relief. Internationally provided food and water became levers of extortion and humanitarian codes of conduct were abandoned. Globalization had made weak governments weaker, the insurgent forces that opposed them stronger and the civil population more vulnerable.

This briefing paper for the 2004 Tswalu Dialogue is partly derived from a previous publication by the same author: Globalization and Insurgency, Adelphi Paper 352 (Oxford: Oxford University Press for the IISS, 2002).

---

[23] The 'economics of civil war' has become a phenomenon with its own genre of literature and research. See David Keen, *The Economic Functions of Violence in Civil Wars*, Adelphi Paper 320 (Oxford: Oxford University Press for the IISS, 1998); Mark R. Duffield, *Global Governance and the New Wars* (London, New York: Zed Books, 2001); William Reno, *Warlord Politics and African States* (Boulder, CO: Lynne Rienner, 1998); Mats Berdal and David Malone (eds), *Greed and Grievance: Economic Agendas in Civil Wars* (Boulder, CO: Lynne Rienner, 2000) and Jakkie Cilliers and Peggy Mason (eds), *Peace, Profit or Plunder?* (Cape Town: Institute for Security Studies, 1999).

Peacekeeping and Peace-Building in the Pacific – Lessons and Trends for International Best Practice

Ian Wilcock

While one must be duly modest about the transferability of the South Pacific's experiences to Africa, it may be of interest that Australia and its partners in the Pacific Islands Forum (PIF) are beginning to develop a wide range of experience in peacekeeping, peace-building and strategies for dealing with failing states. They have had to respond to four serious challenges to internal peace and security: Vanuatu in 1980; the Fiji political crises of 1987 and 2000; the Bougainville conflict; and the Solomon Islands conflict. There are now also serious issues being addressed in Papua New Guinea and Nauru.

Some Trends

While each of these situations has its own dynamics, some general observations can be made. First, challenges have become more difficult and more complicated. Two reasons for this stand out: one is the erosion in many countries of the capabilities of key institutions of state. This puts governance and institution-strengthening at the centre of any successful attempt to restore order. The other is that, compared to twenty-five years ago, weapons – small arms in particular – have become much more widespread and this has made disarmament more important than ever.

Second, the implicit understandings about regional responsibility for the neighbourhood which existed at the time of the Vanuatu crisis in 1980 have become more explicit and formalized. This is best seen in the Biketawa Declaration of October 2000, in which PIF leaders committed themselves collectively to democratic values and to upholding the security

---

His Excellency **Ian Wilcock** is the Australian High Commissioner to South Africa.

of the region, including in particular from non-traditional threats such as terrorism and transnational crime.

Lessons Learned and Preventive Strategies

The Pacific experience is not one of unmitigated success. Looking back, the key weakness in the Pacific approach has been one of timing and anticipation. In the future more efforts will be needed to identify factors that pre-dispose countries to conflict. For example, conflict is more likely where income is derived from extractive, export-oriented industries. If we had been more alert to this, we might have seen earlier the likely risk of conflict emerging in Bougainville.

Similarly, it appears there is a close correlation between the numbers of ethnic groupings and conflict (multiple groups or a single dominant group usually result in less conflict, whereas the presence of two large groups usually results in more conflict.). This could have told us much about the risk of conflict in Fiji, the Solomon Islands and Vanuatu.

What does the Pacific Experience mean more generally?

The main message from the Pacific experience is a hopeful one: remedial actions by regions acting co-operatively can stop conflict and can turn around bad situations. But to be effective, some pre-conditions need to exist – or to be created. These include:

- *A shared sense of responsibility for the region* based on shared political values. We were lucky to have this as an important historical bequest to our region but it is also necessary to build it up and sustain it through intensive engagement on the part of leaders and foreign ministers.
- *A can-do approach to problem solving*, leading to prompt regional initiatives rather than waiting for problems to drift up to the agenda of the Security Council. It is instructive in this regard to compare the regional response to the Solomon Islands with the UN's response to the Liberian and Haitian crises, where waiting for the emergence of Security Council consensus led to costly delays.
- *A willingness to encourage wide regional participation in solutions*, including that of less well-endowed states. The contribution of almost all 16 PIF countries to the Solomon Islands mission is a good example (Australia and New Zealand are the only developed country PIF members).

- *Selective engagement of the UN.* Regional initiatives do not preclude UN action in parallel where this is helpful (Bougainville is a case in point) but even with UN involvement, the outcomes are better when the region remains heavily engaged, as happened in both Bougainville and the Solomon Islands.
- *A commitment to creating regional capacity to deal with governance and policing issues.* In the Pacific we are evolving new ways of responding. The concept of 'pooled governance' is a significant one and can be developed elsewhere. So too is the Australian initiative in creating its 500-strong international police deployment group. Developed countries have to make real and long-term commitments to governance. In some cases this will involve 'embedded support' through long-term placement of personnel in the government structures of recipient countries.
- *A willingness to mobilize civil society* is important in the peace-building process. Women in particular have a crucial role to play in the Pacific, as do church-based organizations.

Conclusion

The actions in the Pacific demonstrate the wisdom of the UN Charter's drafters in encouraging, in Chapter VIII, the development of 'pacific settlement of local disputes through ... regional arrangements or by ... regional agencies'. The challenge is how to make Chapter VIII work well all the time. The UN will continue to be preoccupied with conflicts that slip from Chapter VIII to Chapters VI and VII but, if we want a stronger conflict prevention and peace-building framework, we also need to focus on what should be done to help regions manage their conflicts.

Old Wine in New Bottles?
US Policy Towards Africa after 9/11 and Iraq

John Prendergast

Introduction

Despite increasingly fashionable rationales focused on countering failed states and other root causes of terrorism or havens for its proliferation, US policy towards Africa remains at the bottom of the list in terms of strategic priorities of the US government. Despite the rhetoric of President Bush on his recent trip to Africa, and that of President Clinton on his visits, the continent figures very little into US geo-strategic calculations.

Finding supportive governments in the war on terror promises to replace Cold War client-building as the dominant paradigm of US foreign policy after 11 September 2001 and the second war in Iraq. The issue will increasingly dictate the level of tolerance for human rights and democracy deficits, and will drive favouritism in the doling out of aid resources.

An increasingly muscular, one-track, militaristic approach marks US involvement in counter-terrorism in Africa. Little diplomatic engagement is involved, as the current administration has de-emphasized high level diplomacy (with the exception of Sudan) and focused its efforts on training and building the capacity of compliant African militaries and border control institutions. On the other side of the coin, the Millennium Challenge Account will focus most development resources on a few high performing African governments, leaving many eroding states with fewer resources than ever before, thus increasing the risk of incurring much greater security, political and humanitarian costs down the road.

Regardless, humanitarian considerations will continue to be the largest factor driving US interest in Africa. The prevention and resolution of war, the amelioration of famine or food crises, and the countering of terrorist havens are the most important US considerations, in general terms, and with specific exceptions when the costs are perceived to be too high to respond meaningfully, as was the case in Liberia last year.

John Prendergast is the Special Advisor to the President of the International Crisis Group.

Counter-Terrorism Policy

The 11 September terrorist attacks have ensured the place of counter-terrorism as the unrivalled global strategic priority of the US government. In fact, much as the Cold War defined US foreign policy from the 1950s until 1990, the global war on terrorism has become the dominant paradigm for Bush administration foreign policy, and Africa is no exception.

This is slowly changing the nature of the Bush administration policy towards Africa. In general terms, overt democratization and human rights objectives appear to have been downgraded, in favour of support to regimes that line up favourably on counter-terrorism objectives and Iraq policy. The similarities between this overarching approach and that which defined policies from Eisenhower to Reagan are striking.

Just as during the Cold War, the Horn of Africa has become the main locus for US strategic policy. In the immediate aftermath of 11 September, US Central Command was combing the region for possibilities for increased counter-terrorism co-operation opportunities. Somalia was of the most immediate concern, and an intelligence net was created (with the support of the governments of Germany and others) to ensure against penetration or infiltration by Al-Qa'ida elements.

Ethiopia is the strategic centre of the US Horn Counter-terrorism policy, and Djibouti is the logistical nerve centre. Ethiopia provides intelligence and other co-operation regarding Al-Itihad and other groups within the region, while Djibouti plays host to an increasing number of US military and intelligence personnel.

With the Sudan peace process making rapid progress, plans are in the works for an expansion of counter-terrorism co-operation with Khartoum. Kenya and Uganda are also closely wrapped into the overall strategy, as Kenya remains the principal target of Al-Qa'ida operations in the region.

As a result of this emphasis on counter-terrorism, other objectives in the region have been downgraded. Democracy promotion has not been emphasized strongly, as evidenced by the reduction in aid to Kenya after the victory of President Mwai Kibaki in the elections, the continuing support for governments in Kampala, Kigali, and Addis Ababa, and the diminution of pressure for presidential elections as part of the Sudan peace deal.

Conflict resolution priorities have also been downgraded in favour of counter-terrorism objectives. In late 2003, Secretary of State Colin Powell told Ethiopia's Foreign Minister that the US would not allow the border issue with Eritrea to overshadow US interests, particularly counter-terrorism. The US has done little to counter the possibility of renewed conflict between those two countries. Similarly, in the aftermath of Rwandan and Ugandan support for the Bush administration's invasion of Iraq, the US invited both governments to the White House despite their continuing involvement in the Democratic Republic of Congo. Only in Sudan did conflict resolution priorities remain high, driven by domestic policy considerations.

The most dramatic example of diplomatic disinterest remains Somalia, where counter-terrorism objectives continue to be undermined by the inability to secure a peace agreement between the contending factions. The US and EU have not invested in the peace process led by the Intergovernmental Authority on Development (IGAD), standing by while divisions among IGAD states have brought down one potential agreement after another.

The Horn is not the only area in which counter-terrorism objectives are making themselves felt. The US European Command, the Pentagon's arm responsible for the rest of sub-Saharan Africa outside the Horn, is increasing both co-operation with friendly governments and direct operations, as was seen earlier this month on the Chadian border. In addition to that Sahel region, issues of concern are the suspected terrorist cells in South Africa, the potential for money laundering and mineral investments in West and Central Africa, and Islamic extremism in northern Nigeria.

Beyond Counter-Terrorism

For the Bush administration, the promotion of free trade and expansion of markets is the next priority in Africa. Assistant Secretary of State for African Affairs Walter Kansteiner made this his personal crusade during his tenure, pushing through the bureaucracy a series of creative measures to expand trade and investment opportunities running in both directions.

However, despite the consensus forged to promote these measures, successive Washington administrations continue to maintain economic policies that have a severely negative effect on Africa's growth prospects. By demanding – through the International Monetary Fund (IMF) – that African governments remove all trade barriers, while at the same time maintaining huge production subsidies, the terms of trade for Africa continue to deteriorate in dramatic fashion. As long as this disconnect continues, it will prevent African growth prospects from improving and ensure that no progress is made in World Trade Organization negotiations.

President Bush himself has made the fight against HIV/AIDS a personal priority. In his most recent State of the Union address, he presented a bold plan to increase spending for prevention and treatment to US$15 billion over five years, far exceeding expectations. However, his initial request to Congress was only US$2 billion for the first year, creating concern that the promises will not be kept. Furthermore, controversy still continues over what percentage of the funds will go to the promotion of abstinence. Currently one-third of US aid is earmarked for abstinence education, raising the ire of activists who believe that the promotion of effective prevention methods such as the use of condoms will be undermined by this strong emphasis on abstinence. This policy, as well as the administration's apparent pursuit of a 'go-it-alone' strategy on AIDS, came under intense criticism in July at the fifteenth International AIDS Conference in Bangkok. Bush was also sharply criticized for rejecting the UN Secretary General's plea for more US money to be injected into the UN-sponsored Global Fund to fight AIDS.

It has also been hypothesized that this strong emphasis on abstinence also serves Bush's interests by shifting the disbursement of aid money from the HIV/AIDS programs administered by organizations such as Planned Parenthood and Population Services International to faith-based organizations. Finally, Bush's choice of a retired executive from Eli Lilly, a pharmaceutical company, to serve as the 'AIDS Czar' signals that Bush's AIDS programme may emphasize the distribution of drugs over prevention education. If the programme does end up funding primarily the distribution of HIV/AIDS drugs, this will represent a major subsidy for an already extremely profitable US pharmaceutical sector.

An issue very much linked to HIV/AIDS is reproductive health. Under the Bush administration's anti-abortion policy, known as the Mexico City rule, groups that have been effective in curbing the spread of HIV/AIDS are now forced to close because they are involved in abortions, referral advice, counselling, or contraceptive distribution. As a result, many communities who depended on these clinics for health care must now go without these services.

Another bold but flawed Bush initiative is the Millennium Challenge Account (MCA). It aims to focus development resources on a few high-performing countries. In the process, the US Agency for International Development is slowly and almost imperceptibly being dismantled, particularly in terms of its diminishing role in providing traditional

developmental assistance. Although it is important to try to shake up the aid industry, there will be a number of negative repercussions resulting from the MCA approach:
- All of the resources will go to few countries, creating islands of stability in highly unstable seas;
- Countries that are trying to enact reforms but run up against significant obstacles will not receive help under the MCA; and
- Excluded countries – which arguably need the most help – will simply fall further and further behind and become a larger threat to stability than they already are.

Oil and mineral interests have had a much less significant impact on US policy than is commonly believed. In Nigeria, the State Department has maintained cool relations with Olesugun Obasanjo's government, and provided very little aid. In Angola, a similar lack of engagement marks the relationship. Although there is a great deal of rhetoric about the importance of the oil wealth of the Gulf of Guinea and the mineral wealth of the DRC, there has been little corresponding political and economic engagement in support of any significant enhancement of those interests.

The Bush administration has not lived up to its stated commitment to the Refugee Resettlement Program. In the past two years, the Bush administration has significantly reduced the refugee admissions ceiling to 70,000, the lowest point in two decades. In 2003, only a quarter of the authorized refugees have arrived in the United States. Since 11 September, the administration has cited security concerns as the reason for decreased US refugee resettlement admissions. However, there remains a delay in processing security clearances for these eligible refugees who languish in refugee camps. The implications of this policy extend beyond refugee camp borders. Refugee resettlement assists some of the world's 13 million refugees, reduces regional instabilities caused by alleviating some pressures to host countries, and demonstrates US commitment to sharing the burden of Africa's immense humanitarian challenges.

Conclusion

The Bush administration's foreign policy is not altogether dissimilar to that of its predecessor. However, the terrorist attacks of 11 September have altered the strategic calculations of the US in peripheral zones throughout the world, in ways very similar to the Cold War period. This has had the most significant impact on US policy toward the Horn of Africa. It remains to be seen whether US policy to the rest of the continent follows suit. If that is the case, it is quite possible that human rights and democracy promotion will again be pushed to the back seat of US policy priorities, just as it was during the era of Soviet containment.

Perspectives on the AU and Nepad – An Elite Survey in Seven African Countries

Hennie Kotzé

Introduction

The considerable growth that has typified the world economy over the past three decades has for the most part passed Africa by.[1] Although much of the structural causes for this economic marginalization can be found in the continent's colonial heritage, the track records of post-colonial governments have left much to be desired.[2] With regards to the latter, a causal link has been drawn between weak states, political instability and the consequent reluctance by developed nations to invest in the continent. Coupled with a lack of economic growth, Africa's increasing reliance on aid has plunged many of its states deeper and deeper into excessive levels of foreign debt. Regrettably the whole continent, including those countries with exemplary democratic credentials, has become tainted as one ravaged by bad governance and a dependency on the developed North. Quite clearly, the need has arisen for Africa to show itself capable of overcoming these adversities. With the rapidly changing nature of global economic and general societal trends, Africa finds itself at a juncture where it has to politically stabilize and show sustained economic growth, or face the real possibility of being left behind.

It was in response to these circumstances that the New Partnership for Africa's Development (Nepad) was launched in Abuja, Nigeria in October 2001, followed by the replacement of the Organization of African Unity by the Constitutive Act of the African Union in July 2002. The African Union (AU) aims to 'promote peace, security and stability on the continent' and reserves the right to 'intervene in member states pursuant to a decision of the assembly in respect of grave circumstances such as war crimes, genocide and crimes against humanity as well as the condemnation and rejection of unconstitutional changes of government'. As the policy

---

Hennie Kotzé is Professor in the Department of Political Science at the University of Stellenbosch, South Africa.

initiative of the African Union, Nepad seeks to promote accelerated growth and sustainable development on the continent, eradicate widespread and severe poverty and halt Africa's marginalization in the globalization process.

There is an urgency about the implementation of these structures which highlights the need for African leaders and opinion leaders to act together in order to ensure the upliftment and rejuvenation of the African continent. In a concerted effort to restore peace on the continent and operationalize the policies of the African Union, discussions revolved around the establishment of a Peace and Security Council, Pan-African Parliament, African Court of Justice, the integration of Nepad into the African Union and the activation of the African Peer Review Mechanism (APRM). In order to succeed, the African Union and the Nepad strategy will require the commitment of African leadership in all social spheres on the continent, since both initiatives rely on the principle of increased African integration and unification, supported by the idea of African ownership and control.

Assuming that elites are those persons who 'hold authoritative positions in powerful public and private organizations and influential movements and who therefore are able to affect strategic decisions regularly'[3] an analysis of elite perceptions regarding the African Union and the Nepad will provide important insights into the future direction of the two initiatives. It was against this background that the Centre for International and Comparative Politics at the University of Stellenbosch, with the support of the Konrad Adenauer Stiftung, conducted a survey focusing on elite perceptions regarding the African Union Nepad and other developmental issues (see the Appendix for the methodology of the survey and the composition of the sample). South Africa, Nigeria, Senegal and Algeria were included in the survey as countries whose presidents are the

---

[1] Richard Cornwell, 'A New Partnership for Africa's Development.' *African Security Review* (Vol. 11 No. 1, 2002), p. 91.

[2] X. P. Guma, 'Economic Recovery in Africa, Regional Integration and Good Governance' in Richard Gibb, Tim Hughes, and Greg Mills and Tapani Vaahtoranta (eds.), *Charting a New Course: Globalization, African Recovery and the New Africa Initiative* (Johannesburg: The South African Institute of International Affairs, 2002), p. 55.

[3] See John Higley et al,. *Elite Structure and Ideology* (New York: Columbia University Press, 1976), p. 17 for the original version of this definition. John Higley and Richard Gunther, *Elites and Democratic Consolidation in Latin America and Southern Europe* (Cambridge: Cambridge University Press, 1992), p. 8.

main drivers of Nepad and which have had a fair amount of exposure to the plan thus far. In addition, Kenya, Uganda and Zimbabwe were selected as 'outside countries' to allow for more accurate and detailed comparisons.

This paper contains findings, in a substantially abbreviated form, of the survey that was conducted in South Africa, Nigeria, Senegal, Algeria, Kenya, Uganda and Zimbabwe a little more than a year ago and is based on the publication *African Elite Perspectives on the AU and Nepad: A comparative study across seven African Countries*. Not only does the survey allow us to analyze and make predictions regarding elite attitudes towards the two most influential bodies in African politics in the last decade (namely the African Union and Nepad) but it also allows us to draw important comparisons between African countries that represent a broad spectrum of African political and social climates.

The Importance of Elites

The role of elites in Africa has become increasingly important over the last decade. They do not only fulfil the crucial function of the allocation of scarce resources and values, but they also play an important role in the problem definition and agenda-setting process of public policy issues. In so doing, they bring the problem to the attention of the policy makers and enhance the salience of some issues over others.

As reflected above, African elites should play an important role in drafting, implementing and evaluating policy throughout the African continent. According to Nel and Taylor[4] the exposure of the African continent to the forces of globalization has resulted in a transnational elite 'comprising of transnational executives and their affiliates, globalizing state bureaucrats, capitalist-inspired politicians and professionals and consumer elites'. The emergence of such an elite in Africa has become increasingly evident over the past number of years, with the emergence of a group of African leaders spearheading negotiations between Africa and the developed world and placing Africa's development challenges on the global agenda. Nepad and the launch of the African Union are two such initiatives forming the pinnacle of efforts by these new African leaders to rejuvenate the African continent.

---

[4] Philip Nel and Ian Taylor, 'New Africa, Globalization and the Confines if Elite Reformism: Getting the rhetoric right, getting the strategy wrong.' *Third World Quarterly* (Vol. 23, No. 1, 2002), pp. 163-180.

The important argument in elite theory is that 'public policy is not determined by the demands and actions of the masses, but by a ruling elite whose preferences are carried into effect by public officials and agencies'.[5] To summarize: public policy is a product of elite interaction, reflecting their attitudes and values and serving their ends.

This paper gauges the attitudinal patterns of the African elite on a selection of important issues regarding the AU and Nepad. Through the use of various attitudinal and value scales, we have attempted to provide a picture of current elite thought regarding these two institutions that may arguably become the cornerstones of African development in the next decade or two.

It should be noted that, unlike public surveys, opinion leader surveys should not be used to draw conclusions about the attitudes of a whole population. Their value lies in their ability to discern particular trends or attitudinal patterns amongst the most influential decision makers in both the public and the private spheres. This paper, therefore, attempts to:

- Provide an analysis of elite confidence and ownership of the AU and Nepad.
- Analyze elite perceptions of the problems and challenges facing the African continent, the goals associated with the African Union and Nepad; globalization and the neo-liberal framework; and the partnership with the developed world.
- Describe elite perceptions regarding the capacity of African states to implement Nepad; the perceived confidence in the African Peer Review Mechanism; and countries that could prove beneficial partners for the African continent.

Confidence and Ownership

Plans towards the regional economic and political integration of Africa have been regarded as paramount by a number of African governments for quite some time and have resulted in the launch of numerous initiatives aimed towards this end. In 1980, the Lagos Plan of Action was directed towards greater market integration on the continent, and in 1991 the Abuja Treaty established plans for the creation of an African Economic Community within thirty-four years. In 1999, the Sirte Declaration pre-empted the dissolution of the Organization of African Unity (OAU) and its

---

[5] See James Anderson, *Public Policy Making: An Introduction*, 2nd ed. (Boston: Houghton-Mifflin, 1994).

replacement by the African Union in July 2002. More recently, however, plans towards continental unity and integration have been extended to include issues of good governance, peace and political stability through the establishment of the New Partnership for African Development (Nepad) – a policy initiative of the African Union.

Various criticisms have, however, been levelled against the African Union and Nepad strategy, which will undoubtedly carry important implications for ownership of and confidence in the two bodies. We have asked: To what extent do the elites in the various African countries surveyed believe in the principles upon which the African Union and Nepad strategy are based? Do the majority of elites believe that Nepad is indeed an elite-driven process that has taken little or no cognizance of the needs of Africa's millions? Do they believe that a common African identity is indeed feasible and that the interests of the continent should receive priority over the national interests of the respective states involved? These and other issues will be dealt with in the sections that follow.

When respondents were asked to specifically indicate their level of knowledge regarding the AU on a scale[6] of 1(nothing at all) to 5(a great deal), all countries except Algeria expressed an above average knowledge of the African Union (**Figure 1**). Nigeria (3.71) and South Africa (3.57) expressed the highest level of knowledge, followed by Senegal (3.36), Kenya (3.45), Zimbabwe (3.50), Uganda (3.38) and Algeria (2.95).

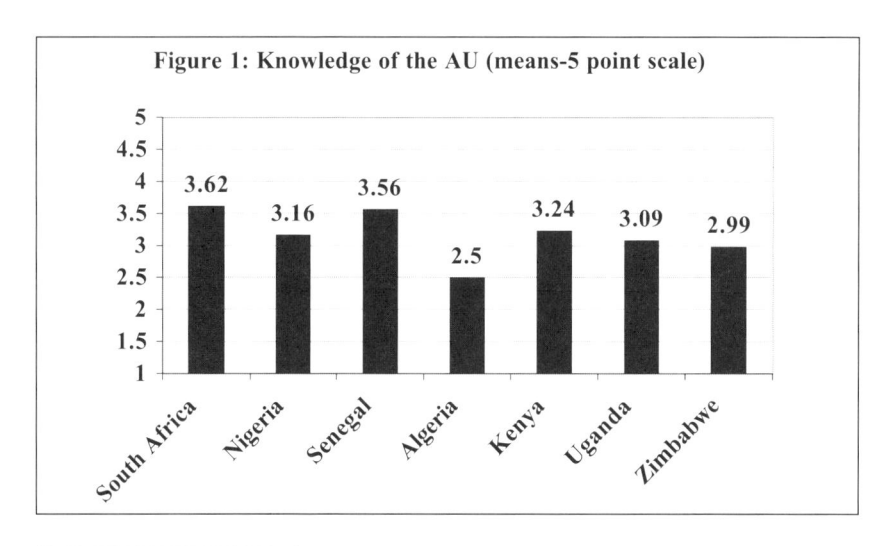

Figure 1: Knowledge of the AU (means-5 point scale)

South Africa	3.62
Nigeria	3.16
Senegal	3.56
Algeria	2.5
Kenya	3.24
Uganda	3.09
Zimbabwe	2.99

---

[6] Responses were recoded in the opposite direction.

When asked to indicate their level of knowledge regarding Nepad[7] (**Fig.2**), only Zimbabwe and Algeria displayed a below average knowledge of the strategy. South Africa (3.62) and Senegal (3.56) expressed slightly higher mean values than the other countries, followed by Kenya (3.24), Nigeria (3.16), Uganda (3.09), Zimbabwe (2.99) and Algeria (2.50).

Figure 2: Knowledge of Nepad (means-5 point scale)

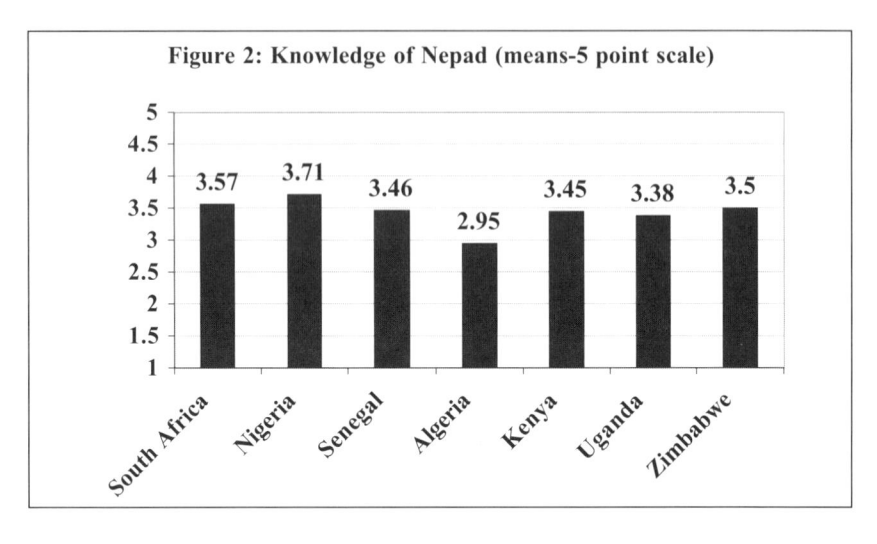

Country	Mean
South Africa	3.57
Nigeria	3.71
Senegal	3.46
Algeria	2.95
Kenya	3.45
Uganda	3.38
Zimbabwe	3.5

Fig 3: Confidence in Nepad to improve the economic prospects of country (means-10 point scale)

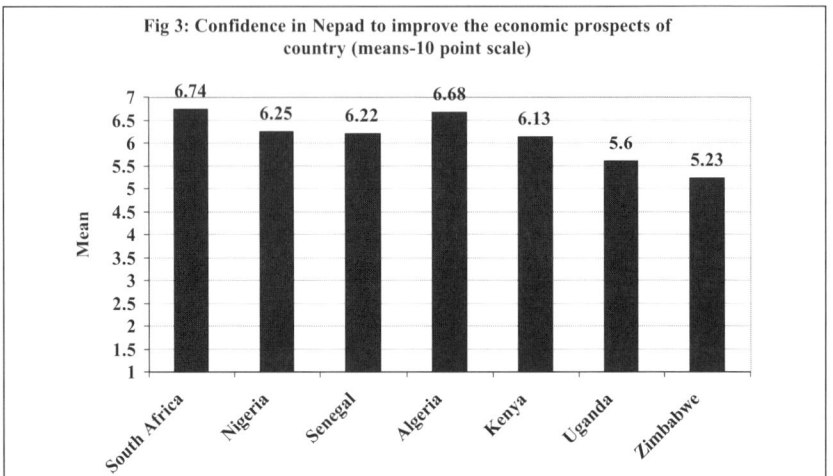

Country	Mean
South Africa	6.74
Nigeria	6.25
Senegal	6.22
Algeria	6.68
Kenya	6.13
Uganda	5.6
Zimbabwe	5.23

---

[7] The elite respondents' academic knowledge concerning the African Union and Nepad was not empirically tested. Responses in this survey merely reflect whether elites claim they have knowledge of the Nepad and AU.

With reference to this issue of confidence, respondents were asked to indicate, on a scale of 1 (no confidence) to 10 (complete confidence) how much confidence they have in Nepad to improve the economic prospects of Africa (**Figure 3**).

Once again, the countries directly involved in the Nepad process have displayed higher levels of confidence than those countries not directly involved in the drafting of the strategy. Interestingly, Algeria displays higher levels of confidence in Nepad's ability to solve the economic problems of the country than in Nepad's ability to solve the economic problems of the continent. South Africa's leading role in the development of the strategy is clearly depicted in the higher levels of confidence expressed by the country's elites when compared to the other countries included in the survey.

When comparing the levels of confidence across the various societal sectors (**Table 1**), civil society's discontentment with the policy becomes evident. In South Africa, Nigeria, Senegal, Uganda and Zimbabwe, civil society displayed lower mean scores than their politician and civil servant counterparts. In Kenya, however, civil society displayed higher levels confidence than politicians and civil servants.

Table 1: Confidence in Nepad to improve economic prospects of continent- Societal Sector (Mean scores on a 10 point scale: 1= no confidence; 10 = complete confidence)

	South Africa	Nigeria	Senegal	Algeria	Kenya	Uganda	Zimbabwe
Civil Society	6.34	6.21	6.08	6.59	6.51	6.51	6.51
Politician	6.89	6.64	7.42		5.80	6.23	6.17
Civil Servants	7.40	6.76	7.09	5.28	6.60	5.67	5.81
N	566	130	136	120	120	97	140

Nepad, as mentioned above, has often been labeled as an elite-driven process due to the lack of public participation and consultation in the process.[8] Such

---

[8] See for instance: *African Scholars' Forum for Envisioning Africa: focus on Nepad* (2002) p.2; collection of conference papers published online at <www.worldsummit2002.org>; P Arthur, Achieving and sustaining African economic recovery through the Nepad, p.17; Ross Herbert, 'Implementing Nepad: A Critical Assessment' in Roy Culpeper (ed). African Report: Assessing the New Partnerships (North-South Institute, 2003), p. 12; 'We do not accept Nepad! Africa is not for sale' Declaration issued by civil society organizations that met in Port Shepstone, Kwazulu-Natal, on 4-8 July, *Global Dialogue* (Vol. 7, No. 2, July 2002), p. 8.

criticisms carry important implications for confidence in and ownership of the Nepad strategy. If perceptions exist that the policy reflects only the interests of a few elites and their partners in the developed world at the expense of the needs of ordinary Africans, successful implementation of the plan may be seriously stymied. To what extent do elites in South Africa, Nigeria, Senegal, Algeria, Kenya, Uganda and Zimbabwe believe that Nepad is indeed an elite-driven initiative that does not take the needs of ordinary Africans into account?

Elites were asked to indicate on a scale of 1 (strongly agree) to 5 (strongly disagree) to what extent they concur with the statement that 'It is only the ruling elite in [country] that is actively involved in promoting Nepad' (**Table 2**).[9]

Table 2: It is only the ruling elite that is actively involved in promoting Nepad (means – 5 point scale)

	Agree	Neutral	Disagree	Mean
South Africa	59.4	14.1	26.5	2.57
Nigeria	71.5	12.3	16.1	2.20
Senegal	66.4	7.5	26.1	2.44
Algeria	39.0	45.1	16.0	2.66
Kenya	53.3	24.2	22.5	2.60
Uganda	71.2	17.5	11.4	2.20
Zimbabwe	34.3	16.1	49.6	3.25

Another important topic is that of African identity and integration: The extent to which the elites believe that an African identity can and should be created carries important implications for confidence in and ownership of the African Union and the Nepad strategy. Respondents were therefore confronted with a number of questions measuring the extent to which they believed that such unity and integration are indeed plausible and possible given the current African context.

Although support for African unification and integration seems quite strong amongst African elites as suggested by the survey data, criticisms have been levelled against the AU and the Nepad initiative, suggesting that they may result in a conflict of interest between the goals

---

[9] The categories 'strongly agree' and 'agree' were collapsed to form a single category, 'agree'. Similarly, 'disagree' and 'strongly disagree' were collapsed to form 'disagree'.

of the continent and the national interests of the respective states. It is clear that the Constitutive Act of the African Union remains ambiguous on issues of state sovereignty, since it proposes the right to intervene in the internal affairs of member states under conditions of autocratic rule.[10] According to articles 4 (h) and (j) of the Act, the AU reserves the 'right to intervene in a member state pursuant to a decision of the Assembly in respect of grave circumstances, namely war crimes, genocide and crimes against humanity'.[11] Similarly, the Nepad structures proposed a Peer Review Mechanism to be adopted by the African Union, which is regarded by some as a possible infringement on the sovereign right of the state. Respondents were asked to indicate the extent to which they agreed with the statement that 'the interests of the continent should receive priority over the national interests of the respective states' (Figure 4). Responses were once again ranked on a scale from 1(strongly agree) to 5 (strongly disagree). The majority of respondents in South Africa, Nigeria and Zimbabwe disagreed with the statement, while the majority of respondents in Senegal, Kenya, Algeria and Uganda agreed with the statement.

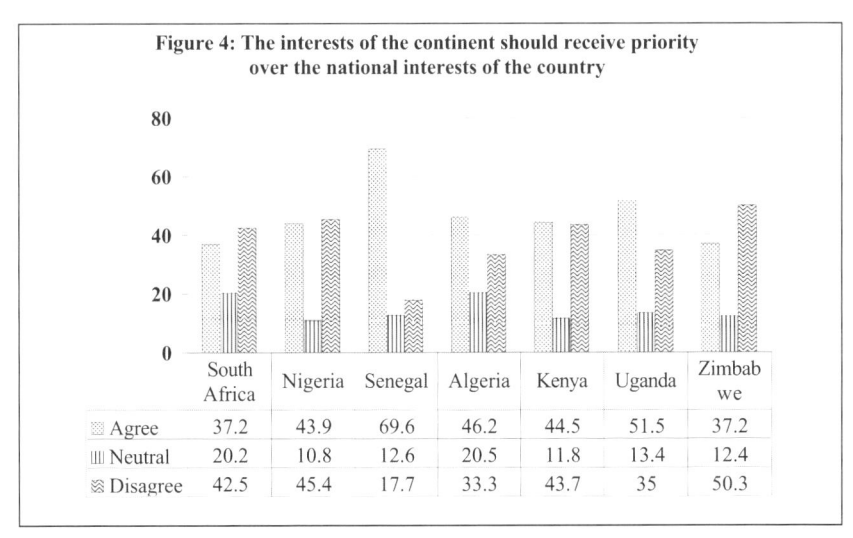

Figure 4: The interests of the continent should receive priority over the national interests of the country

	South Africa	Nigeria	Senegal	Algeria	Kenya	Uganda	Zimbabwe
Agree	37.2	43.9	69.6	46.2	44.5	51.5	37.2
Neutral	20.2	10.8	12.6	20.5	11.8	13.4	12.4
Disagree	42.5	45.4	17.7	33.3	43.7	35	50.3

The data presented above therefore suggests that although the majority of African elites do, in principle, ascribe to the value of African identity, they

---

[10] Meyns 2002 as cited in W. J. Breytenbach, 'The African Renaissance and Nepad.' (Cape Town: Stellenbosch University, 2003)

[11] Baffour Ankomah, 'African Union in danger of being stillborn', *New African*, June 2002.

are aware of the possible problems of implementation associated with a potential clash between the national interests and continental interests.

Although architects of the Nepad initiative have succeeded in gaining support for the initiative amongst Western partners, support for and confidence in the initiative amongst their own publics has left much to be desired. The elite perceptions presented in this section should hint towards possible problems which may arise during policy articulation, implementation and evaluation, and as such, provide an invaluable point of departure from which to proceed.

Goal and Principles

Although arguing that the policies resulting from an increasingly globalized economic system have resulted in the marginalization of Africa, the Nepad policy does stress that the current economic revolution could provide the very environment and instruments with which Africa can liberate herself from the chains of poverty, famine, lawlessness and war.[12]

A number of debates surrounding the goals and means with which the Nepad policy attempts to achieve these goals have emerged in the literature. The neo-liberal framework embraced by the Nepad policy has come under severe criticism from various camps that assert that the alignment of African developmental goals with the Northern paradigm of globalization may result in the neglect of the local needs and aspirations of the African people.[13] Further concern has been expressed surrounding the goals and objectives contained in the document, with numerous complaints regarding the marginal role that gender equality has been relegated within the policy.[14] Apprehension has also been expressed that safety and security issues may receive priority over issues of development and social welfare; due to the increased importance that security is currently afforded on the

---

[12] Page 6, paragraph.28 of the Nepad document states: 'The world has entered the new millennium in the midst of an economic revolution. This revolution could provide both the context and the means for Africa's rejuvenation. While globalization has increased the cost of Africa's ability to compete, we hold that the advantages of an effectively managed integration present the best prospects for future economic prosperity and poverty reduction.'

[13] 'Issues Briefing 38', Institute for Democracy in South Africa. September 2002.

[14] L. Dupree and K Ogunsanya, 2003. Mainstreaming women into Nepad: Invisible Progress. Peace and Governance Program. Briefing Paper No. 8. Olofi, I. 2002. 'Nepad and Globalization: Matters arising', p. 4.

global agenda.[15]

In the light of these arguments, respondents were asked to judge on a 7-point scale[16] how problematic they thought a number of issues were for Africa's future, with 1 being not problematic at all and 7 being extremely problematic.[17] (See **Table 3** for the results)

Table 3: Problems facing the African continent (Comparison of means on a 7-point scale, where 7 = most problematic)

Rank	South Africa	Nigeria	Senegal	Algeria	Kenya	Uganda	Zimbabwe
1	HIV/AIDS (6.55)	Income disparities (6.04)	HIV/AIDS (6.28)	HIV/AIDS	HIV/AIDS (6.63)	HIV/AIDS (6.32)	HIV/AIDS (6.74)
2	Income disparities (6.02)	HIV/AIDS (5.95)	Secessionist movements (6.07)	Income disparities (5.83)	Income disparities (6.34)	Income disparities (5.84)	Income disparities (6.38)
3	Gender Equality (5.00)	Ecological problems (5.11)	Income disparities (6.00)	Ecological problems (5.52)	Stable and democratic govts (5.70)	Ecological problems (5.11)	Domestic order and stability (5.42)
4	Globlization (4.98)	Secessionist movements (5.04)	Domestic order and stability (5.54)	Secessionist movements (5.34)	Ecological problems (5.22)	Secessionist movements (4.93)	Secessionist movements (5.39)
5	Ecological problems (4.70)	Stable and accountable democratic govts. (4.88)	Stable and democratic govts (5.53)	Domestic order and stability (5.26)	Globalization (4.98)	Domestic order and stability (4.88)	Stable and democratic govts (5.22)
6	Secessionist movements (4.68)	Domestic order and stability (4.66)	Ecological problems (5.51)	Stable and democratic govts (5.25)	Gender Equality (4.94)	Globalization (4.85)	Globalization (4.98)
7	Stable and democratic govts (4.51)	Globalization (4.14)	Globalization (5.17)	Globalization (4.78)	Secessionist movements (4.71)	Stable and democratic govts (4.75)	Ecological problems (4.71)
8	Clash between modern and traditional (4.06)	Clash between modern and traditional (3.93)	Gender Equality (4.86)	Gender Equality (4.74)	Clash between modern and traditional (4.55)	Clash between modern and traditional (4.67)	Gender Equality (4.43)
9	Domestic order and stability (3.64)	Gender Equality (3.85)	Clash between modern and traditional (4.01)	Clash between modern and traditional (4.05)	Domestic order and stability (4.53)	Gender Equality (4.45)	Clash between modern and traditional (3.80)

---

[15] Janis Van der Westhuizen, 'Selling Nepad after 9/11: Can global security be linked to global welfare?' Paper prepared for 'Studies of Development in an Era of Globalization' research workshop, Dalhousie University, Halifax, Canada, 9-10 August 2002.

The data presented in **Table 3** suggests that HIV/AIDS and the large income disparities between rich and poor are perceived as the most problematic issues facing the African continent. World ecological problems were regarded as relatively important, ranking within the top 5 issues by respondents in South Africa, Nigeria, Algeria, Kenya and Uganda, while secessionist movements also ranked within the top 5 of the majority of countries surveyed, i.e. Nigeria, Senegal, Algeria, Uganda and Zimbabwe. Globalization was only placed in the top 5 problems in Kenya and South Africa, while importance placed on domestic order/stability and stable and accountable democratic governments varied considerably between countries. Although regarded as the most important problem facing the African continent by all countries except Nigeria, the issue of HIV/AIDS has received scant attention within the Nepad document. According to Herbert[18] 'Nepad's blind spot is the social, economic and governance impact of HIV/AIDS' since the document 'accords HIV/AIDS no greater status than that of a problem of health'. Considering that the percentage of adults (age 15-49) living with HIV/AIDS is more than 15 per cent in South Africa and Zimbabwe, and between 5 and 10 per cent in Uganda, Kenya and Nigeria[19], one would assume the issue to receive greater priority within the Nepad framework.

Of further concern, however, is the relatively low importance accorded to the issue of gender equality amongst the African elites. Such perceptions would echo the relatively low importance afforded to issues relating to gender equality within the Nepad document.[20]

Respondents were also asked to select the five biggest obstacles that would inhibit the development of the African continent and rank them in order of importance.[21] According to the data, political instability can be

---

[16] In the case of no answer, responses were recoded as system missing and then replaced with the series mean

[17] Items listed included: globalization; secessionist movements; world ecological problems; domestic order and stability in your own country; the clash between tradition and modernization; stable and accountable democratic governments; large income disparities between rich and poor; the equality between men and women; HIV/AIDS.

[18] R. Herbert, 'Implementing Nepad: A Critical Assessment' in Roy Culpeper (ed). African Report: Assessing the New Partnerships (North-South Institute, 2003), p. 15

[19] Africa Institute of South Africa. *Africa at a Glance: Facts and Figures 2001/2002*, p. 38.

[20] Ross Herbert, *Implementing Nepad*: A Critical Assessment, 2002, p. 473

[21] The obstacles listed included: HIV/AIDS; corruption; a lack of accountable African leaders; political instability; an unfair international trade regime; poverty; insufficient infrastructure; debt; negative stereotypes of the continent; ineffective bureaucracy; gender inequality; income inequality between the very rich and very poor Africans.

regarded as the most challenging issue facing the African continent, since it appears in the top three of all countries surveyed. Similarly, corruption also appears in the top three of most challenging issues identified of all countries surveyed, except Zimbabwe. Poverty was placed in the top 5 issues of all countries surveyed, while a lack of accountable governments was placed in the top 5 of South Africa, Nigeria, Senegal, Algeria and Uganda. Interestingly, HIV/AIDS loses its importance in relation to other issues identified, and is only regarded in the top three by South Africa and Kenya. Once again, gender inequality is not regarded as a challenge facing the African continent, along with negative stereotypes of the continent.

The data with reference to the biggest obstacles highlights the importance placed by African elites on issues of good governance. As mentioned at the outset of this section, problems in Africa can not exclusively be attributed to issues of globalization, but also stem from the large scale neo-patrimonial policies introduced by African governments in an attempt to gain constituent support.

Respondents were then asked to indicate how important (1 being very unimportant and 5 being very important)[22] they believed it to be for the African Union to pursue a number of goals[23] (**Table 4**) overleaf.

---

[22] Responses were recoded in the opposite direction. In the case of no answer, responses were recoded as system missing and replaced with the series mean.

[23] The goals listed included: working for peace in Africa; working to discourage human rights violations; working to solve environmental problems; promoting trade among African states; developing mechanisms to combat corrupt and accountable governments; improving the situation of women; participation of all interest groups in governing the country; working to punish all African states that cause human rights violations.

Table 4: Goals of the African Union (Comparison of means on a 5-point scale, where 5=very important)

Rank	South Africa	Nigeria	Senegal	Algeria	Kenya	Uganda	Zimbabwe
1	Peace in Africa (4.87)	Peace in Africa (4.91)	Peace in Africa (4.84)	Peace in Africa (4.79)	Peace in Africa (4.95)	Peace in Africa (4.86)	Peace in Africa (4.87)
2	Discourage Human rights violations (4.81)	Discourage Human rights violations (4.69)	Discourage Human rights violations (4.63)	Discourage Human rights violations (4.60)	Discourage Human rights violations (4.80)	Discourage Human rights violations (4.84)	Discourage Human rights violations (4.81)
3	Combat corruption (4.75)	Combat corruption (4.67)	Encourage trade among African states (4.61)	Combat corruption (4.47)	Combat corruption (4.76)	Combat corruption (4.72)	Encourage trade among African states (4.73)
4	Improve situation of women (4.62)	Encourage trade among African states (4.59)	Combat corruption (4.51)	Improve situation of women (4.40)	Promote trade amongst African states (4.73)	Promote trade amongst African states (4.70)	Discourage Human rights violations (4.69)
5	Encourage trade among African states (4.59)	Solve environmental problems (4.48)	Improve situation of women (4.92)	Solve environmental problems (4.38)	Solve environmental problems (4.62)	Solve environmental problems (4.52)	Solve environmental problems (4.48)
6	Solve environmental problems (4.45)	Punish states that violate human rights (4.45)	Solve environmental problems (4.48)	Promote trade amongst African states (4.31)	Punish states that violate human rights (4.37)	Improve situation of women (4.49)	Punish states that violate human rights (4.45)
7	Punish states that violate human rights (4.35)	Improve situation of women (4.16)	Punish states that violate human rights (4.16)	Punish states that violate human rights (4.25)	Improve situation of women (4.34)	Punish states that violate human rights (4.47)	Improve situation of women (4.42)
8	Participation of interest groups (4.07)	Participation of interest groups (4.03)	Participation of interest groups (3.26)	Participation of interest groups (3.56)	Participation of interest groups (4.27)	Participation of interest groups (4.15)	Participation of interest groups (4.33)

Table 4 indicates that African elites perceive issues of governance in Africa to be of primary concern for the African Union.

An important previously mentioned debate surrounding the goals and objectives upon which the Nepad policy is based is the extent to which the Nepad policy embraces the neo-liberal paradigm, the proposed partnership with the developed world and the subsequent conditionalities evident within this agreement. It is against the background of these arguments that respondents were asked to indicate to what extent they felt that globalization poses a threat to Africa's economic reconstruction (Figure 5). Responses were once again plotted on a scale of 1(strongly agree) to 5 (strongly disagree) and then collapsed to include three categories, namely agree, neutral and disagree.

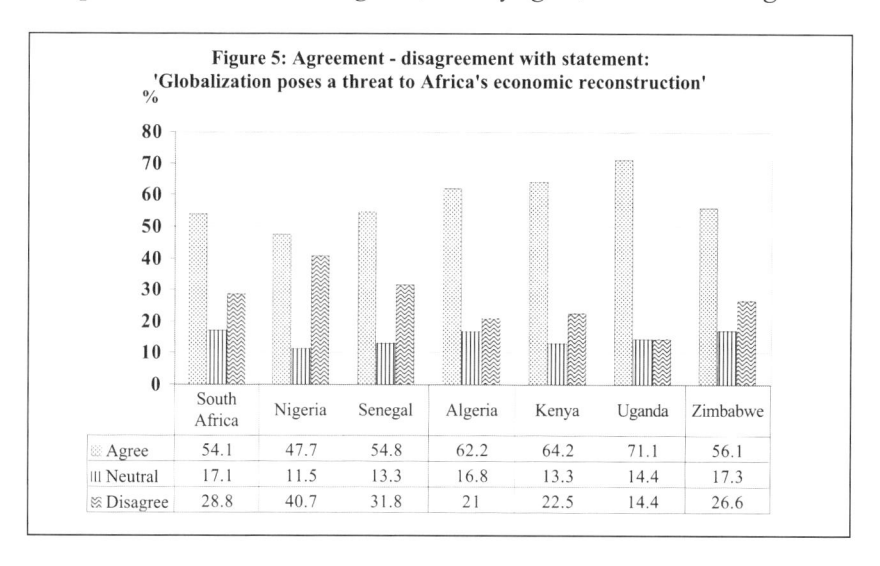

Figure 5: Agreement - disagreement with statement: 'Globalization poses a threat to Africa's economic reconstruction'

	South Africa	Nigeria	Senegal	Algeria	Kenya	Uganda	Zimbabwe
Agree	54.1	47.7	54.8	62.2	64.2	71.1	56.1
Neutral	17.1	11.5	13.3	16.8	13.3	14.4	17.3
Disagree	28.8	40.7	31.8	21	22.5	14.4	26.6

Quite clearly the majority of respondents in all countries surveyed agreed with the statement, thereby displaying a strong level of distrust for the impact of globalization on Africa. An interesting finding in the light of what can be arguably called Nepad's embrace of neo-liberal policies.

Implementation of Nepad

It is quite clear that the successful implementation of the Nepad initiative depends firstly on the extent to which the African leadership believes that African states possess the necessary capacity to implement the Nepad strategies; whether these strategies are indeed in line with national development needs and goals; and whether a political will to implement the policies successfully exists. Against this background we asked respondents to indicate to what extent they believed that their country has the capacity to implement Nepad policies.

Figure 6: Country has the capacity to implement NEPAD policies

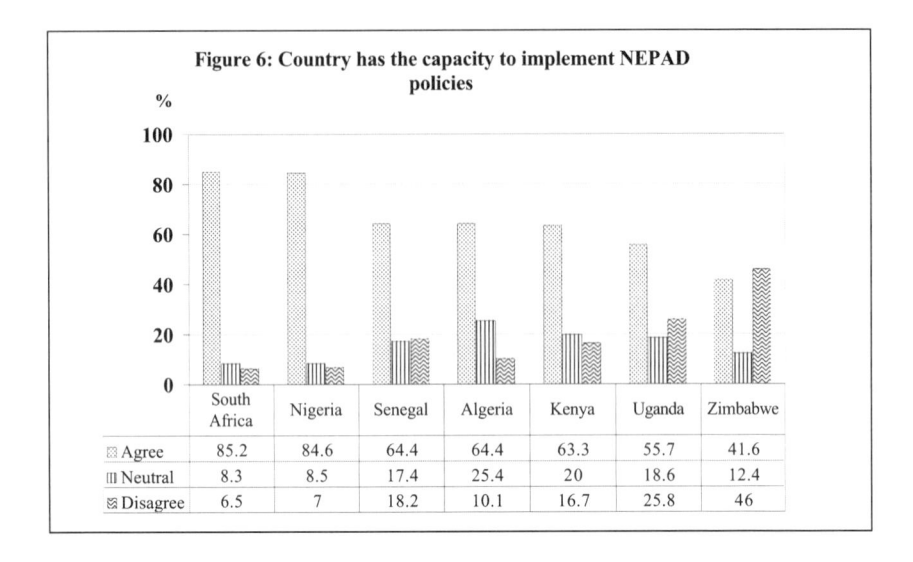

	South Africa	Nigeria	Senegal	Algeria	Kenya	Uganda	Zimbabwe
Agree	85.2	84.6	64.4	64.4	63.3	55.7	41.6
Neutral	8.3	8.5	17.4	25.4	20	18.6	12.4
Disagree	6.5	7	18.2	10.1	16.7	25.8	46

The data in Figure 6 suggests that the majority of elite respondents in all the countries surveyed except Zimbabwe agreed with the statement, thereby displaying a high degree of confidence in the ability of their respective countries to implement the Nepad strategies effectively. Interestingly, countries not directly involved in the drafting of the Nepad process display somewhat lower levels of agreement than those countries directly involved in the drafting process.

Although the majority of the elites in six of the seven countries surveyed believe that their countries have the necessary capacity to implement the Nepad policies, the actual implementation of the plan has been slow and often fraught with difficulties. At a Black Management Forum in Cape Town on 10 October 2003, President Mbeki expressed concern that some of the Nepad projects were in danger of not being properly implemented. President Mbeki was reported[24] as saying:

> We are not going to achieve some of the programmes we have set [out] to [achieve] because of the lack of capacity…Even if we do have the resources, the institutions do not have the capacity, and African renewal needs capacity… The embarrassing thing is that they [developed nations] have committed resources, but we do not have the capacity to implement [them].

The success with which the Nepad initiative will be implemented would

---

[24] *Cape Argus*, 10 October 2003.

therefore also largely depend on the extent to which the institutions of state in the respective African countries can indeed establish an implementation framework for the policy and whether such structures can be maintained in the long-term. Elite respondents were therefore asked to indicate the level of confidence they had in the institutions of state. An 'institutions of state index' was constructed by combining the confidence levels respondents expressed in the government, civil service and parliament. Unfortunately, these questions of elite confidence were not included in the Nigerian survey, due to cost constraints. In the index 'a great deal' and 'quite a lot' were combined in 'quite a lot' in Figure 7 and 'not very much' and 'none at all' were combined to form the category 'not very much'. Since the state is largely responsible for the successful drafting, implementation, propagating and funding of state policies, the perceived confidence expressed by elites in the state institutions should carry important implications for the implementation of Nepad.

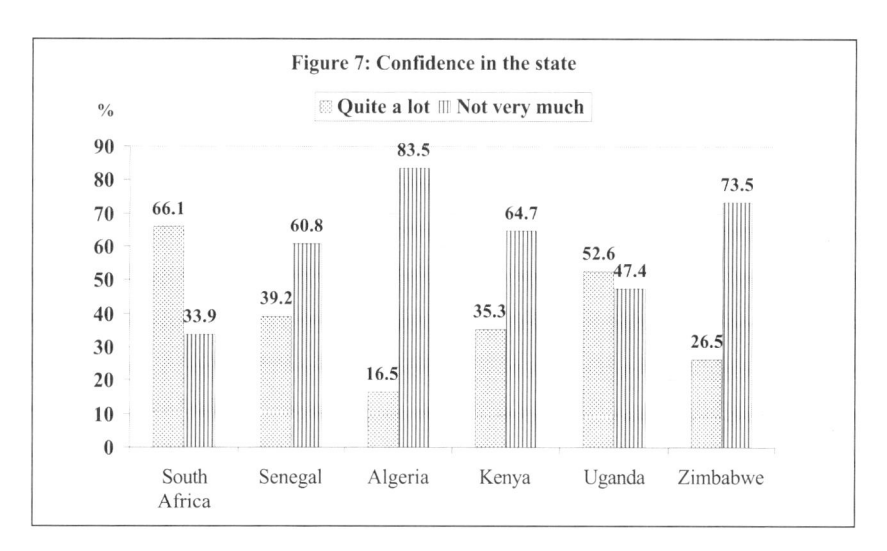

Figure 7: Confidence in the state

Country	Quite a lot	Not very much
South Africa	66.1	33.9
Senegal	39.2	60.8
Algeria	16.5	83.5
Kenya	35.3	64.7
Uganda	52.6	47.4
Zimbabwe	26.5	73.5

When asked to indicate their level of confidence in the state, only the majority of respondent elites in South Africa (66.1 per cent) and Uganda (52.6 per cent) expressed quite a lot of confidence (**Figure 7**).[25] The majori-

---

[25] Unfortunately, these questions of elite confidence were not included in the Nigerian survey, due to cost constraints. In the index 'a great deal' and 'quite a lot' were combined in 'quite a lot' in Figure 7 and 'not very much' and 'none at all' were combined to form the category 'not very much'.

ty of respondents in Senegal (60.8 per cent) and Kenya (64.7 per cent), however, expressed little confidence in the institutions of state, while over 70 per cent of respondents in both Algeria and Zimbabwe expressed low levels of confidence in the institutions of state. Arguably, such low levels of confidence reflect elite perceptions regarding the inability of state institutions to draft and implement state policies successfully. If such perceptions are indeed grounded in reality, then the drafting and implementation of Nepad policies may be fraught with numerous difficulties.

Another element of the implementation of Nepad is the APRM. Approved by the African Union Summit in July 2002, it is regarded as the true test as to whether the Nepad policies can indeed be successfully implemented throughout the African continent. The aim of the APRM is to 'ensure that the policies and practices of participating states conform to the codes and standards contained in the Declaration on democratic, political, economic and corporate governance that was approved by the African Union Summit in July 2002.'[26]

Peer Review can generally be described as the 'systematic examination and assessment of the performance of a state by other states, with the ultimate goal of helping the reviewed state improve its policy making, adopt best practices and comply with established standards and principles.'[27] They are generally performed on a non-adversarial basis and rely on the persuasion and influence of peer states involved in the process.

The situation in Zimbabwe and African states' inability to deal with the crisis has made it increasingly difficult to promote the policy. Furthermore, the lack of interest expressed by many African Heads of State in the design and implementation of the mechanism has raised doubts about the validity of the mechanism, as only one third of invited African presidents deemed it important enough to attend a weekend meeting (8 and 9 March 2003) in Abuja, Nigeria.[28]

To what extent do the African elite display confidence in the peer review mechanism? Respondents were asked to indicate on a scale of 1(strongly agree) to 5 (strongly disagree) the extent to which they agreed with the following statement: The APRM will not lead to improved levels of good governance (**Figure 8**).

---

[26] United Nations Economic Commission for Africa. 'The African Peer Review Mechanism: Process and Procedures.' *African Security Review* (Vol. 11, No. 4, 2002), p. 7.

[27] Fabricio Pagani, 'Peer Review as a tool for co-operation and change', *African Security Review* (Vol.11, No. 2, 2002), p. 16.

[28] Business Day, 11 March 2003.

Figure 8: The APRM will not lead to improved levels of good governance on the continent

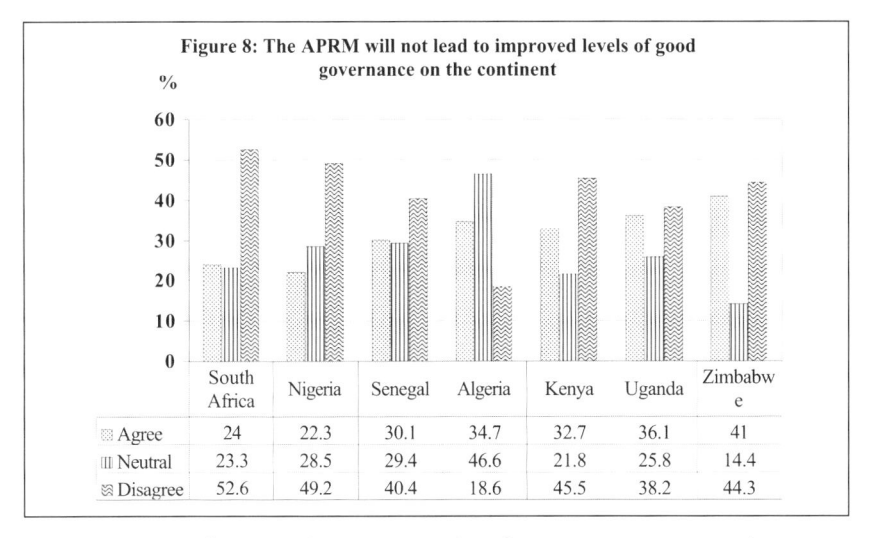

%	South Africa	Nigeria	Senegal	Algeria	Kenya	Uganda	Zimbabwe
Agree	24	22.3	30.1	34.7	32.7	36.1	41
Neutral	23.3	28.5	29.4	46.6	21.8	25.8	14.4
Disagree	52.6	49.2	40.4	18.6	45.5	38.2	44.3

The majority of respondents in South Africa, Nigeria, Senegal, Kenya, Uganda and Zimbabwe disagreed with the statement, thereby expressing support for the APRM as proposed by Nepad. The majority of respondents in Algeria, however, expressed a neutral opinion towards the statement, although more respondents in Algeria agreed with the statement than disagreed with it.

One could therefore conclude that the majority of elite respondents in all countries surveyed do believe that the APRM will indeed prove successful and lead to stronger levels of democratic governance on the continent. Most of the goals as outlined by the Nepad policy document require action on the part of national governments.

Although the presence of a co-ordinated African leadership is crucial to the successful implementation of Nepad, the plan also relies heavily on the notion of productive partnership, a principle which many believe to be in direct contradiction with the idea of African ownership and control. Partnership on various levels as suggested by Nepad is also a concept connected to the issue of globalization.

Firstly, it proposes increased integration and co-operation within the African continent itself. But probably the most contentious issue of partnership is that with the developed world. To what extent do African elites believe that the developed world has a moral responsibility to uplift the people of Africa, and do they believe that the notion of a partnership with the developed world may indeed threaten Africa with a new form of colonization? Respondents were asked to indicate their level of support (1=strongly agree; 5=strongly disagree) for the following statement: The developed world has a moral responsibility to uplift Africa's people (**Figure 9**).[29]

Figure 9: The developed world has a moral responsibility to uplift Africa's people

	South Africa	Nigeria	Senegal	Algeria	Kenya	Uganda	Zimbabwe
Agree	75.8	77.7	77.8	83.8	81.7	76.3	72.7
Neutral	9.2	3.8	8.9	8.5	7.5	8.2	10.1
Disagree	15	18.5	11.9	7.7	10.8	15.4	17.2

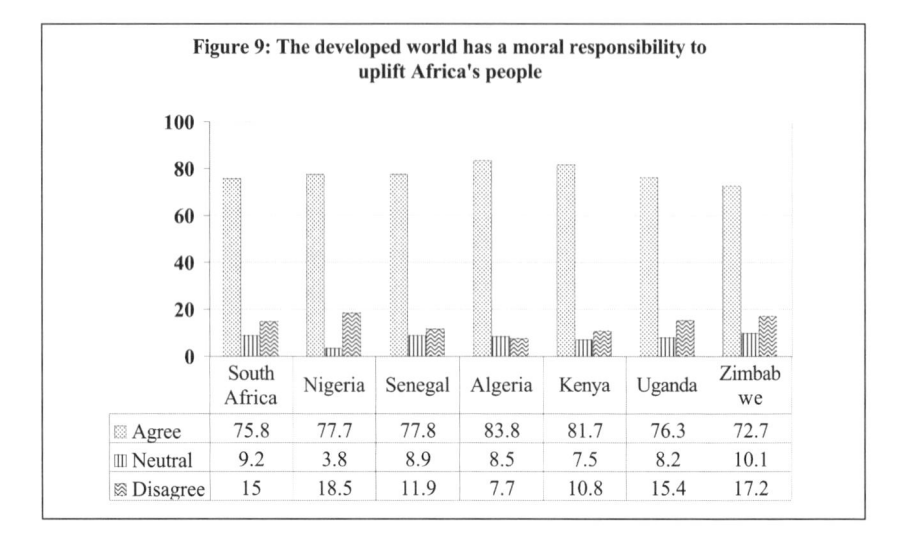

Figure 9 indicates that the majority of respondents in all countries surveyed agreed with the statement that the developed world has a moral responsibility to uplift the people of Africa.

Again with the principle of 'partnership' in mind, respondents were asked to indicate to what extent they agreed with the statement that the following economic blocks could be relied upon to support the economic revival of the African continent.[30] The economic blocks listed included: the European Union, the United States of America; the ASEAN states (South-East Asia); the Gulf states (Arab oil-producing states of the Middle East); the G8 (group of most industrialized countries); Latin America; other African states and the Scandinavian states.

---

[29] Responses were one again collapsed to include: agree, neutral and disagree.

[30] The question was phrased as follows: We would like to know your reaction to each of the economic blocks mentioned in the statement: The following economic blocks can be relied on to support the economic revival of the African continent. Respondents were asked whether they strongly agree, agree, neither agree nor disagree; disagree; strongly disagree.

Table 5: Economic blocks that can be relied upon to support the economic revival of the African continent[31]

	South Africa	Nigeria	Senegal	Algeria	Kenya	Uganda	Zimbabwe
1	Scandinavian States	African States	EU	EU	African States	African States	African States
2	European Union	G8	African States	G8	G8	EU	Scandinavian States
3	African States	US	G8	US	EU	Scandinavian States	G8
4	G8	EU	US	African States	US	G8	EU
5	ASEAN States	ASEAN States	Gulf States	Gulf States	Scandinavian States	US	ASEAN States
6	Gulf States	Gulf States	ASEAN States	ASEAN States	ASEAN States	ASEAN States	US
7	US	Scandinavian States	Scandinavian States	Scandinavian States	Gulf States	Gulf States	Gulf States
8	Latin America	Latin America	Latin America	Latin America	Latin America	Latin America	Latin America

The trends reflected in Table 5 are largely reflective of the historical ties between the African countries and the respective blocs and the idiosyncratic nature that these ties took.

Respondents were also asked to indicate to what extent they approved or disapproved of the following countries as reliable partners for the Nepad process. According to the data presented in **Table 6**, Japan was ranked as the most reliable partner for Nepad in all countries surveyed, except South Africa, where it was ranked second. The very high overall

---

[31] The table was compiled by ranking the items according to the mean values calculated per country.

ranking of Japan is significant and most probably based on Japan's very active role since the mid-90's, both politically and economically, in the African continent.[32]

Table 6: Reliable Partners for Nepad

	South Africa	Nigeria	Senegal	Algeria	Kenya	Uganda	Zimbabwe
1	Sweden	Japan	Japan	Japan	Japan	Japan	Japan
2	Japan	Britain	Canada	Germany	Britain	Denmark	Sweden
3	Denmark	USA	France	Canada	China	Sweden	Denmark
4	Britain	Canada	Germany	France	Canada	China	Netherlands
5	Germany	China	USA	Italy	France	Netherlands	France
6	Canada	France	Taiwan	China	Sweden	Britain	Canada
7	Netherlands	Germany	Netherlands	Switzerland	Denmark	Canada	Switzerland
8	China	Netherlands	Denmark	Sweden	Switzerland	USA	Germany
9	France	Switzerland	Italy	USA	Netherlands	Malaysia	Italy
10	Switzerland	Taiwan	China	Denmark	Germany	France	China
11	Malaysia	Malaysia	Switzerland	Britain	Italy	Germany	Britain
12	Italy	Sweden	Sweden	Netherlands	Taiwan	Italy	USA
13	USA	Italy	Britain	Russia	USA	Switzerland	Malaysia
14	Taiwan	Russia	Malaysia	Malaysia	Malaysia	Taiwan	Taiwan
15	Russia	Denmark	Russia	Taiwan	Russia	Russia	Russia

Assuming that the majority of African elites in the countries surveyed are not threatened by a partnership with the developed world, what conditionalities are these elites willing to accept? When asked to indicate the relative importance they believed the G8 countries should attach, in general, to a number of policy objectives and rank them in order of importance (1=most important; 5=least important), all countries surveyed agreed that the G8 should place the most importance on stable governments and eco-

---

[32] In 1990, Japan became the top aid donor in the world and during the 1990s sponsored two conferences on African development focusing on self-help and partnerships with the developed world. And it may also be that Africa's renewed enthusiasm to seek 'African solutions to African problems' resonates with Japan's own development philosophy. The prominence of Japan as a reliable partner for Nepad may therefore be explained through reference to the dominant position the country has grafted for itself through multi-lateral initiatives (such as the Tokyo International Conference on African Development held in 1993, 1998, and later in 2003) and bilaterally, through large disbursals to key African countries.

nomic growth (Table 7). In a PhD dissertation entitled 'Measuring Political Risks as Risks to Foreign Investment', Brink[33] identifies a number of factors that are taken into account when considering political risk. According to her analysis, political stability was regarded as one of the primary indicators of political risks. The majority of elites in the current study therefore recognize the fact that political stability should play an important role when establishing conditionalities.

Table 7: Conditionalities linked to aid (Ranked on a scale of 1-5)
The percentages listed in the table refer to the percentage of respondents within each country that regarded the specific conditionality as the most important one to be considered.

	South Africa	Nigeria	Senegal	Algeria	Kenya	Uganda	Zimbabwe
1	Stable governments (42.9%)	Stable governments (46.9%)	Stable governments (49.25%)	Stable governments (52.5%)	Rapid economic Growth (45%)	Rapid economic Growth (33%)	Stable governments (42.1%)
2	Rapid economic Growth (23.7%)	Rapid economic Growth (32.3%)	Rapid economic Growth (18.2%)	Rapid economic Growth (18.2%)	Stable governments (30.8%)	Stable governments (32%)	Rapid economic Growth (20%)
3	Maintenance of civil liberties (16.8%)	Attitude towards G8 (6.9%)	Maintenance of civil liberties (15.9%)	Maintenance of civil liberties (13.3%)	Attitude towards G8 (11.7%)	Maintenance of civil liberties (13.4%)	Maintenance of civil liberties (18.6%)
4	Support of free enterprise (6%)	Support of free enterprise (5.4%)	Free enterprise (6.1%)	Avoid unprovoked aggression (5.8%)	Maintenance of civil liberties (8.3%)	Avoid unprovoked aggression (9.3%)	Support of free enterprise (9.3%)
5	Avoid unprovoked aggression (5.7%)	Maintenance of civil liberties (4.6%)	Avoid unprovoked aggression (3.8%)	Attitude towards G8 (5%)	Support of free enterprise (7.5%)	Attitude towards G8 (7.2%)	Avoid unprovoked aggression (7.1%)
6	Attitude towards G8 (3.5%)	Avoid unprovoked aggression (3.8%)	Attitude towards G8 (3%)	Support of free enterprise (4.2%)	Avoid unprovoked aggression (0.8%)	Support of free enterprise (5.2%)	Attitude towards G8 (1.4%)

---

[33] C. Brink, *Measuring Political Risk as Risks to Foreign Investment : A computer-assisted model for analyzing and managing political risk*, PhD dissertation (Cape Town: University of Stellenbosch, 2002), p. 191.

Finally, although the Nepad document acknowledges the fact that efforts to realize the renewal of the African continent would probably be greatly enhanced through co-ordinated collaboration with the developed world, such efforts would, however, prove futile if African states themselves were unable to secure structures through which to implement the Nepad processes. During the G8 Summit in Evian in June 2003, substantial funds were committed by the developed countries to improve peace and security, health and agriculture on the African continent. Such commitments from the developed world do, however, place a burden on the African continent to ensure the implementation of the development plans as outlined in Nepad. President Mbeki expressed such a view following the Summit, when he commented on the commitments made by the G8 by saying that 'if we had taken a bigger bite we would not have been able to process it and it would create disappointment.' He referred to the potential of such commitments placing a 'burden' on Africa to produce results and called on African leaders to improve the capacity of their implementation structures, so as to ensure the success of Nepad.[34]

The fact that the majority of elite respondents in the various countries surveyed have regarded the European Union, the G8 and other African states as economic blocs that can be relied upon to support the economic revival of the African continent bodes well for the partnership upon which Nepad is largely based. Of particular importance, however, is the fact the African elites surveyed have also displayed a great deal of confidence in the reliability of other African states to improve the economic prospects in Africa – a perception which ultimately reinforces the concept of African ownership and control through the implementation process.

Conclusion

Some of the most interesting and relevant findings discussed in the report are highlighted below:
- The success of Nepad and the African Union depends to a large degree on the extent to which African ownership and control of the two initiatives can be created and maintained. The data presented in the study shows, however, that those countries directly involved in the drafting and implementation of the Nepad initiative display significantly higher levels of confidence in Nepad than those countries

---

[34] *Cape Times*, 4 June 2003.

not directly involved. Both Uganda and Zimbabwe displayed relatively lower levels of confidence in the strategy and may, as such, view the policies associated with Nepad with a certain degree of distrust and caution.
- In the majority of instances, civil society support for the initiative has also been less than impressive when compared to the support expressed by their civil servant and politician counterparts.
- The success of both Nepad and the African Union rests on the extent to which a common African identity can be called upon to uplift the continent, and finds realization in the Pan African concepts of African Unification and integration. Although respondents included in the survey supported the general principles of African unification and integration, only the majority of elite respondents in Senegal, Algeria and Uganda believed that the interests of the continent should receive priority over the national interests of the country.
- The extent to which African leaders can reach consensus on the goals of the African Union and Nepad and prioritize these goals accordingly will undoubtedly have an impact on the successful implementation of Nepad. As the current study has shown, issues of political stability and corruption have repeatedly been regarded as paramount by the African elite included in the survey and should thus contribute to the coherence of goal prioritization.
- The issue of HIV/AIDS was also regarded as an important obstacle to African development by the elites included in the survey. Unfortunately, AIDS has received scant attention within the Nepad document, to the disappointment of numerous civil society organizations.
- Unfortunately, only a minority of elite respondents included in the survey regarded the improved position of women and gender equality as important goals for the African Union and Nepad. The Nepad document does recognize gender inequality as a development challenge, but criticisms suggest that the issue does not receive the attention that it deserves.
- The eventual success of Nepad and the African Union will, however, ultimately depend on whether, once all the structures are in place, they are eventually efficiently implemented. In one of the most striking findings of the current study, it was reported that elite respondents in all countries surveyed except Zimbabwe believed that their countries have the capacity to implement the Nepad policies.

But when asked how much confidence they have in the institutions of state, only the majority of elites in South Africa and Uganda displayed quite a lot of confidence. This disturbing trend forces one to ask whether the institutions responsible for drafting, implementing, propagating and funding the Nepad policies do, in fact, possess the capacity to implement the policies.

The fact remains, however, that Nepad and the African Union represent bold initiatives designed 'for Africans by Africans' that have the potential to uplift and revive the African continent. The time has come, however, to move beyond mere rhetoric and to ensure that the principles and goals enshrined within the two bodies are successfully brought to fruition. In the words of South African president Thabo Mkebi: 'the ball is now in Africa's court.'

Appendix: Methodology
With the operational definition, where the elite is defined as comprising those people who fill top positions in the 'largest and most resource-rich political, governmental, economic, professional, communications and cultural institutions in society' as starting point, a positional sample was employed to select the respondents in the different countries for the particular survey.[35]

Such a procedure implies that individuals holding the most authoritative positions in influential institutions are approached to participate as respondents in the survey. The sectors from which respondents were selected include: the private sector, Non Governmental Organizations (NGOs), Community-based organizations (CBOs), civic organizations, public sector, professional, academic or analyst sector, trade union sector, political sector, media and church sectors. Respondents were interviewed using a structured questionnaire on key issues relating to the African Union and Nepad.

---

[35] See G. Lowell Field et al, 'A new elite framework for political sociology', *Revue Européene de Sciences Sociales* (Vol. 28, No. 1, 1990), p. 153. Other authors that use closely related operationalizations of national elites include: R. Putman, *The Comparative Study of Elites* (Englewood Cliffs, N.J: Prentice Hall, 1976) and P. McDonough, *Power and Ideology in Brazil* (Princeton: Princeton University Press, 1981).

Table 8: Composition of the Sample

Sector	South Africa		Nigeria		Senegal		Kenya		Algeria		Uganda		Zimbabwe	
	No	%	No	%	No	%	No	%	No	%	No	%	No	%
Private Sector	91	16.1	11	8.5	33	24.3	18	15.0	17	14.3	5	5.2	32	22.9
NGO, CBO	84	14.8	4	3.1	22	16.2	22	18.3	9	7.6	10	10.3	17	12.1
Public Sector	98	17.3	34	26.2	22	16.2	15	12.5	39	32.8	18	18.6	16	11.4
Prof. Anal./acad.	77	13.6	10	7.7	21	15.4	22	18.3	19	16.0	29	29.9	31	22.1
Trade Union	50	8.8	5	3.8	1	0.7	5	4.2	2	1.7			10	7.1
Politician	64	11.3	42	32.3	12	8.8	10	8.3			22	22.7	12	8.6
Media	49	8.7	15	11.5	12	8.8	12	10.0	27	22.7	4	4.1	14	10.0
Church	42	7.4	8	6.2	1	0.7	10	8.3			2	2.1	4	2.9
Other	10	1.8	1	0.8	5	3.7	6	5.0	4	3.4	6	6.2	4.	2.9
Not Class.	1	0.2			7	5.1			2	1.7	1	1.0		
Total	566	100	130	100	136	100	120	100	120	100	97	100	140	100

It should be pointed out, however, that it is virtually impossible to determine the boundaries of some sectors. The selection of the number of persons depended on certain assumptions about the configuration of power and influence on the national level as well as within sectors themselves, the grand total as well as the number of persons selected per sector may be regarded as arbitrary. Furthermore, cost factors also played an important part in the size of the sample. Carefully chosen survey institutions were contracted to carry out the survey in the different countries.

The occasional paper by Hennie Kotzé & Carly Steyn, African Elite Perspectives: AU and Nepad *(Johannesburg: Konrad Adenauer-Stiftung, 2003) forms the basis of this paper.*

Section 4

The Impact of Global Developments on Africa

A Safer World After Saddam?
Richard Cobbold

Saddam Hussein was captured by US forces on 14 December 2003. Is the world a safer place since then? To answer that we need to parse the question.

Safer
To calculate the mean risk of preventable death to an individual is not good enough. Safety from preventable death is as much a subjective judgement as a quantitative assessment. The risks of a fatal incident have to be set against its impact. Thus the impact of daily road deaths in South Africa or Britain is minimal; the impact of the same number of people dying in one railway accident is greater and lasts longer; deaths from an air crash may be greater again; a major terrorist attack has the greatest impact. The aftershocks of the atrocities of 11 September 2001, when some 3000 people died, will be with us for years, indeed decades, to come. During the 1991 flooding of Bangladesh over 139,000 died. This was at least partially a manmade disaster, but the statistics have hardly been remembered. A war in the Democratic Republic of the Congo can rumble on for years, with millions of casualties, without causing a tremor in first world stock exchanges. Impact changes with time, circumstances, geography and interest to the media. In the first Gulf War, the 500,000 US soldiers deployed suffered fewer casualties than the same number would have been expected to suffer had they remained in their home towns in continental USA. 19,000 British troops were killed on the first day of the Battle of the Somme, yet the First World War staggered on; the first US soldiers killed during the early fighting in Operation Iraqi Freedom were mourned in heroic headlines, yet today many more are killed, hardly meriting a foot-note. The deaths of

---

Rear Admiral **Richard Cobbold** is Director of the Royal United Services Institute for Defence and Security Studies.

Iraqi civilians have been uncounted except by their families, and therefore never aggregated, yet in their killings today may be sown the dangers for tomorrow, just as much as the sacrifices of Coalition forces may have helped to build a safer future both for Iraq and the countries of the Coalition.

We take comfort that the spread of democracy and the increased pace of globalization should lead to more value being placed on individuals and that for each individual the world will become safer. This is not necessarily so, for the waves of change are not uniform. There will be discontinuities. 9/11 was not just a statistical spike: because of actions on that day, and because of the reactions to them and even the reactions to the reactions, the world has changed irreversibly.

World

Amongst experts on African security, I stand out as ill-informed. Yet in the wider world, I probably score above average. Africa is an esoteric continent, known to insiders and the cognoscenti, yet still dark and different to outsiders. To many it can be contained, treated as a special case away from the mainstream of world affairs. Subjectively, safety looks different in Britain from Europe as a whole, just as it looks different in South Africa from Africa as a whole. Both Africa and Europe have different perspectives from each other. Yet increasingly, if I may corrupt John Donne, 'no continent is an island entire of itself', and thus subjective values of safety in Africa should be seen in a global perspective. Equally, the particular values and foibles of Africa should be acknowledged.

After

The 2003 war in Iraq, which resulted in regime change and Saddam's capture, followed the conflict in Afghanistan against the Taliban and Al-Qa'ida; whether the former happened because of the latter is a matter for debate. Since the end of the war-fighting in Iraq against Saddam's forces, there has been an active insurgency against the Coalition forces; taking part in it have been fighters who might belong, albeit loosely, to Al-Qa'ida. In slightly different circumstances they might be described as terrorists, thereby closing the loop, for those who want to close it, between the war against Saddam and counter-terrorism post-9/11. We should beware the ancient fallacy of 'post hoc, ergo propter hoc'.

Saddam

Saddam is now in the custody of Iraqi authorities. Some Iraqis are not persuaded that he has gone for good, they fear still the banging on the door. Soon he will have his day, or maybe his year or two, in court. A prolonged legal defence could see Saddam take on the mantle of the under-dog and the 'devil the Iraqis knew'; he could yet become a fashion icon on a million T-shirts. His ousting is certainly not the sole determinant of whether we are a safer place.

Events in Iraq

Events in Iraq are going through a bad patch, and some of the Coalition wounds are self-inflicted. The insurgents show agility in changing tactics and targets that upsets both the Coalition and public opinion back home. There is a link with Al-Qa'ida and they may have good reason to be satisfied. On 11 March 2004, a connected group bombed Madrid, changed the Spanish Government, caused the Spanish military contingent to be removed from Iraq and panicked the European Union into bringing forward deliberations over their Constitution. As a result, the United Kingdom is sending out more troops to Iraq, and will probably keep them there until 2006, or longer. This will overstretch the British Army and the Royal Marines, and there will be fewer of them around for peacekeeping and peace-support operations elsewhere. Other countries also may get peacekeeping fatigue. So Africa may be less safe.

If the US and UK suffer a disastrous reversal in Iraq during the next year or two – and it is certainly not inevitable – then one outcome could be that the world is less safe. But that would imply that that the US and UK stop trying to manage outcomes.

However, if we look at Iraq from the point of view of the insurgents or terrorists, it does not look so good either. They may be causing disruption to the Coalition, but their frequent changes of tactics and targets could be desperation. Certainly Moqtada al-Sadr is defiant and aggressive, but is he living his dream? As the summer heat rises over Basra, and the need for electrical power to run all the new air conditioning plants becomes an imperative, the outcome may reduce to a question of whether the Coalition can advance the political agenda and reconstruction faster than the opposition can damage military and political cohesion. As long as we do not get too disappointed by a failure to get quick results, and do not become too concerned about not being liked, then the Coalition can leave behind a viable government when it leaves Iraq.

Iraq and Global Terrorism

Much of the evidence now points to there being a link between Iraq and Al-Qa'ida, but whether it is strong or enduring is more doubtful. Al-Qa'ida is an opportunistic franchise, so we can assume that some Al-Qa'ida elements are stirring up trouble in Iraq. There too, 'the enemy of my enemy is my friend'. Any success they may get in Iraq could help Al-Qa'ida towards some intermediate objectives, such as undermining the House of Saud, and their longer-term aim of establishing a Militant Islamic Caliphate stretching in an irregular ellipse from Morocco to Indonesia.

Global terrorism, exemplified by Al-Qa'ida, is different because it apparently cannot be negotiated with, cannot be deterred, and has no self-imposed limitations. That may not be so. A suicide bomber may not be deterred, but there are twenty or so in each support team, that may want to enjoy the good life a little longer.

Global terrorism is exportable to Africa, and has been; but maybe it is geographically limited, containable, and equally unsustainable. But good governance in affected countries is needed to stop terrorism becoming endemic. Global terrorists are not defined by 'weapons of mass destruction', meaning anything that is a nuclear, radiological, biological or chemical agent, but which could cause less carnage than a large high explosive warhead. In 2002, ricin, a toxin derived from castor oil pods and therefore a bio-chemical weapon, was found in West London. Famous for being used by a Bulgarian assassin in 1978 when stabbing the dissident Georgi Markov with an umbrella on Waterloo Bridge, ricin has all the lethality of a handgun. Even if developed for aerosol delivery, it would have no more effect than a sub machine-gun. Many people in London were frightened and fascinated until, after a few days, the alarm wore off.

The 9/11 terrorists hijacked fully fuelled passenger aircraft using stanley knives. The knives, the aircraft and the hijackers came together to form a system for a 'weapon of mass effect', and this is the preferred weapon of the global terrorist. Any terrorist attack seeks to cause terror, but not all the terror that is caused follows inevitably from the activity. The terror in the US after 9/11 was undoubtedly heightened by the short if deadly series of anthrax attacks that followed close behind. There is a special terror factor attached to some biological weapons, out of proportion to the likely danger, especially when combined with other means of attack.

During the same period, there were a number of 'white powder' incidents in Britain that caused high if localized alarm. They were all false, but the terror was infectious enough to cross the Atlantic. An aircraft accident in New York in November 2001, when another passenger aircraft took off from Kennedy Airport, and crashed into the suburb of Queens, initially caused acute alarm. All on board were killed, but the country breathed a palpable sigh of relief when it was shown to be an accident, rather than terrorist action. The tragedy stayed the same, but the terror had gone. When the emergency services can demonstrate competence in the face of sustained terrorist attacks – for example in the summer of 1974 when the PIRA moved their terror campaign to London – the population can become resilient and terror can lose its virulence. Then terrorism is seen in perspective, and the shock of terror is mitigated.

We must also deal with those who harbour and sustain terrorists; those who provide the water in which Mao's famous fish can swim. They may be as guilty as the terrorists, or they may be dupes. They threaten the fabric of society. To defeat terrorism comprehensively at an acceptable price to our society, we have to get the right balance between effective counter-terrorism and civil rights. This is not just bleeding hearts morality; if the balance is right, then the flow of accurate intelligence will increase, prevention and prosecution should follow, and the fishes' water will dry up. If the balance is wrong, then the fish will flourish and public confidence in authority will crumble.

Terrorism in Perspective

We have to keep terrorism in perspective. 9/11 changed the world and since then the world has embarked on a stormy and bloody passage. The 3000 killed on 9/11 was a terrible figure, but the effect was more extensive than that, and the damage to the national structure of the US could have been far worse even than it was. But 3000 killed was a bad but not catastrophic day for the allies in the First World War. And it was the average daily killing each day for five years during the Holocaust. And an average of 8000 people were killed each day during the Rwanda genocide for 100 days. 3000 people are killed each day on the world's roads: 1.2 million people are killed each year. These figures are expected to increase by 60 per cent by 2020, to become the third biggest cause of preventable deaths. African roads are amongst the most dangerous, averaging 28.3 deaths per 100,000 of the population. While road deaths are highest in developing countries, traffic accidents are the leading cause of death for Americans under the age of thirty-five.[1]

Road traffic deaths in 2002 ranked eleventh in the list of the world's top killers – at 2.1 per cent of preventable deaths. Heart disease is first at 12.6 per cent; HIV/AIDS is fourth at 4.9 per cent. I hardly need to rehearse here how terrible the current WHO statistics are for HIV in Sub-Saharan Africa. Nearly two-thirds of the people who die from AIDS in the world come from Sub-Saharan Africa: some 30 million cases in 2002, with a further 20 million expected by 2010. It will be scant comfort that by then, India, China, Russia, Eastern Europe and the Central Asian Republics will have a higher rate of increase; India for example, by then, may have 20-25 million cases.[2] Work to suppress the HIV virus lags massively behind the need. The South African Government's target of getting anti-retroviral drugs to 53000 sufferers (out of a total of some 5 million) by the end of March 2004, was missed; the Treatment Action Campaign say that only 2700 people received the drugs.[3]

South Africa is still a dangerous place to live in, with 115 murders per 100,000 people/year. Next is Brazil, followed by Russia, each with about twenty-two per 100,000. Other African countries listed include Botswana at twelve, Zambia at eleven, Angola at nine, and Ghana at two. The United States by comparison has six. The less bad news for South Africa is that the annual total of murders has topped out, and with a rising population, the per capita figures are falling.[4]

Against these figures, terrorist statistics seem less bad. Since 1996, the average annual global number of terrorist attacks has been 312: with the most in 2000 (426) and the least in 2002 (199), with no significant trend. There is again no significant trend in casualty figures, with a high peak in 2001 (3547 killed of which 90 per cent occurred in the 9/11 attacks). Of those injured, the peak (5952) occurred in 1998 mainly from the attacks on

---

[1] WHO (2002) figures quoted in
http://newsvote.bbc.co.uk/mpapps/pagetools/print/news.bbc.co.uk/1/hi/health/360343.
[2] WHO, UN, US Intelligence figures quoted in
http://news.bbc.co.uk/1/shared/spl/hi/africa/03/aids_debate/html/key_countries.stm. 05 Apr 04.
[3] http://newsvote.bbc.co.uk/mpapps/pagetools/print/news/.bbc.co.uk/1/hi/world/africa/3, 05 Apr 04.
[4] Interpol figures quoted in *The Economist*, 11 October 2003, p. 66.

US Embassies in East Africa.[5]

So in terms of actual preventable deaths and based on current and recent figures, the world is getting rather more dangerous, but not as a result of what is happening in Iraq, nor from terrorism.

Looking Ahead

Potentially, the future is bleak, if one looks at worst case scenarios including the use of weapons of mass destruction in general and nuclear weapons in particular. But the world has eye-balled nuclear threats for almost sixty years and has become accustomed to nuclear stress. I am edgily sanguine, and the acquisition of nuclear weapons by India and Pakistan seems to have produced a stressed form of stability. There are other countries coming up behind – Iran and North Korea are two – but the record since 1945 is positive, and the engagement of North Korea in dialogue is at least hopeful.

In Africa the graver danger remains 'weapons of aggregated individual destruction': small arms, machetes and other farm instruments. One may take issue with the prophet Isaiah who urged us to beat our swords into plowshares and our spears into pruning hooks... neither should we learn war any more.[6] Farm implements have killed far more people than nuclear weapons during the last sixty years, and anyway one does not want to confront a fast moving plowshare or a well-swung pruning hook. Equally the appropriate use of military forces in skilled and wise hands can keep, support and make peace, deliver humanitarian relief, prevent and resolve conflict and enable reconstruction afterwards. It can prevent and resolve conflict. The armed forces must study their full profession if they are to be a force for good. If a secure environment is a pre-requisite for development, then the application of military capability is a potent enabler.

The causes of violence are myriad, and to develop the words of Tony Blair when Shadow Home Secretary, we should be tough on violence and tough on the causes of violence. Achieving this is not a trivial undertaking, but it calls prosaically for balance, pragmatism and investment. Preventing violence is usually more cost-effective than reacting to it. But it may be hard to demonstrate that convincingly.

Like most of the world, I look in on Africa as an outsider, from the

---

[5] US State Department figures.
[6] Isaiah Ch 2 v 4.

periphery. There is fog over Africa, reminiscent of the famous British newspaper headline: 'Fog in Channel, Continent Isolated.' There are few 'good-news' stories coming out of Africa; the international media are lethargic, so the oxygen of publicity that could help to burn up troublemakers is seldom available. Africa is given insufficient attention from the outside, and inside the authorities may be over-committed, and beset by many problems. Much is said about forgiveness and reconciliation, but it is not always available. Resilience is also much needed. When the world looks at Africa, perceptions are reality. The dark continent is becoming translucent, but not yet transparent. But the fires of war in Africa may just be dampening down as light percolates through the smoke.

The need for good, though not necessarily strong, governance is clear. Weak or bad governments are linked to corruption, criminality, the trafficking of every conceivable commodity including people, organized crime, terrorism and ethnic conflict. Weak government can make life unsafe for the people. As most governments agree in public, 'the security of the people is its first duty'. But the principle tends to decompose into a platitude, often as a preamble to cost-cutting. But from security (with the levers of power under accountable civil control) all else follows.

Globalization of information is a force for good, although in many parts of Africa, the spread of basic IT is constrained by poverty. But the continuing development of IT offers reassurance backed by experience. The power of a computer chip is still doubling every 18-21 months, while the price of a unit of computing power drops by 50 per cent.[7] This trend has been maintained since 1960 and is expected to continue for another twenty years. Furthermore, early mass provisions of IT will result in the greatest advances. Finally poverty can be eased over time. So IT, together with the globalization of travel, trade, television, goods and media, can all act to produce a levelling in Africa. But they will not necessarily do so. Unfair internal subsidies in the European Union and the United States, for example, can keep Africa poor.

The military can be a force for good in many ways, and intelligence remains the key to every defence and security function. In trying to collect, analyze and use intelligence, African countries must confront real issues about where intelligence comes from, how it is used, and how to share it with other countries. The same applies for countries from outside Africa, operating inside, whether the intelligence is at a high security level or

---

[7] Moore's Law. For explanation see http://webopedia.com/TERM/M/Moores_Law

drawn from open sources. The crucial criterion is whether or not the armed forces can make the environment safer. African countries have to make their forces effective for what they need to do, often operating in the complex areas below war-fighting and above criminality, against opposition that will use global systems to make themselves more challenging, adaptable and mobile. Governments need forces that can do all necessary tasks, can co-operate across borders, and carry the consent of the people.

There is a functional spectrum from conflict prevention and defence diplomacy through to peace enforcement and war-fighting; these functions have fuzzy edges, and the nature of the tasks at any one moment can swoop up and down the ladder of escalation. When outside forces have operated in Africa, they have not always had the right capabilities and it may not be getting better. Urban counter-insurgency differs from desert operations, and again from the jungle. It will get more complex and will be exacerbated as more actors join in: international agencies, contractors, more allies, police, private military companies, and NGOs – all with a say and each with a different angle.

There could be four trends:

- the effectiveness of an international force may be in inverse proportion to the number of countries taking part.
- the legitimacy will be in proportion to the number of countries taking part.
- the number of actors will increase as the activity reduces in intensity from war-fighting.
- command and control will get more difficult and more important.[8]

Conclusions

Countries need to invest in safety, and to afford the measures that will increase safety. Any security activity takes place in a political framework, but the political will to afford security cannot be assumed. The need to educate to survive will become stronger.

Terrorism is a threat to us all, but not the only threat, nor necessarily the biggest. Killing does not require high technology systems.

---

[8] This also includes C4ISR: command, control, communications, computers, intelligence, surveillance and reconnaissance.

Richard Cobbold

Globalization offers a tool-kit for security. There are not good nor bad tools, just good and bad users. Tools should be kept away from bad users. The world can be safer after Saddam, but not necessarily because he has gone. It depends on whether we want a safer world enough, and whether we are smart.

The Role of External Actors in Combating Corruption

Jeffrey Herbst

Given the continuing focus on governance, it was inevitable that the high level of corruption in many African countries would eventually become central to the agenda of donors. However, while the World Bank and various Western governments have highlighted corruption as an issue in Africa, donors have developed very different approaches. Unfortunately, as corruption is such a politically sensitive topic, most donors have announced policies without explicating their underlying political assumptions. In this brief paper, I assess two of the contrasting approaches and attempt to explore the implications of current trends for the future of anti-corruption efforts in Africa.

The Millennium Challenge Account and the World Bank

There are probably almost as many approaches to corruption as there are donors. One of special interest is the Millennium Challenge Account (MCA), the new American initiative announced in March 2002 by President George Bush. As proposed, the MCA would increase American spending on foreign aid by US$5 billion over three years. The new initiative was meant not only to be a significant new financial contribution but also to have a different methodology to past aid efforts. In particular, participants are to be selected based 'on a transparent evaluation of a country's performance on sixteen economic and political indicators, divided into three clusters corresponding to the three policy areas of governance, economic policy, and investment in people'.[1] To qualify, a country must score above the median on half of the indicators. However, corruption is treated differently: A country that scores at or below the median on control of corruption is automatically disqualified, irrespective of how it does on the other fifteen scores. The MCA essentially makes above-the-median perfor-

---

Jeffrey Herbst is Professor of Politics and International Affairs at Princeton University.

mance on control of corruption the necessary condition for increased assistance.

Not surprisingly, the corruption 'pass/fail' test may have a significant impact on the distribution of aid. Many of Africa's large countries have especially poor corruption records. For instance, a majority of the twenty most populous countries on the continent (displayed in the following chart) do significantly worse than the African average when measured on controlling corruption. While many of these large countries would have not qualified for MCA funding because of their miserable performance on the other indicators, it is likely, if the MCA were to begin as scheduled, that some countries would be disqualified solely because of their corruption score.[2]

Control of Corruption, Comparison across selected countries

Country	Percentile Rank (0-100)	Standard Deviation	Regional Average
Angola	7.2	0.17	32.4
Burkina Faso	57.7	0.27	32.4
Cameroon	8.8	0.20	32.4
Congo, Demo Rep.	1.5	0.19	32.4
Cote D'Ivoire	22.7	0.19	32.4
Ethiopia	44.8	0.25	32.4
Ghana	42.8	0.16	32.4
Kenya	11.3	0.17	32.4
Madagascar	61.9	0.27	32.4
Malawi	19.6	0.18	32.4
Mali	46.4	0.24	32.4
Mozambique	14.9	0.21	32.4
Niger	8.2	0.27	32.4
Nigeria	3.1	0.16	32.4
South Africa	67.5	0.15	32.4
Sudan	9.3	0.19	32.4
Tanzania	15.5	0.16	32.4
Uganda	19.1	0.16	32.4
Zambia	17.0	0.16	32.4
Zimbabwe	6.2	0.16	32.4

Calculated from the World Bank's Governance Research Indicator Country Snapshot found at http://info.worldbank.org/governance/kkz2002/mc_chart.asp.

---

[1] For a review, see Congressional Research Service, *The Millennium Challenge Account: Congressional Consideration of a New Foreign Aid Initiative* (Washington, DC: CRS, 2003), p. 1.

[2] For some initial estimates, see Steve Radelet, 'Qualifying for the Millennium Challenge Account' (draft), (Center for Global Development, December 2002), p18 found at: http://www.cgdev.org/docs/Choosing_MCA_Countries.pdf.

The Bank adds the following proviso: 'The governance indicators presented here reflect the statistical compilation of responses on the quality of governance given by a large number of enterprise, citizen and expert survey respondents in industrial and developing countries, as reported by a number of survey institutes, think-tanks, non-governmental organizations, and international organizations. The aggregate indicators in no way reflect the official position of the World Bank, its Executive Directors, or the countries they represent'. The Bank also notes that 'countries' relative positions on these indicators are subject to margins of error that are clearly indicated. Consequently, precise country rankings should not be inferred from this data'.

Indeed, the 'hard hurdle' approach on corruption is a particularly blunt weapon. The architects of the World Bank's corruption indicators suggest that the data on corruption control is so bad that there is only a 90 per cent certainty that many countries near the median are actually between the 40th and 60th percentile.[3] This data, of course, does not actually measure corruption but *perceptions* about corruption, a more difficult and problematic concept. It is possible that the MCA's approach to corruption will evolve, especially as the initiative has only recently begun. However, it is interesting to spotlight the MCA because it has taken such a radical and direct approach in linking control of corruption to further assistance. One of the problems in taking a tough line on corruption and highlighting it as perhaps the critical issue in governance is that the data is so poor and the concept so underdeveloped that it is not clear what 'control of corruption' means. It also may not be possible to develop objective measures of corruption. As a result, the US and other donors who want to focus on this issue may find their aims frustrated by operationalization failures.

A final interesting question is how credible the MCA incentives are to improve corruption, given the uncertainty of the statistical measure and that countries are competing against others for the above-the-median ranking. Some countries that are, in fact, improving their corruption performance may still find themselves moving down the tables, instead of up, because others are doing relatively more. As important, some countries will, perhaps inevitably, find themselves moving down the tables, no matter what they are actually doing, simply because of the imprecision of the data. Of course, some countries may improve in the standings

---

[3] Ibid.

simply because other countries are doing worse or because the underlying statistical imprecision worked in their favour. There are ways of dealing with this problem, especially by looking at how robust performance is measured over time, but the admirable goal of being transparent inevitably runs into difficulties when trying to decide precisely what to measure.

The World Bank has developed a different approach. There is no doubt that the Bank has led a massive intellectual effort aimed at diagnosing, understanding, and fighting corruption in recent years. The turning point may have been Bank President James Wolfensohn's 1997 address to the joint Bank/Fund meetings when he urged the organizations to fight what he called the 'cancer of corruption'.[4] However, the Bank has not adopted the 'pass/fail' approach of the MCA, indicating that it is more willing to accept corruption when lending. This is not to imply that the Bank approves of corruption (far from it) but that it is has not explicitly elevated fighting corruption to a necessary condition for receipt of funding.

For instance, the Bank has begun lending a large amount of money to the Democratic Republic of Congo, even though the Kabila government is in many ways a regime devoted to sharing the spoils. Indeed, it appears that Congo will soon again be one of the major Bank customers in Africa, despite a track record and future prospects that are highly problematic. Many will not believe, for example, that the recent credit of US$410 million and grant of US$44 million for rehabilitation and reconstruction given to the government in Kinshasa will be used in a particularly impressive manner. Many would also disagree with the World Bank's country director for Congo when he argued that, 'the Government has demonstrated its commitment to implementing economic reforms and tackling governance issues'.[5] Indeed, Congo scores miserably on the Bank's own corruption index (see chart).

While the Bank is too politic to explain its lending to the Kabila government, it is clear that it has not adopted the 'hard hurdle' approach to corruption that is so central to the MCA. President Bush apparently per-

---

[4] http://www1.worldbank.org/publicsector/anticorrupt/efforts.htm
[5] See the World Bank announcement 'Democratic Republic of Congo: World Bank Supports the Country's Emergency Rehabilitation Program', 6 August 2002, at: http://web.worldbank.org/WBSITE/EXTERNAL/NEWS/0,,contentMDK:20060699~menuPK:34466~pagePK:64003015~piPK:64003012~theSitePK:4607,00.html.

sonally inserted the MCA's language on corruption.[6] He had the luxury of doing so, in part, because the MCA was from the start supposed to be a new way of doing business. The Bank, on the other hand, has always had to deal with the dilemma of both spending money to promote development while providing certification of good economic behaviour. As a multilateral organization with a majority of members from the developing world, and a staff that may not always have incentives not to give money, the Bank would necessarily find the 'hard hurdle' approach to corruption difficult. To be fair, there has also been technical criticism of the MCA's 'hard hurdle' approach, some of it from the Bank itself, given the imprecision of most of the data on corruption.

Hard Hurdles and Soft

The MCA approach has the clear advantage of being an unambiguous signal about corruption. In this regard, it probably is most useful in preventing the US itself from giving money to regimes that are corrupt (however imperfectly measured), despite other pressing strategic and political interests. This is part of the MCA philosophy of transparency. Given the overall dependence on quantitative indicators, it should be easy to determine if the US is, in fact, giving money to regimes who have not achieved the necessary scores.

The corruption indicators will therefore matter immensely to those countries that are at or close to the median. Indeed, given the significant amount of money that the MCA promises and what appears to be the limited number of countries that can qualify, the incentive for at least some countries to improve on corruption perceptions will be very significant. These countries will, given that they have to perform above the median on many scores to qualify for MCA aid, are already doing well, on average, and are almost certainly likely to have relatively high per capita incomes by African standards. They would especially benefit from being certified by MCA because they could use this status to further differentiate themselves from other, poorer African countries while seeking development aid from donors and when trying to recruit foreign investors. Ghana would certainly be one example of a country that could benefit from being able to jump

---

[6] See, for instance, the testimony of Under Secretary of the Treasury John Taylor before the Senate Foreign Relations Committee on 4 March 2003, at: http://www.treasury.gov/press/releases/js80.htm

the MCA's hard corruption hurdle.

What the MCA does not do, and what the Bank must therefore be forced to confront, is responding to corruption in Africa's poor performers. By design, significantly more than 50 per cent of the countries in Africa will not qualify for the MCA because they will not perform well enough on enough indicators across several different areas as well as being in the top 50 per cent on control of corruption. It is hard for donors to threaten to walk away from these countries because the humanitarian needs are so great and because corruption is so embedded in the political systems of poor performers that it is unlikely that significant improvement is gong to happen in the short term. The Kabila government may score badly on all of the governance and corruption indicators, but it is also probably the best chance that the Democratic Republic of Congo has had in some time to make progress. Indeed, few would disagree with the World Bank's country director when he argues that a 'peace dividend' is needed for countries such as Congo that are emerging from conflict.[7]

What the MCA and the World Bank approaches imply is a division of labour when it comes to combating corruption. The US, perhaps joined by an increasing number of other donors annoyed by the continual waste of their money, may increasingly seek to funnel development funds to a relatively small group of countries that can clearly make use of these monies, without the obnoxious panoply of conditionalities that increasingly annoy both donors and recipients. The World Bank, and a few other donors, would then be left with a relatively large number of countries (including a substantial number of Africa's big countries) that are not performing well on most indicators but could conceivably benefit from development assistance, while wasting substantial portions of the money they receive. This division of labour might actually retard external efforts to curb corruption in the more poorly performing countries because they might not fear that many donors would be willing to cut funding in the face of poor performance on corruption.

Such a division of labour, and the resulting incentives facing different recipient governments, is perhaps not surprising given that Africa is becoming more heterogeneous. With great difficulty, there are some countries that are now making significant, albeit halting, gains in both democratization and economic governance. There are also a perhaps growing number of countries that face crises of an institutional order; that is, the

---

[7] World Bank anncouncement, 'Democratic Republic of the Congo', *op. cit.*

very existence of the state as an institution, as opposed to its day-to-day performance, is now in question. African leaders have been reluctant to highlight this differentiation because they feel that it will be an excuse for the world to abandon significant portions of the continent that are not doing well. Donors are responding to the differentiation slowly but there is no doubt that they will continue to adapt their strategies to the changing trajectories of African countries. It will be necessary for donors of all types to be much more explicit in how they are addressing corruption in the particular African countries, lest incentives lead to unintended consequences.

Corruption, Hurdles and Nepad

Finally, the MCA approach is a profound challenge to the New Partnership for Africa's Development (Nepad). This new initiative hopes to shift the enforcement of conditionality from the Washington-based international financial institutions and the donors to the African continent by instituting peer review amongst African governments. The Africans have also promised transparent criteria but, since Nepad is still a work in progress, their work cannot be evaluated yet. The MCA is an example of a set of tough and transparent criteria on corruption, with all the difficulties that such a metric implies. When the Nepad criteria are finally developed, they will inevitably be compared to what the US has done to see how the Africans balance transparency, sensitivity to the underlying data, and toughness in response to imperfect performance.

Impact of Global Developments on Africa
Richard Bouma

Introduction

In October 2003, World Bank President James Wolfensohn wrote that 'Africa as a whole is better governed and is in better economic shape than at any time in living memory'.[1] To the casual observer, such a statement might evoke surprise and the informed consensus does not give much cause for hope or celebration. However, Wolfensohn's statement is factually correct. It simply demonstrates that when you start from such a low base, any progress can be made to look statistically impressive. What it cannot do is disguise the enormity of the challenge this continent is facing to provide its citizens with the political, legal, social and economic framework that is taken for granted in many other parts of the world.

Global developments have had a major impact on Africa ever since it was colonized, but the question addressed in this paper is whether recent events, including and post-11 September 2001, have shifted the mindset to such an extent that it could affect the continent's potential to achieve what President Mbeki has symbolized as the 'African Renaissance'. My perspective is that of a banker who has practiced his profession in some thirty-four of the fifty-three countries of this continent over the past twenty-five years. Inevitably, this will involve my opining on political, economic and military developments, for which I ask the reader's forbearance.

The interventions that have been made in Africa over the years by countries, economic blocs, multilateral agencies and numerous other entities are well known. However, the following quote from the Council on Foreign Relations' publication of the *1998 Africa Task Force Report*, comprising a study of events relating to the introduction of the African Growth and Opportunity Act (AGOA), summarizes eloquently the effects of these

---

Richard Bouma is the Head of Business Development (Africa) for HSBC in South Africa.

interventions not only by the United States but all Western interests:

> But regardless of the particular orientation of the US economic policy toward Africa over the years, its effectiveness has always suffered from the low priority it received within the prevailing foreign policy agenda and within the foreign policy bureaucracy. Moreover, by limiting US economic policy relations with Africa to those of aid donor and aid recipient, instead of promoting real partnerships utilizing a full range of aid, trade, investment and debt management instruments to promote development, Africa was wrongly cast as a region of little economic significance or potential.[2]

While the African Growth and Opportunity Act (AGOA) has, without question, helped certain sectors in Africa, notably textiles, it has not yet fundamentally changed Africa's situation.

11 September and Beyond

The events of 11 September 2001 and the subsequent 'war on terrorism' have cast Africa in a new light, especially for the US. This fact, together with a number of events (some related and some not), could have a fundamental effect on Africa's renaissance.

Africa is now perceived as a significant security risk by the United States and Europe and, given the continent's size, diverse populations and the porosity of its borders, one cannot deal with this risk in any conventional sense. Approximately one third of Africa's population of more than 700 million is Muslim, many living in poor circumstances. Sudan provided a refuge for Osama bin Laden, until pressured to expel him, and the bombing of the US embassies in Kenya and Tanzania are testimony to the fact that Al-Qa'ida has networks in the region. It is also relevant that most of the suspects in the Madrid bombing are Moroccan.

In addition to being a potential recruiting ground and refuge for terrorists, Africa has the potential to fund their activities through the smuggling of diamonds and other precious metals, money laundering, drugs and other criminal activities. It also provides numerous soft targets for terrorist activities.

It is evident that these problems cannot be addressed in the old Cold

---

[1] James Wolfensohn, 'Africa getting it right', *Sunday Times*, 19 October 2003.
[2] Peggy Dulany, Frank Savage and Salih Booker, *Promoting US Economic Relations with Africa: Report of an Independent Task Force* (Council on Foreign Relations Press, 1999).

War style but must involve a comprehensive, long term approach that will lead to improvement in the socio-economic state of the majority of Africans to the extent that they can see the benefit of living and working in a democracy within the rule of law. This will be an enormous task and may not be achievable, but it would appear there is now a new determination at least to try.

On the diplomatic front, considerable progress has been made at ending the civil war in Sudan. Although the talks are currently stalled and there are serious humanitarian problems in the Western Darfur, continued high level pressure from the external parties involved should achieve a positive result. Perhaps even more significant is the progress made by Libya with its likely re-emergence onto the world stage following its agreement to dismantle its weapons of mass destruction (WMD). Not only will this have a positive impact on the Libyan economy, with the ending of sanctions, but it should bring an end to the Libyan support of rebel movements and undemocratic regimes throughout the continent.

It will be very important, however, that the opening of the economies in Libya and (hopefully) Sudan be accompanied by strong international pressure to establish the institutions to ensure good governance of this newfound wealth, so it can benefit the whole population. This pressure should not only be brought to bear on the host governments but on the multinationals seeking to take advantage of these new opportunities.

Equatorial Guinea, for example, has just held elections, that have been won once again by President Teodoro Obiang's Democratic Party. One would have hoped that a country of 500,000 people that has seen its oil revenues increase from US$3 million in 1993 to US$700 million would have resulted in some improvement in the socio-economic condition of its population, but sadly this is not yet evident.

A demonstration of the increased emphasis being placed on Africa by the US is the establishment of the Africa Policy Advisory Panel mandated by the US Congress to advise the Secretary of State on US Policy on Africa. The fifteen-member panel was meant to focus on six key areas: the HIV/AIDs pandemic, capital markets, environmental sustainability, US counter-terrorism efforts, diplomacy and peace operations and US energy policy [as of May 2004 the panel had not yet reported its findings].

In the UK, Prime Minister Tony Blair has recently established the Commission for Africa to demonstrate the political will to place Africa at the forefront of the international development agenda and to ensure international focus remains on Africa's development problems. Blair will chair the commission and African representatives include South African Finance Minister Trevor Manuel, Tanzanian President Benjamin Mkapa and Ethiopian Prime Minister Meles Zenawi. The commission has a mandate to address the economy, including finance for development, trade and the economic integration of developing countries in globalization, natural resources, agriculture and the environment, investing in people, governance and effective states, and building on Africa's heritage and participation.

These two entities will complement the New Partnership for Africa's Development (Nepad), a programme conceived, developed and managed by Africans to facilitate the renaissance of this continent. This programme was met with some cynicism when it was announced, especially the peer review mechanism, as it was considered that as with the Organization of African Unity (OAU), and it replacement, the African Union (AU), the tendency would be for an 'all for one and one for all' approach, refusing to condemn the actions of any single African government.

What will the establishment of an Advisory Panel, a Commission and a New Partnership achieve for Africa's future? With memberships comprising eminent experts on Africa, all desirous of improving the continent's lot, how can their joint views and recommendations be translated into meaningful action? The answer is: with great difficulty, but it is not an impossible task if all the stakeholders are genuinely committed to making a difference and are prepared to take some pain in the process. The following are four steps that, in my opinion, would go a long way in achieving the African Renaissance:

1. Recognition of Africa's Potential

First, there needs to be recognition that, notwithstanding the commonly-held perception that Africa has little economic potential, it is in fact generously endowed with a vast array of natural resources which, if appropriately managed, would achieve the growth rates necessary to get Africa out of its poverty trap.

- **Energy:** As is becoming increasingly apparent to the West, given the events in the Persian Gulf, Africa is not only, currently, a significant producer of oil but it is likely to have substantial reserves that are yet to be discovered. Accordingly, in addition to increased activity along the west coast, Libya and Sudan will see a number of the major oil companies seeking exploration licences as sanctions are lifted.

Natural gas, currently associated mainly with Algeria, is being discovered in increasing quantities off the coast of Tanzania, Mozambique, South Africa and Namibia and will challenge coal as the feedstock for power generation in South and Southern Africa. What is perhaps less well known is the continent's enormous potential for the production of hydro electric power with the Inga hydroelectric facility, at the mouth of the Congo River in the Democratic Republic of Congo, having the capacity to supply Africa's needs twice over.
- **Minerals:** Africa contains 30 per cent of the world's mineral resources: gold (40 per cent), platinum group metals (90 per cent), diamonds, uranium, manganese, chromium, nickel, bauxite and cobalt (60 per cent).
- **Agriculture:** Again, tremendous under utilized potential with a range of soil types and climatic conditions.
- **People:** Africa is producing a new generation of foreign-educated, worldly-wise professionals, many of whom are returning home determined to change the perception and the reality of the way Africa conducts its affairs.

To date, only South Africa has begun to realize its potential in a coherent manner and it has replaced England and France as the primary base for investment into the rest of Africa. South African companies are becoming increasingly active across the continent joining what many would find a surprisingly large number of multinationals who have been active in these markets over many years. More than 20 per cent of HSBC's top multinational client base, for example, has a presence in Africa.

2. Lowering of Trade Barriers

The United States and the European Union need to take the very painful steps of abolishing tariffs and subsidies and give preferential access for African products to their markets at realistic prices. In addition, this cannot be reciprocal. While opening up their markets, the US and EU must allow Africa to protect its producers until their industries have been revitalized and are growing.

A form of 'affirmative action' is needed until the balance between production costs have reached equilibrium. I acknowledge that with the strength of the agricultural lobby in the United States, the French government's position, not to mention an enlarged EU with its ten new members, the chance of wholesale abolition of tariffs and subsidies is remote. However, developing countries are beginning to organize and take a stronger stand in this area. In Cancun, South Africa played a leading role together with China, India and Brazil in pressing for a more equitable world economic trading system.

3. Share the Pain to Share the Gain

If, against the odds, the US and EU made substantial trade concessions in favour of Africa then, in return, they would be entitled to demand economic and political reforms before any country could benefit from them (so called 'Hard Power'). To benefit from beneficial trade concessions, a country would have to demonstrate commitment to basic democratic principles, guarantee rule of law, and support institutions to create an environment in which a market economy could grow and develop.

Such conditionality would have to be agreed and accepted by the AU/Nepad as a prerequisite to the US and EU initiating their part of the bargain. The newly-launched Millennium Challenge Account is a concrete initiative designed to link aid with good governance and sound policies. Although only in the first stages of implementation, the lack of comprehensive buy-in as well as some of its conditions, such as the opening up of Africa's markets, could limit its impact.

4. Engagement with banks and business to facilitate the growth and development of market economies

Both foreign and African governments need to engage with business and the financial sector so that they are apprised of these developments and commit to take advantage of them. In fact, they will not take much persuading. Emerging markets are once again becoming attractive to investors and their bankers are prepared to follow them. South Africa's trade and investment throughout Africa is growing rapidly, creating jobs and opportunities throughout the region.

Advances in technology are assisting this process and are changing the face of Africa and the way its people live and work. For example, Africa has the highest proportion of mobile phone users among all telephone subscribers (more than 60 per cent), and mobile phone growth on the continent has averaged 78 per cent per year over the last seven years. In two years, Nigeria's GSM phone market has grown from zero to two million, four times the number of land lines installed over the past century. More importantly, this growth is being led by African companies.

Such developments require financial services of various kinds and are therefore attracting international banks with emerging market appetites who wish to grow their presence in Africa. Standard Chartered and HSBC were granted banking licenses in South Africa last year and Barclay's has recently moved its Africa office to South Africa. Like most banks, we have established rigorous money laundering prevention systems, including comprehensive 'know your client' requirements that will make it virtually impossible for terrorists and other criminal elements to facilitate such activities with legitimate players.

Conclusion

For reasons we would not have chosen, Africa has again become strategically important to the West, which is now prepared to commit significant resources in an attempt to neutralize the risk that the continent poses to its way of life. Will this shift in strategic focus and commitment of resources be significant enough to achieve an African Renaissance – a renaissance that both creates wealth and opportunity as well as enabling a majority of African peoples to live in an environment of peace and stability?

It is too soon to tell. Based on past experience, the prognosis is not good although the confluence of events – the war on terror, recognition of the importance of Africa's resource base, increased global acceptance that the disparity between the haves and have-nots must be addressed, enhanced business activity driven by South Africa's emergence as the continent's growth engine, greater pressure for multinationals to operate with standards of good governance and the new generation of well-educated worldly-wise African professionals – may just conspire as such a positive force for change that, at last, Africa's place in the sun may be approaching.

The Importance of Partnership for Peace and Development

Tekeda Alemu

One of the most effective ways to address the challenges that Africa faces is through partnership. This is also one of the fundamental assumptions on which the New Partnership for Africa's Development (Nepad) is based. Three levels or types of partnership need to be considered:
- The country level
- The sub-regional level
- The international level

In order to be effective and meaningful, all three levels of partnership must be based on certain values and principles to which there is strict adherence.

Partnerships are effective only when based on mutual obligations, whether or not the parties are equal in terms of power, influence and level of development. Accordingly, the contribution of the more powerful or more developed party to the partnership should not be seen as an altruistic gesture. In the present world, where security concerns are increasingly universal, even the most powerful need the co-operation of the manifestly weak. We either swim together or we shall sink together. But the relatively weak should not view the benefits of partnership as entitlements. They also have an obligation to be worthy of the partnership – to contribute to the building of effective partnership.

Partnership at the Country Level

The most important partnership for peace and development is that which should pertain to the country level. Africa will have little hope of achieving economic development and ensuring durable peace without strong partnership among governments, civil society and the private sector. There is even a need for partnership between ruling and opposition parties on matters affecting national interests. Without loyal opposition, there can be no

---

His Excellency **Dr Tekeda Alemu** is the State Minister of Foreign Affairs of Ethiopia.

meaningful politics.

Economic development will remain a chimera in the absence of partnership between governments and the private sector. It is now becoming clear that foreign investors take their cues from domestic confidence: if the local private sector disinvests, international scepticism rises. The problems that we in Africa face in this regard are significant. Often, parties belonging to the same country show greater mutual confidence with foreign parties than they do among themselves.

Partnership at the Sub-Regional and Continental Level

No country can isolate itself from regional turmoil. When a neighbourhood is troubled by conflict, individual state and collective economic development is disrupted. The Horn of Africa illustrates this. It is therefore in the mutual interest of neighbouring countries to create and consolidate partnerships for peace and stability, regardless of how well they manage their domestic affairs or how much co-operation they receive from international partners.

We in Africa, however, struggle to create effective partnerships within our own sub-regions. The inability of neighbouring countries in the Horn to help resolve Somalia's 13-year crisis reflects a weakness of regional partnerships, and the costs are high. Instability in one country, as we have noted, tends to have broader consequences for prosperity across its borders.

Once again, the tendency to prefer international to regional engagement affects the formation of effective partnership at this level. This must change. Africa needs to have partnership for peace at the level of the various sub-regions as well as the continental level. It is to be hoped that at the level of the African Union, the Peace and Security Council will help to facilitate a more effective partnership for peace among African countries.

Partnership at the International Level

No country can presently claim that it can ensure its security without co-operation from of the international community. Big or small, all states have become vulnerable. The globalization of terrorism provides a self-evident rationale for international co-operation on security issues.

While at the general theoretical and abstract level not too many people may question this claim, it is nonetheless true that at the practical level not too many countries have been ready to establish effective 'partnership for peace' arrangements with Africa based on commitments to mutual obligations. A critical question follows: would entities engaging in terrorist activities and whose operations are confined within Africa or individual African countries – and not, therefore, deemed a threat to the developed world – be as vigorously pursued and targeted as those that are considered more dangerous to international or Western security? From past experience, one cannot dismiss the possibility.

Failure to foster economic development through partnership between the international community and Africa is particularly evident. Obviously, Africa bears the primary responsibility for its progress. Africans should put their house in order, both in the political and economic arenas. It is the obligation of African governments and private sectors to create more enabling conditions for growth and prosperity.

But Africa's economic recovery is also an international concern, and not just for ethical or philanthropic reasons. This is the essence of Nepad. It is naïve to believe that the international community will not feel the negative consequences – ranging from refugee flows to increased threats of terrorism – of Africa's decline. Accordingly, Africa's developmental challenges must also belong to the international community.

Conclusion

The Tswalu Dialogue is also a forum intended to foster partnership among those who have the interests of Africa at heart. All those associated with this process should be commended. Sincere thanks and appreciation must be extended to the hosts of the Tswalu Dialogue – Jennifer and Jonathan Oppenheimer – for making this forum possible. Tswalu is a partnership. Long may it thrive.

Bridging Global and National Divides – What Needs to be done?

Paul Kagame

The topic 'Bridging the Global and National Divides' concerns the very survival of our people. There is no doubt that these divides are growing. In fact, never have the divides seemed so intractable as the divide between developed and developing countries, the divides between those who have access to information technology and benefit from the Internet revolution, and those for whom the Internet is still a very distant dream.

The levels of poverty are increasing faster than new technologies can reach them. Meanwhile, the rich are getting even richer, as they amass more wealth and can afford to use more technology to get still further ahead. In this regard, a few statistics illustrate this point, to set alarm bells ringing in some quarters of the international community.

- Half the people in developing countries have never used a telephone;
- The total population with phone lines in Africa is smaller than in Manhattan or Tokyo, and 80 per cent of those lines are in only six countries;
- The GDP of countries like the Netherlands is bigger than that of sub-Saharan African countries combined, excluding South Africa;
- The number of engineers who graduate in Japan every year is about ten times that of the whole of Africa.

What these statistics show vividly is that crossing the global and national divides is indeed, as someone has put it, like a race between lions and gazelles. Lions only need to run as fast as the slowest gazelle in order to survive, while the gazelles must run faster than the fastest lion in order to survive. We in Africa do not only need to run faster than those in the developed world, we must leap frog if we are to survive in the so-called digital village!

His Excellency **Paul Kagame** is President of the Republic of Rwanda.

Some people have argued that the technology required and the resources involved to narrow the divides are out of reach for most ordinary people in developing countries. There is even a further argument that we should get our priorities right. That for the price of one computer, you could vaccinate 2 000 children against six killer diseases. In other words, that in some instances the choice may be between a Pentium and penicillin. In my humble view, bridging the divides starts with a change of that kind of mindset.

Sometimes, the key factor is not resources, but rather raising awareness that only technology and value-adding will lead to the socio-economic transformation of the developing world. What is crucial in this race is the ability to spread and acquire knowledge and bring relevant information and appropriate technology to the people. Technology should permeate every aspect of our development agenda, and seek to give it added value. For example, we know that in many developing countries the vast majority of people depend on agriculture, which for many years has been subsistence agriculture. There is a pressing need to add value to this sector by modernizing agriculture and animal husbandry, especially by pursuing the agro-processing route. It is true that the necessary infrastructure, particularly in rural areas, in an expensive enterprise, but long-term investment is of the essence.

In many ways, the economic condition of the citizens in the rural sector cannot improve, and divides bridged, until and unless their economic activities are monetarized and contribute to the economic growth of the country in general. The first step is to have a leadership that is *pro-people*, a leadership that focuses on human resources and skills development.

We cannot begin to bridge the global and national divides without investing in education and skills development. For example, even if telecommunication systems were in place, most people on the African continent would be excluded from the information revolution because of illiteracy and lack of basic computer skills. So closing the digital divide starts with closing the educational gap.

In Rwanda, our *Vision 2020* programme is very clear in that respect. Its pillars include, among others, the development of human resources and a knowledge-based economy, and it seeks to promote literacy and basic education for all, gender equity, science and technology, and professional and managerial training. It also seeks to promote good governance and encourage the values of transparency, honesty, trust and democracy in governments. We in Rwanda started by sorting out our national problems.

We restored peace and national stability; we fought inequality and injustice and restored the rights of all our citizens; and we embarked on what we believe is an irreversible course of unity and reconciliation. Ultimately, these create an environment conducive to fostering reforms that close the divides between countries.

Another step that governments have to take is the liberalization of the economy in general. Our experience has shown that such deregulation promotes the development of entrepreneurship and the private sector, which are the real engines for long-term economic growth. Job opportunities, too, open up once such liberalization takes place, and not just for the well-educated.

Needless to say, the development of Information Communication Technology (ICT) plays a pivotal role in bridging not only the digital divide, but also other divides in political, economic and social domains. As things stand, however, only a small percentage of our literate population have access to a computer, and a still smaller percentage are connected to the Internet.

In Rwanda, in order to improve access, we are in the process of setting up Internet centres in schools and other strategic places. Once they are fully operational, it is expected that these facilities will enable students to access information from reputable institutions in remote places anywhere in the world. They will enable peasant farmers to access markets that pay better for their products. The centres will enable the same farmers to telecommute globally, so that a Rwandan farmer can get tips on how to improve their yield from a farmer in Brazil; or enable a Rwandan tour company to get tips from a company in Tswalu, or how to better preserve their tourist site or attraction.

Similarly, it is hoped that our people will be able to get access to broader markets by advertising their products on Internet sites, just as they may be able to get access to financial services. Alternatively, our people can better solve their needs and do business globally through e-mail, voicemail, and short messaging services. More importantly, it is through trade, exchange of technology, and the free movement of our people at regional levels that we can hope to bridge the national and global divides.

Our individual economies are still very weak and are not in a position to compete. But if we can form strong partnerships regionally, and are able to trade among ourselves, we will be able to pool our limited resources and achieve needed economies of scale. That is why we in Rwanda are keen to see vibrant and viable regional groupings.

The issue of fair access to the world markets is also crucial. We cannot bridge the divides if the industrialized nations seek to maximize benefits from the developing countries, if our products continue to have limited access to world markets and, where they do have access, fetch prices that are well below their value. It is only when access to such markets is readily available that it will be possible to reduce the huge gap between the poor and the rich in our countries, and the gap between the developing and developed nations.

Another issue that needs consideration is infrastructure development as a means of bridging national and global divides. Lack of infrastructure is a major impediment to trade, competitiveness and sustainable development, especially in a landlocked country like Rwanda. Besides, infrastructure development is one of the major contributors to poverty reduction strategies. At the macro level, investment in infrastructure enhances growth integration in the global economy, thereby reducing the global divide. At the micro level, access to infrastructure reduces poverty by providing easy access to markets and even increasing productivity.

I am convinced that bridging the national and global divide is possible and is critical not just for moral reasons, but for economic ones as well. In 1960, South Korea's economy was similar to that of many African countries. Now its economy is among the fifteen biggest economies of the world. It is envisaged that by the end of 2004, half of South Korea's population will have access to the Internet. Clearly what this means is that once the proper policies are put in place, it is possible to bridge the global and national divides.

In conclusion, let me emphasize the need to promote the philosophy of a borderless Africa, and to promote integrated regional markets as a means of devising strategic steps to build effective bridges to lessen the gap between the 'haves' and 'have-nots'. This will also put us in a strong negotiating position, particularly when it comes to dealing with the powerful nations. Nepad is there as our tool to move forward our development agenda of uplifting our people from poverty, and in so doing bridging global and national divides.

Appendix

2004 TSWALU DIALOGUE

Global Challenges and Africa
Bridging Divides, Dealing with Perceptions, Rebuilding Societies

Participants

Akwasi Aidoo (Dr), Ford Foundation Special Initiative for Africa, Ghana
Carlton Fulford (General), African Centre for Strategic Studies, US
Charles Murigande (The Hon Dr), Foreign Minister, Rwanda
Christopher Clapham (Professor), Cambridge University, UK
David Richards (General), Deputy Chief of British Army, UK
Fred Phaswana (Mr), BP Africa, SA
Gerry Salole (Dr), Ford Foundation, US
Greg Mills (Dr), SAIIA National Director, SA
Helena Nilsson (HE Ms), Ambassador of Sweden to SA
Hennie Kotzé (Professor), University of Stellenbosch, SA
Ian Wilcock (HE Mr), Australian High Commissioner to SA
Jeffrey Herbst (Professor and Department Head), Princeton University, US
Jennifer Oppenheimer (Ms), Chair: De Beers Fund, SA
Jeremiah Mamabolo (HE Amb), Deputy Director-General (Africa), SA Dept of Foreign Affairs
John Angol (The Hon Mr), State Minister for Health, Sudan
John Mackinlay (Dr), King's College London/RUSI, UK
John Makumbe (Professor), Zimbabwe
John Prendergast (Mr), International Crisis Group, US
John Robertson (Mr), Zimbabwe
Jon Bech (HE Mr), Ambassador of Norway to SA
Jonathan Oppenheimer (Mr), De Beers, SA

Appendix

Joseph Karemera, (HE Dr), Rwandan Ambassador to SA.
Kirsti Lintonen (HE Ms), Ambassador of Finland to SA
Kurt Shillinger (Mr), SAIIA NEPAD Project, SA
Lynda Chalker (Baroness), Unilever, UK
Madawi El-Turabi (Dr), Assistant Secretary-General National Unionist Party, Sudan
Mark Bellamy (HE Mr), US Ambassador to Kenya
Michael Lake (HE Mr), Representative of the European Commission, Pretoria
Moeletsi Mbeki (Mr), Endemol, SA
Peter Fabricius (Mr), Editor: Independent Foreign Service, SA
Peter Ondgeng (Mr), Director: NEPAD Eastern Africa, Kenya
Rakiah Omaar (Ms), Africa Rights, Somalia
Richard Bouma, Head: African Business Development, HSBC, SA
Richard Cobbold (Admiral), United Services Inst. for Defence and Security Studies, UK
Richard Dowden (Mr), Royal Africa Society, UK
Robert Schrire (Prof), University of Cape Town, SA
Samuel Jonah (Sir), Ashanti Goldfields, Ghana
Steve Karangizi (Mr), Head: Peace and Security Sector, COMESA
Steve Morrison (Dr), Centre for Strategic and International Studies, US
Tekeda Alemu (The Hon Mr), State Minister of Foreign Affairs, Ethiopia
Theresa Whelan (Ms), Deputy Assistant Secretary of Defence for Africa, US
Thomas Knirsch (Dr), Konrad Adenauer Stiftung, Germany
Tim Hughes (Mr), SAIIA Parliamentary Research Fellow, SA
William Swing (HE Amb), UN Special Representative to MONUC

PROGRAMME

Thursday 29 April 2004
17h30-18h30 Drinks
19h00-19h15 Introduction Greg Mills; Welcome Jonathan Oppenheimer
20h00 Keynote Evening Talk: Charles Murigande, "The Rwanda Genocide: Ten Years On".

Friday 30 April 2004 Motse
07h00-onwards Breakfast

09h00 Session One: African Conflict Resolution (Chair: Jonathan Oppenheimer)
David Richards (Sierra Leone)
Steve Morrison, Madawi El-Turabi and John Angol (Sudan)
John Makumbe and John Robertson (Zimbabwe)

There is hopeful evidence that Africa is experiencing a continent-wide decline in conflict. There are a number of countries that are on the cusp of a possible solution but where continued violence is still possible. This session will review the domestic and international determinants of conflict resolution in a number of critical countries.

10h45 Tea
11h00 Session Two: Democratisation in Africa (Chair: Jennifer Oppenheimer)
Mark Bellamy (Kenya)
Christopher Clapham and Tekeda Alemu (Ethiopia)
Rakiah Omaar (Somaliland and Somalia)

Most African countries now conduct elections on a regular basis and a plurality of elections world-wide are now found in Africa. However, the quality of these elections varies enormously In addition, many countries still have extremely weak democratic institutions: parliaments, parties, courts, and the press are often unable to play their democratic roles. This session will focus on how to improve Africa's democratic institutions.

13h30 Lunch
14h30 Session Three: Responses to Promote African Peace (Chair: Greg Mills)
Sam Jonah
Lynda Chalker
John Prendergast
Steve Karangizi
Bill Swing

Peace in Africa will depend on the immediate cessation of hostilities, the institutionalisation of democratic institutions, and a halt in cross-border hostilities. African and western governments and international organisations all have roles to play in order to move all these issues forward. This session will discussion the division of labour in promoting peace.

Appendix

20h00 Dinner Address: Hennie Kotze, "Elite Opinion Survey on NEPAD". (Chair: Jennifer Oppenheimer)

Saturday 1 May 2004 Motse
07h00-onwards Breakfast
09h00 Session Four: African Security Challenges (Chair: Lynda Chalker)
Jeremiah Mamabolo
Moeletsi Mbeki
Carlton Fulford
Peter Ondeng
John Mackinlay

African police, military and intelligence agencies often function poorly. As a result, many governments are continually at risk from small groups of rebels, organised crime faces little resistance, and terrorists are able to find sanctuary. This session will discuss how to promote the effectiveness of African security organizations.

11h15 Tea
11h30 Session Five: The Impact of Global Developments on Africa (Chair: Gerry Salole)
Theresa Whelan
Richard Cobbold
Jeffrey Herbst
Richard Bouma

Invariably, international developments affect the poor countries of Africa. New approaches to fighting corruption will affect attempts at governance reform. How Western countries conceptualize security challenges will also alter the opportunities and constraints faced by African leaders. Finally, Western evaluations of the international trade regime will have a potentially dramatic effect on the international orientations of many countries in sub-Saharan Africa.

13h00 Lunch
13h45 Keynote Lunchtime Talk: Robert Schrire, "SA after 10 years of democracy". (Chair: Jonathan Oppenheimer)
Afternoon Free/Game Drives
17h00 Walk/Drive to Dune for Supper
20h30 Talk on Stars by Tswalu Staff

Sunday 2 May 2004 Lekhaba
07h00-onwards Breakfast
08h15 Depart for Lekhaba (Chair: Fred Phaswana)
09h30 Keynote Concluding Talk: Tekeda Alemu, "The Importance of Partnership for Peace and Development".
10h00 Concluding Discussion.
11h30 Brunch at Waterhole; Group Photo
13h00/14h00 Depart